SHREWSBURY COLLEGE OF ARTS & TECHNOLOGY
RADBROOK COLLEGE

Telephone 01743 232686 Ext 642

To Renew Book Quote No:
and last date stamped.

010839

D1355919

SHREWSBURY COLLEGE

010839

DEPRESSION AND HOW TO SURVIVE IT

A grief without a pang, void dark and drear,
A drowsy, stifled, unimpassioned grief,
Which finds no natural outlet or relief
In word, or sigh, or tear.

'Dejection', Samuel Taylor Coleridge

DEPRESSION AND HOW TO SURVIVE IT

Spike Milligan and Anthony Clare

EBURY PRESS
LONDON

First published 1993 by Ebury Press
an imprint of the Random House Group
Random House
20 Vauxhall Bridge Road
London SW1V 2SA

5th Impression 1993

Copyright © 1993 Spike Milligan Productions Ltd and Anthony Clare

The right of Spike Milligan and Anthony Clare to be identified as the authors of this work
has been asserted by them in accordance with the Copyright, Designs and Patents Act
1988.

All rights reserved. No part of the publication may be reproduced, stored in a retrieval
system, or transmitted in any form or by any means, electronic, mechanical,
photocopying, recording or otherwise, without prior permission of the copyright
owners.

Designer: Bob Vickers

Cataloguing in Publication Data is available from the British Library.

ISBN 0 09177019X

Typeset in Century Old Style by SX Composing Ltd, Rayleigh, England
Printed and bound in Great Britain by Mackays of Chatham PLC, Kent

SHREWSBURY COLLEGE LIBRARY

INV No. 5414 980   DATE 3/6/93

OR   00519   DATE 5.5.93
Acc. No.   930818

CLASS No. 616.8527 MIL

PRICE £14.99   CHECKED CT

CONTENTS

MANIC DEPRESSION

The pain is too much
A thousand grim winters
   grow in my head
In my ears
   the sound of the
   coming dead.
All seasons
All sane
All living
All pain.
No opiate to lock still
   my senses
Only left.
   The body locked tenses.

Spike Milligan
St Luke's Hospital,
Psychiatric Wing
1953/4

INTRODUCTION

*I*T is one of the most commonly occurring disorders – and also one of the most distressing. At any one time about three million people in Britain are suffering from it. Every year in Britain nearly 4000 people kill themselves while experiencing its severest symptoms. It is easily diagnosed, yet in as many as one-third of sufferers it remains undetected. Although it is eminently treatable, many sufferers never receive any adequate therapy whatsoever. It is hidden, misunderstood and feared. It is depression.

Some years ago, Pat Phoenix, celebrated for her role as Elsie Tanner in the long-running television soap opera *Coronation Street*, died of cancer. The occasion of national mourning was used to put across a message to the public concerning the prevalence of the disease, the current state of the battle against it and the need for greater public understanding and commitment.

Around the same time, the television personality Ted Moult shot himself. The media were dumbfounded. Testimonies to Moult's love of life, vigour, energy and commitment flowed in such profusion as to make his suicide all the more arbitrary, incomprehensible and irrational. In fact, Ted Moult had suffered an attack of depression and had killed himself in a torment of despair.

When a well-known figure dies of cancer, the opportunity is taken to educate the general public concerning this awesome disease. Newspapers offer updates on what is known about it, and there is advice on prevention, early detection, energetic treatment, the general outcome.

Yet when a seriously depressed individual dies by his or her own hand, the media are mute as if with embarrassment and shame, and the public are left bemused, suspicious, uncomprehending. Nobody learns anything about the disorder depression save that it is inexplicable. As a result, this common, debilitating and, in certain instances, deadly condition has languished, its sufferers silent and ignored, their families shamed and guilty, their friends baffled and uneasy. Such voices as are raised on their behalf are largely those of professionals and the growing number of voluntary associations dedicated to raising the profile of psychiatric ill-health.

The inability of people to admit to a history of psychiatric ill-health for fear of discrimination, dislike or isolation has deprived psychiatry of an important source of public education, information and demystification which is available to other branches of medicine, such as cardiology or cancer research. Cardiac bypass and transplantation surgery, for example, have benefited enormously from the public testimony of grateful and successfully treated patients. Illnesses such as diabetes, asthma, disseminated sclerosis and Parkinson's disease have been rendered less mysterious and perhaps even less frightening by people who have these illnesses speaking up and bearing witness to the effectiveness of modern treatment, the progress in understanding the disease and the need for further research.

In 1992 the Royal College of Psychiatrists began a five-year Defeat Depression Campaign to raise public awareness concerning the condition. A series of surveys of the general population that it commissioned MORI to conduct as part of this campaign revealed the extent of the problem. Most of the people surveyed had considerable difficulty defining clinical depression. There is clearly a stigma attached to psychiatric problems; sufferers are presumed to be weak, abnormal and unstable. Most people felt that physical illness is easier to sympathize with because it is easier to see than mental illness. Events thought likely to cause depression included having a baby, marital breakdown and loss of a job, but few people in the survey acknowledged the possibility of a physical cause.

Given that people see depression as linked with the individual's ability to cope with life, it is perhaps not surprising that they regarded counselling as the most important form of treatment. Counselling ranged from talking to a friend or family member to consulting a general practitioner or psychiatrist. Antidepressants were not understood at all; confused with tranquillizers, they were believed to be addictive. Hence, drug treatment was not generally favoured.

A series of surveys of non-medical professionals involved in health care, also commissioned in 1992 by the Royal College of Psychiatrists, revealed a very similar picture. Depression was not seen as a serious illness and the potential risk was missed by many.

There were, however, some hopeful findings too in these surveys. In the MORI poll, over 90 per cent of the public polled agreed that people suffering from depression deserve more understanding from their family and friends than they get at present. Over 90 per cent agreed that anybody can suffer from depression – indeed, 54 per cent revealed that they, a close relative or a friend had suffered from depression. Over 70 per cent believed that depression is a medical condition, like bronchitis or arthritis.

A survey of public attitudes to depression in the Irish Republic revealed somewhat more positive findings. Carried out by AWARE, a voluntary organization which has as one of its goals the provision of greater information concerning mood disorders, it involved the interviewing of over

1400 people. The great majority of those interviewed regarded depression as a treatable condition; however two-thirds did not regard it as a mental illness. The majority believed it was caused by stress and relieved by counselling, although a significant number of respondents identified drug therapy as an important and useful approach. One third of the sample reported that somebody close to them had been treated for depression. The more personal contact respondents had had with depression the more positive were their attitudes. Two in every three respondents disagreed with the view that sufferers from the condition are either weak-willed or tend to feel sorry for themselves.

Another recent survey, looking at public attitudes to psychiatric illness in Europe, reveals interesting differences across the continent. The results suggest that as one moves from southern to northern Europe one moves from a less tolerant and less informed attitude to a more accepting and progressive one. Respondents from a variety of countries were asked whether they agreed or disagreed with a series of statements concerning the psychiatrically ill and psychiatric illness. For example, provided with the statement 'It is only people with a weak psyche who develop psychiatric illness', 8 per cent of Swedes, 19 per cent of Britons, 58 per cent of Italians and 68 per cent of Greeks agreed. The statement 'Anyone can become psychiatrically ill' was assented to by 90 per cent of Swedes and 88 per cent of Britons but by only 31 per cent of Italians and 34 per cent of Greeks. Only 8 per cent of Britons admitted that psychiatrically ill people scared them, compared with 65 per cent of Italians and 63 per cent of Greeks. A very high proportion of Swedes and Britons, 27 per cent and 37 per cent respectively, claimed that a relative had been psychiatrically ill, compared with only 13 per cent of Italians and 4 per cent of Greeks.

There are, of course, many different explanations for these findings. Perhaps the steady drip drip of public information, discussion and education carried through a variety of media – radio discussions, television documentaries, magazine articles, even soap operas – has helped slowly to dissipate some of our more established ideas concerning psychiatric illness and the psychiatrically ill.

Another possible explanation is that northern Europeans experience less of a sense of threat in the face of psychological disorder. It is certainly interesting to note that Greece, the country in this survey where psychiatric illness appears most denied and most feared, is the country in which Europe's greatest modern psychiatric scandal has occurred – namely the recent revelations that over 3000 patients were being held, half-naked and untreated, in medieval conditions on the Greek island of Leros.

There have been stirrings of a change. A number of sufferers have 'come out' as it were and admitted to suffering from clinical depression. Many of these are artists: the Tchaikovsky Prize-winning pianist John Ogdon, the

Oscar-winning actress Brenda Fricker, the poet Robert Lowell, the writer William Styron. It has been said, a trifle cynically, that the artist has less to lose by admitting to psychiatric disturbance, given the long-held yet arguable view that mental illness and genius go hand in hand. But others of a more prosaic background have also testified to the fact that depression respects no boundaries of class or creed, occupation or status. Prominent people in public life are beginning to identify themselves as sufferers. These include the former President of the Royal College of General Practitioners, Dr John Horder, and the Leader of the House of Lords, David Waddington.

In 1982, I met Spike Milligan. I had asked to interview him for my series *In the Psychiatrist's Chair* broadcast on BBC Radio 4 that year. Milligan's manic punning, deliriously fertile imagination and anarchic sense of the absurd had fuelled the rise of *The Goon Show*, arguably the most innovative comedy series in the history of British radio. Geoffrey Wansell in *The Sunday Telegraph* declared him to be 'one of the few comic geniuses to have emerged in the second half of this century'. A whole generation of comedians, including John Cleese, Eric Idle, Peter Sellers, Rowan Atkinson, Michael Palin and Peter Cook, have acknowledged his influence. He has been admired by the ordinary and by the great – Prince Charles is a devoted fan, and the late novelist and poet Robert Graves conducted with him a long, rich and affectionate correspondence.

Yet Spike Milligan suffers from recurrent bouts of manic depression. The illness has been so severe on occasions that he has had to be admitted to hospital and receive treatment, including electroconvulsive therapy (ECT). In 1982, he and I discussed his psychiatric illness and the fact that he had publicly identified himself as a manic-depressive. Nearly ten years later, I began to think of writing a book on the subject of depression, not merely from the perspective of a psychiatrist who has spent nearly 25 years diagnosing and treating it, nor indeed from the perspective of an individual suffering from the condition, but from both perspectives. Spike Milligan seemed the obvious collaborator.

It is not that his illness is classic in form and content. In a sense nobody suffers from classic depression. There are, of course, core symptoms and similarities, but every individual's illness has individual characteristics, and Milligan's is no exception. Nor is it because Spike Milligan's story is one of a triumphant cure, a tale of dramatically effective treatment eradicating the illness and restoring him to excellent mental health, a heroic tale of victory over adversity. It is not. He still suffers from time to time quite dreadfully, and indeed during interviews for this book he experienced a particularly debilitating depressive episode which required him to return to hospital for further treatment.

I chose to work with him because Spike Milligan describes in a particularly powerful and reflective way what it is like to be depressed, and the factors in his make-up which may or may not have contributed to his experience of depression. He considers whether, looking back, such mood swings have proved of any benefit, or whether they have disfigured in an irredeemable way what would otherwise have been a happy and fulfilling life.

It has not been an easy book to write. Depression is a grim disorder, and describing it as it is while maintaining and encouraging hope in readers – particularly readers who suffer from it or know friends or relatives who are sufferers – poses a considerable challenge. Many sufferers obtain little relief, while many of those who do recover nevertheless experience distressing relapses. Such facts cannot be shirked in any account that aspires to being honest.

At the same time, the story of depression is one of hope. New methods of physical and psychological treatments are being tested. New methods of studying brain function as it relates to mood are being explored. New insights into the psychological and social as well as the biological factors in depression are being described. Professionals engaged in the recognition and treatment of depression – hospital physicians, general practitioners, social workers, psychologists, nurses, health visitors, pharmacists, midwives and others – are beginning to receive better training.

But certain misconceptions relating to psychiatric illness in general, and depression in particular, remain. Among the most persistent and confusing are the following:

Error 1: 'Depression is mild, a passing mood, a personal weakness.' Untrue. Depressive illness is one of the major public health problems facing our society today. It is the most common of all psychiatric disorders, affecting between three and four million people in Britain at any one time.

Error 2: 'Depression is not a life-threatening disorder like cancer or heart disease.' It is. The majority of the 4000 people who commit suicide in Britain every year suffer from severe depression. A significant proportion too of the 1900 deaths associated with alcohol abuse are of individuals suffering from depression. Depression is also commonly associated with many serious illnesses, including dementia, Parkinson's disease and stroke.

Error 3: 'Depression is untreatable. All one can do is encourage the sufferer to buck up, pull himself or herself together and fight on.' Untrue. There are effective treatments for the disorder – physical, such as drugs and ECT; psychological, such as counselling and psychotherapy; and social, including facilitating personal and occupational development.

The amount of money we personally contribute to psychiatric health, compared with donations to other health charities, provides some insight into public attitudes. Figures published in January 1992 by *Today* show that the annual charity donations to mental health contributed by the general public in Britain amount to £6 million. The figure is dwarfed by the amounts contributed to cancer (£82 million), animals (£43 million), the blind (£40 million) and chest and heart disease (£13 million). Thus, the magnitude of the task involved in raising public awareness and concern can be appreciated.

It is not as if psychiatric illness were uncommon; it is exceedingly common. Current estimates are that one person in 32,000 suffers from Aids, one person in 50 is affected by mental handicap, one person in 30 suffers from cancer, one person in 10 suffers from heart and circulatory disease, and one person in 10 suffers from psychiatric ill-health.

Of those suffering from psychiatric ill-health, the great majority suffer from depression. One in 20 adults suffers from it at any one time. One in 10 men and one in five women will experience a severe depressive episode in their lifetime. 70 per cent of all sufferers remain untreated. 80 million working days are lost every year through depression, and the financial cost to business and industry has been reckoned at around £4 billion a year. The toll taken of personal, marital and family relationships is incalculable.

The American Pulitzer Prize-winning novelist, William Styron, himself a sufferer, wrote in 1991:

> Depression is a disorder of mood, so mysteriously painful and elusive in the way it becomes known to the self – to the mediating intellect – as to verge close to being beyond description. It thus remains nearly incomprehensible to those who have not experienced it in its extreme mode, although the gloom, 'the blues' which people go through occasionally and associate with the general hassle of everyday existence are of such prevalence that they do give many individuals a hint of the illness in its catastrophic form.

Depression, as Styron says, borders on being beyond description. But it is important to struggle, as he has done, to describe it. In our book, we attempt to describe depression from the vantage points of a psychiatrist and a patient – from someone who has suffered from it for much of his professional life and from someone who has attempted to treat it for much of his. It is not a definitive account. Depression is too variable and elusive for that.

During the time it took to write this book, Spike Milligan suffered a severe attack of depression, one of the worst of his entire life. For over a year he remained depressed and anxious, lacking motivation, zest and energy, a shadow of his normal self. This episode proved particularly resistant to various forms of treatment – hospitalization, drugs, electroconvulsive therapy (ECT), reassurance, counselling. Then, about one month before Christmas 1991, the depression lifted as suddenly and as inexplicably as it had originally struck, and the old, humorous, outgoing, enthusiastic and sociable Spike returned.

Both sides of Spike – the ill and the well – are reflected in this book. We hope that reading it will help people begin to obtain a clearer idea of what depression is and what it is not, what treatment can offer and what it cannot, what can be done to help sufferers cope and what cannot, and what we are beginning to discover about the causes of one of the most common and distressing disorders of our time.

1

SPIKE MILLIGAN: THE PATIENT

*T*HE basic details of Spike Milligan's life, and much else besides, are well known, thanks to a splendidly informative and sympathetic biography by Pauline Scudamore which was published in 1985 and to Milligan's autobiographical writings, in particular *Adolf Hitler: My Part in His Downfall, Rommel? Gunner Who?, It Ends with Magic* and his most recent book, *Peace Work*. Contained within these works are the details of his early life in India, his period in the army, his career as a scriptwriter and performer with the legendary Goons, his three marriages and his four legitimate children. There are references, though less detailed, to his psychiatric illness and hospitalizations and to his complex, idiosyncratic personality.

It is with Spike Milligan's illness that this book is centrally concerned. There is no great argument about the diagnosis: he suffers from manic depression. The illness has exacted a fierce toll of the man and of those around him, and it continues to dog him relentlessly. He has become the patron of the Manic Depression Fellowship, a voluntary organization composed of sufferers and their relatives dedicated to improving public knowledge concerning the disorder.

A PSYCHIATRIC ASSESSMENT

If Milligan's own life were to be laid out in the form of a typical psychiatric assessment drawn up by a psychiatrist such as myself, this is how it would look. It is based on the first visit I paid Milligan to talk to him about his life, in November 1990.

Patient's name: Terence Alan ('Spike') Milligan
Date of birth: 16th April 1918
Place of birth: Ahmednagar Military Hospital, Bombay Province, India

Presenting problem

This patient has a long-standing history of recurrent mood swings dating back to 1952 when he was first hospitalized in St Luke's Hospital, Muswell Hill, London, and treated for manic-depressive psychosis. He has had numerous relapses since, although between these episodes he appears to have maintained a remarkable level of psychological and physical health and a prodigious creative output as a comedian, writer, actor and broadcaster. In recent years, his depressive swings have become more frequent and more resistant to treatment.

When depressed, he becomes more socially withdrawn, finds it increasingly difficult to write and perform, expresses marked feelings of futility and worthlessness and at times feels suicidal. Although he has experienced suicidal thoughts from time to time, he has not acted on such feelings in recent years. Currently he sleeps only with the help of medication, has great difficulty concentrating and relaxing, is hypersensitive to noise and has profound doubts that he will ever recover.

His most recent episode of depression, which lasted over 12 months, appears to have been precipitated by the death of his mother, at the age of 97 years, and by difficulties in his relationship with his only brother, Desmond. However, he himself is of the opinion that his depressive swings can occur in the absence of any obvious precipitating factor.

Personal history

The patient was born in India in 1918. There is evidence that his mother endured a prolonged labour. There were early feeding difficulties – mother and baby were sent on hospital leave in 1919. At that time the patient's mother was quite seriously ill; her sight became impaired for a period and she may well have been depressed. After a period in hospital, she returned with her son to India. However, there is some evidence that he was an anxious child – he wet his bed intermittently till he was 10 and was inclined to temper tantrums.

Family history

Father: Leo Alphonsus Milligan was born in Sligo, Ireland. He died 14th January 1969 in his late 70s of a stroke. He was the sixth child of a large family and he joined the Royal Artillery aged 14 years. He was discharged from the army in 1933. Spike Milligan describes his father as 'temperamental' and 'dramatic' and he appears to have been prone to occasional 'rages'. Leo Milligan loved theatricals and was a fine singer, dancer and actor. In 1949 he moved with his wife to Australia in search of work. His marriage, however, was not a happy one and there appear to have been many disagreements. Leo suffered intermittently from depressive mood swings but never received treatment. His relationship with his son was a reasonably affectionate one.

Mother: Florence Kettleband died aged 97 in June 1990 in Australia. She married Leo Milligan in India in 1914. She was in her youth a fine contralto singer and had a dramatic, 'neurotic' temperament. She appears to have been a possessive, protective mother who, while not particularly ambitious for her sons, was not happy with Spike's choice of career in his early years. Nevertheless, she was proud of his achievements. She had few friends in England but many in Australia. Her relationship with Spike became closer in later years.

Siblings: Spike has one brother, Desmond, who is seven years younger. Twice married, Desmond is a painter and lives in Sydney, Australia. His relationship with Spike was strong and positive while they were growing up but in recent years has deteriorated. He has one son, Michael. There is no history of psychiatric ill-health.

The Milligan family atmosphere was affectionate, although the patient was aware of marital strains between his parents from quite a young age. There appear to have been sexual difficulties between his parents, which may have been a consequence of the lengthy periods away from home that his father's military duties demanded. Spike's early years were unsettled – as an infant, he came with his sick mother to Britain and was looked after by an aunt. His eventual and permanent return to London in 1933 was particularly traumatic, such that recollection even now remains painful.

History of psychiatric ill-health in extended family

Spike Milligan's maternal grandmother suffered from depression and made at least one unsuccessful suicide attempt. His own mother may have had an episode of depression during the year following Spike's birth. His father never underwent formal treatment for depression but was a moody man and was prone to fits of morbid introspection.

School and occupational history

The patient attended the Convent of Jesus and Mary at Poona between 1924 and 1930 and then St Paul's High School, Rangoon, between 1930 and 1933. On coming to Britain, he went to Greenwich and Woolwich Day School for six months in 1933. He left school at the age of 15 and worked in a variety of jobs including storeman, packer, doorman. In 1940 he was called up and saw active service in North Africa and Sicily. After being wounded in action in 1944, he was moved from front-line service and spent the remainder of the war with the Entertainments Group until he was demobbed in 1946. He began his career as musician, comedian and scriptwriter while in the army and in 1953 began a comedy series with the BBC – *The Goons* – which ran until 1959. He has since worked as stage, television and film actor, author, poet and musician.

Psychosexual/marital history

He describes a normal if somewhat protected adolescence, and in late adolescence and his early 20s he had several heterosexual relationships. His first serious relationship occurred while he was in Italy with the British Army and involved an Italian ballet dancer. He married his first wife, June Marlowe, in 1952. They divorced in 1959 and he was granted custody of the children. He married his second wife, Patricia Ridgeway, in 1962. She died of breast cancer in 1977. He has been married to Shelagh Sinclair since 1983 and lives in Sussex. He has three children by his first wife – Laura, Sean and Sile – and one by his second wife – Jane. During the 1970s he had an affair with artist Margaret Maughan, and a son, James, was born in 1976. This affair and the existence of a son came to public notice in January 1992.

Previous medical history

In general, Spike Milligan's health is good and he possesses remarkable stamina for a man of his age. As a child he had malaria in India and while in Italy with the army had sandfly fever and bronchitis. In 1944 he was wounded in the left leg. During April 1992 he had a thrombosis of his left leg which has responded to treatment.

Previous psychiatric history

There is a history of bedwetting until the age of 10. In 1953 he suffered a severe attack of manic depression and was hospitalized and treated with drugs and bedrest. Since that time he has been hospitalized for severe depressive mood-swings. In 1955 he was treated with hypnotherapy for insomnia. His most recent hospital admission was in September 1990 to a private nursing home in Sussex. The diagnosis was severe depression and he was treated with antidepressants and ECT. During this admission he was put on lithium, in an attempt to prevent further relapses.

Personality

His wife, Shelagh, Norma Farnes, his agent for nearly 30 years, and Milligan himself describe him as a sensitive and easily hurt man, a perfectionist who is easily moved to anger and tears. Others have described him as unforgiving and pessimistic by temperament. He is inclined to nostalgia and is an ardent collector of memorabilia, particularly family records and heirlooms. He can be demanding, particularly in friendship and when ill. He does not smoke and drinks alcohol moderately. A Roman Catholic, he is active in a number of charitable causes and is an active campaigner for the environment. He loves classical music and jazz (he did play the trumpet professionally), has a number of close, loyal friends, including the Prince of Wales, and is a devoted family man.

On examination

Appearance: He is a tired-looking, frail, elderly man, silver-haired, casually dressed, predominantly in black. He wears spectacles for reading. He looks extremely depressed.

Behaviour: He is markedly lacking in spontaneity, sitting quietly, responding to questions but initiating little conversation. There is a noticeable lack of facial expression and little extraneous movement.

Speech: There is some delay in responding and his flow of speech is slow and halting. The tone is monotonous and the whole impression is of someone struggling to make the effort to respond and converse.

Mood: He is clearly depressed. His mood changes little during the interview, and while he is still capable of wry, ironic shafts of wit he smiles wanly and with effort. Although he does not cry during the interview, he appears to be on the verge of tears. He admits to feeling pessimistic about the future and believing that there is little hope that he will feel better. He worries that he will be depressed until he dies and doubts that anyone can help. He feels guilty that he is a burden to his wife and to his children. Currently he wishes for relief and occasionally wonders about suicide, but he doubts that he would do anything because of the distress it would cause others. He feels apprehensive and worries about the future and whether he will be able to work again, and he worries about his financial status. He does not, however, complain of any physical symptoms of anxiety, such as palpitations, abdominal discomfort, dry mouth, dizziness or headache. He sleeps poorly without medication. His appetite is poor and he has lost about 14 pounds in weight in one year. He has lost all his zest for life and feels lethargic, disinterested and apathetic.

Thought content: He is preoccupied with the past, constantly thinking of his past life with his parents and with his own children. He worries about the possibility that he has, through his genes, transmitted his illness to one or more of his own children. He is profoundly, almost morbidly nostalgic, showing me mementoes of his children – their toys, baby shoes, school reports – but the net effect on him seems to be as a poignant and painful reminder that the best of his life is over.

Perception: He is clearly in touch with reality, and no psychotic symptoms such as delusions or hallucinations are present.

Intellectual functions: He is correctly oriented to time, place and person, and his recent and long-term memory are excellent. His concentration is, however, variable – he subjectively complains of poor concentration and of being easily distracted. Nevertheless, objective testing reveals little evidence of significant impairment.

Insight: He accepts that he is ill and realizes that he has felt like this before and has recovered. He is, however, very doubtful that he can recover again, on account of his age, but he acknowledges that these doubts may reflect the fact that he is profoundly depressed at the present time.

Diagnosis: Recurrent severe depression in an elderly man with an established 35-year history of manic-depressive illness.

Thus would Spike Milligan's history and mental state appear on the average psychiatric report – a crude and compressed summary of many years of suffering and achievement, of pain and pleasure, of family joy and personal tragedy. Each line or statement contains enough for an entire analytical session. Elsewhere in this book various elements are examined in more detail: his personality, early childhood experiences, creativity, relationships with family and friends. In this chapter, it is psychiatric illness which merits particular scrutiny.

MY FIRST MEETING WITH MILLIGAN

I first met Spike Milligan in 1982 when he agreed to be interviewed in the series *In the Psychiatrist's Chair*, which I had just started doing for BBC Radio 4. He was reasonably well at the time, although he had been quite seriously depressed not long before. I asked him on that occasion to try to describe what it felt like to be depressed. He described it as follows:

MILLIGAN: Sometimes I just turn out the light, take these tablets and go to sleep, totally blacked out. When I get depressed I try to get something for the terrible sadness that comes over me and create something in terms of poetry.

CLARE: Do you know when it is coming on or do you get depressed overnight?

MILLIGAN: It can be triggered. I was doing a television show on Saturday and I was trying, in all the chaos that goes on in making a show, to get a message across to the actors, and every time I spoke one of them would start telling funny jokes. It drove me stark raving mad and that depressed me so much that I just switched off being me and didn't give a very good performance; but I came out of it by next morning.

CLARE: That's an example of you controlling it to some extent.

MILLIGAN: Yes, I'm getting better at controlling it now.

CLARE: But what about when you're busy and you get depressed and you can't snap out of it? After all, you're like so many people who suffer from this; you must get very irritated with people who say 'Snap out of it'.

MILLIGAN: That's silly.

CLARE: Yes.

MILLIGAN: Going round with a broken leg – 'Come on, walk, you'll be all right.'

CLARE: It's silly because . . . ?

MILLIGAN: Because they don't understand. It's an emotional language.

CLARE: You mean you can't do it, you can't snap out of it?

MILLIGAN: No, you can't. Neurosis, as I say, is an emotional language. You must understand: a person who has suffered it will never say to you 'Come on, snap out of it'. Immediately he'll reach out emotionally and say 'What can I do to help? Let me sit and talk to you for a while.'

CLARE: But most people get depressed.

MILLIGAN: Not to the extent that a neurotic does. You can tell it. It's the mere fact you haven't been this side of the emotional fence. I can tell you've never been this deep down yourself. I can tell it. Difficult to describe.

CLARE: Why is it so difficult to describe?

MILLIGAN: It's invisible. There's no written diagrams. It's an abstract, it's a sensation, and if you ask people to paint it most depressives will draw black. Have you noticed that? Black paintings all over the place, so we know it has no colour for a start.

A DECADE LATER

In November 1990, I talked to Spike in the penthouse room of the Gresham Hotel in Dublin. He was in Ireland to launch his latest book, *It Ends with Magic*, which required him, among other things, to sign copies for several hours in a prominent bookshop and to be interviewed on the live Irish television chat programme *The Late Late Show* by its host, Gay Byrne. Spike had gamely completed both tasks when I saw him. He was in the grip of a depressive swing which had started some time before. He looked wretched, with drooping posture and lack-lustre eyes. He found it difficult to lift himself and appeared as flat as an exhausted battery. His mind was sluggish, his speech without its usual sparkle, his normally mobile and expressive face bleak and morose. Struggling to describe his feelings he identified several characteristic features of severe depression which are described, somewhat more prosaically, in every classic textbook.

> I have got so low that I have asked to be hospitalized and for deep narcosis [sleep]. I cannot stand being awake. The pain is too much. I have had thoughts of suicide. I get depressed that I am old. Something has happened to me – this vital spark has stopped burning – I go to a dinner table now and I don't say a word, just sit there like a dodo. Normally I am the centre of attention, keep the conversation going – so that is depressing in itself. It's like another person taking over, very strange. The most important thing I say is 'good evening' and then I go quiet and other people will talk. It must be a bit unbalanced at the table with me just sitting there dead-silent.

Seriously depressed individuals describe an overall deadening of sensation.

Food becomes bland, dry, tasteless. Sound becomes either distant or horrendously loud and intrusive. For Milligan, the merest sound when he is depressed can render him immobile with pain. Colour, as he observes above, drains from the environment – grey-black predominates. Smell fades. Touch dulls. The emotions drain away such that the truly depressed fear they have lost the power to respond to concern, affection, love with any human feeling whatever.

We met again that month. He was now in the grip of a severe depression. It was so crippling that he had been forced to withdraw from the forthcoming pantomime in Tunbridge Wells. He had never had to do this before and it was clearly causing him guilt and anguish. He worried whether it marked the beginning of the end of his career as a performer, fearing that it would signal to producers and directors that Spike had become unreliable – a massive blow to his professional pride. He was exceedingly difficult to console.

HOW DEPRESSION FEELS

I asked him to try to describe how he felt when he was depressed. Just answering the question was a struggle. This man, normally fast and furious with words, had to make a Herculean effort just to make conversation. Responding to questions about how he felt took an almost physical struggle.

> There is this terrible emptiness. I just want to go away, disappear, cover myself up until it goes away. It is like pain yet it is not a physical pain. I cannot describe it. It is like every fibre in your body is screaming for relief yet there is no relief. How can I describe it? I cannot really. I cannot, of course, escape because I have to keep working, which I just about do – though once or twice I have had to stop, had to just hide away and wait till I could summon up the energy just to keep going.

When, eventually, that paralysing state eased, I returned to the issue of what depression is like. When he is feeling better, feeling well, I asked him, can he recall how he felt when he was depressed?

MILLIGAN: Yes, I can. The fact that you are constantly thnking of suicide reminds me how fatal depression can be. People do die. In fact, insurance companies are reluctant to extend cover to people who have unsuccessfully attempted suicide in the past. They increase the premiums. When I am depressed I find my mind preoccupied with the past. I seek out nostalgic occasions – my children, when I was a little boy, my grandmother telling me fairy stories. I seek out something that may be totally unproductive. I go backwards into time, my grandmother singing a French lullaby when I was a child going to bed in Poona – and that becomes even more depressing, the fact that she is gone, that occasion is gone.

When I am depressed, having been a person who likes to be creative, I try and remain creative, but it is like changing from a fast horse to a slow horse. I start writing poetry and when I look back at it some of it is bloody good. But it only comes out when I am in depression. I only write it when I am depressed. I have no idea why.

CLARE: When did you realize that you suffered from depression, that you were a depressive?

MILLIGAN: When I first had it, in 1953-4, I thought, 'This is just a one-off.' But of course as I kept having episodes of depression I realized that it was not a one-off, that I had, well, not a disease really, more an illness. I suppose I felt it really started when I got blown up in 1944 and I started to stutter and feel anxious. I did seem to settle down after that but I do wonder whether that triggered off something that was latent in me.

CLARE: How does it start? How do you know it is starting again?

MILLIGAN: It is like a light switch. I feel suddenly turned off. There is a tiredness, a feeling of complete lethargy. There may be something unexpectedly stressful – one of my daughters having a row with my wife, not talking to each other, something like that, which I find grossly unsettling. What I think should be occurring quite naturally, my wife and my daughter talking together, isn't happening and it upsets me and then I find I am getting depressed. Something like that might start it. It doesn't so much develop. It just goes 'bang' like that and I find I am in the grip of it again and I just can't shrug it off. For instance, I had to fly to Australia to see my mother, who was ill. My brother suddenly decided, out of the blue, that I had been throwing away valuable family photographs. Finally he served me with a writ! The whole thing eventually smoothed over. Then I gave my mother £400 to buy a washing machine. Unfortunately she became ill and had to go into hospital. He gave me back the cheque saying, 'We don't want your money.' Now I had been on pretty bad terms with him and I was pretty down, and this reinforced it. I don't know if that makes me depressed but it doesn't help.

CLARE: Would that sort of experience be enough to trigger a depression?

MILLIGAN: Well, it hurt damnably. But I am strong enough to take it now. But if I were to become a little depressed that might be enough. It would be like a switch. I'd be gone. I'd be gone. A sort of hibernation.

CLARE: Some people might see this as a kind of escape – hiding away from trouble?

MILLIGAN: They would be wrong. It is no escape. It is a torture much worse than any problem you might face.

CLARE: But do you retreat? Do you close the door behind you?

MILLIGAN: Yes. The whole world is taken away and all there is is this black void, this terrible, terrible, empty, aching, black void and the only thing that helps is the psychiatrist coming in with the right tablet. But of course there isn't really a right tablet. It is a little like jacking a car. The psychiatrist can jack up the car but he can't change the tyre. You have to wait. You need tremendous patience. You need the patience. You need the patience of Job.

CLARE: Do you ever lose heart and feel you are not going to get well? When I saw you when you were seriously depressed you did seem to have lost hope.

MILLIGAN: Did I? I don't think I really completely lose hope. I wrote my last book [*Peace Work*] in my semi-depressed state. I think I hang on. Shelagh [his wife] helps. Knowing that with time it has passed before helps.

CLARE: Does the presence of other people who are depressed, does that depress you?

MILLIGAN: No. I feel empathy, sympathy. I don't think of depression as contagious. Other depressed people challenge the idea, which can be very persistent and irritating, that there is something odd about you, that you are unique with regard to this wretched state.

In the depressed state, mood rarely fluctuates and is usually unaffected by environmental changes, although Spike's own account suggests that some domestic, personal or professional setback can trigger off an attack. The question of what causes his depressions is considered again in Chapters 4 and 5 of this book. What can be said, certainly in relation to this episode, is that once underway it seemed relatively unaffected by happenings or events going on around him. Spike remained more or less miserable whether he sat in his hotel room alone or whether friends were around him. Neither good nor bad news affected his melancholy. He did, however, note one characteristic feature of depression, namely a tendency for it to be worse in the morning and to ease slightly towards evening – so-called 'diurnal variation' of mood.

DARKENED PERCEPTION

Depression darkens the sufferer's perception of the world. Spike, when depressed, cannot be convinced that the world isn't a doomed and disastrous place. Not at the best of times a particularly optimistic man, when depressed he is gripped by a bleak and pitiless vision. Everything appears hopeless, the future pointless, and past achievements worthless for being just that – past achievements. His thinking becomes dominated by one or more of three major themes: guilt, worry about illness and poverty.

One of the most distressing features of depression is the evaporation of feeling. Spike, in common with many depressives, describes himself as devoid of any feeling except pain. Sexual feelings simply disappear.

MILLIGAN: I have reached an age when I am not sexual any more. I am in my 70s. It has just stopped.

CLARE: Before – when you were ill before?

MILLIGAN: It would just go. I would lose all interest, all drive. It would be the last thing to come back – my sex drive – and the first to go. But it doesn't affect me now because I am 75 and sex has gone completely.

But what about Spike Milligan's personality in all of this? Is he prone to depression because he is 'that kind of person'? Surely personality has a great deal to do with whether, say, a row with one's brother triggers a profound depressive swing, or a crisis over work or money leads to crippling, suicidal worry?

A TEMPESTUOUS INTOLERANCE

Spike Milligan's own portrait of himself is interesting and revealing as far as it goes. He describes himself as tempestuous and, in his early years, an exceedingly jealous and insecure man.

I had cause to note during my interviews with him how demanding he can be of other people – a trait exacerbated by his depression. So striking can this be that at times it made me wonder whether he liked people at all. Our very first interview for this book, undertaken when he was clearly depressed, started badly. He became quite irritated when I revealed I had seven children. This revelation provoked a tirade about over-population, global contamination, environmental pollution, despoliation of the planet. His views – uncomfortably reasonable in many ways, indeed quite conventional by today's standards – were expressed with extraordinary vehemence, an almost personal hostility which was extremely disconcerting. At times he appeared to be suggesting that humanity itself is garbage, effluent by virtue of its effects on the environment. He took a certain lugubrious satisfaction in reciting, 'I wish I loved the human race, I wished I loved its silly face.'

He admitted to an intolerance of stupid people, defining them somewhat menacingly as people who like contemporary music, architecture or cities, or who proffer unsolicited comments on his radio or television performances (unsolicited praise being every bit as unwelcome, every bit as much an invasion of his privacy as criticism).

It is certainly true that the fallibility of ordinary mortals tries his patience sorely. He can get exceedingly upset by unpunctuality; people who are late appear to insult him personally – like those who kept him waiting at the book-signing in Dublin. My reassurance at the time that there was nothing personal, that unpunctuality in Dublin is a trait like queueing in London, mollified him not one whit.

During the same interview, he became particularly incensed about people who approve of multiracialism. During a discussion about his brother Desmond, he became upset about the fact that Desmond's son, Michael, who lives in Sydney, Australia, is married to a Chinese girl. If she has a son he will be a Chinese-Irish Milligan. 'The races as we know them will disappear,' Spike observed mournfully. 'There will be someone called Patrick Milligan and he will be Chinese. What will happen to our songs, the stories, the music?' I protested that he himself was the product of an Irish-English union, but he would have none of it. 'I am not an ethnic mess,' he replied, by which he appeared to mean someone like Trevor McDonald, the ITN newsreader – 'The man is African but he has a Scottish name.'

In an interview given around the same time to Lynn Barber in *The Independent on Sunday*, Milligan repeated the self-same observation. Lynn Barber concluded that he had a 'hatred of other human beings' and that it was no coincidence that he 'campaigns most vociferously for population control'.

ECHOES OF JONATHAN SWIFT

But if Milligan does have a hatred of humanity, it has more than a touch of Swiftian hate. It was, after all, Jonathan Swift who declared:

> I hate and detest the animal called man although
> I heartily love John, Peter, Thomas and so forth . . .

Compare such sentiments with a comment Spike made in a letter to the poet and novelist Robert Graves in 1969, around the time of the first moon landing:

> I love my fellow-man but he's a two-faced bastard. I'm sorry for him principally because he can't change, he's reached the end of the line, and going to the moon smacks of 'I climbed the tree first, so there'. Aren't I in a grim mood.

Like Swift, Spike Milligan has fought vigorous, turbulent, often savage campaigns on behalf of great causes – in Milligan's case, endangered species, historic buildings, the earth itself. One campaign of which Swift would himself have been proud was Spike's participation in a protest to save one of Dublin's two major canals, which the Government in 1970 wanted to fill in and replace with a road. There is in Spike something of the savage indignation that lacerated the great Dean's heart.

Yet, like Swift, Spike Milligan has many close friends and, when he is well, a lively social life. His extraordinary, revealing, intense friendship with Robert Graves, which began in 1964 and lasted right up to Graves's tragic development of Alzheimer's disease and death in 1985, has recently been movingly revealed with the publication of their correspondence by Pauline Scudamore, in *Dear Robert, Dear Spike*.

FALLING OUT WITH FRIENDS

Again like Swift, Spike seems to have a penchant for falling out with people. During a succession of interviews I was struck by the number of people who had been close but had fallen into disfavour. For instance, there was the disagreement with his brother Desmond described earlier in this chapter. Another example relates to a best friend from Milligan's schooldays in Poona. Spike told me how 'before we parted we swore we would be friends forever'. Two years ago they met and Spike asked him, 'Can you get me a photograph of the house where I lived in Poona?' The friend replied, 'Don't worry. I'll get it to you in the post.' He didn't. For Spike his failure was tantamount to an unforgivable betrayal.

Another very good friend took exception to what Spike insists was a harmless remark passed after Spike's *This Is Your Life*. The friend had given a short speech, and Spike said good-humouredly during the applause, 'Good old Harry, you'll get the Queen's award for this.' The friend took this to mean that Spike was suggesting he was a homosexual. 'How can you have a mind like that?' demands Spike. 'I said, "Well, fuck you." When you love somebody, have total confidence in them, lean on them, say that you like them and all of that and then suddenly . . . '

Spike remarked to me, 'My father said to me before he died, "Spike, people are made of shit, yes, every little tiny bit."' He went on:

I am afraid that like Timon of Athens I just cannot let go of my friendships. So when you, Anthony Clare, appear in front of me I say to myself 'This joker is going to write something about me in a book. He goes out of my room and goes out of my life.' I don't like it like that but my only safety lies in feeling like now because that is how I feel . . . I love to love people and give them everything I've got in return for everything that they've got. That is how I like it to be in long-term friendships. I don't suppose that you can say that you have long-term friendships . . . Everybody is so passing through.'

He expressed these views in a manner which suggests that despite his best efforts people, all people, will let him down, cannot be trusted, are profoundly and unforgivably flawed.

FAILURE TO RECOGNIZE FLAWS

Milligan appears genuinely baffled by any suggestion that he might not be the easiest person in the world to live with. In our encounter for *In the Psychiatrist's Chair*, I asked him whether he might be 'bloody difficult' on occasion. The exchange went as follows:

MILLIGAN: Yes, perhaps I might be difficult at times, but I am not known as a difficult person. I'm not an exceptionally difficult person – not really, I don't think so. If they find me difficult they must be an awful pain in the arse themselves.

CLARE: Why are you so frightened of being thought of as bloody difficult?

MILLIGAN: That's a very good question. I suppose because I want to be a decent person. I don't want to make life painful for people because a lot of people made life painful for me and I know how bloody awful it can be to have a painful life and I try to avoid that. For instance, I've never struck my children.

CLARE: It would be very difficult for you to cope with the notion that, despite all your efforts, you've failed?

MILLIGAN: I'm not saying I'm a prophet or an apostle or a disciple or a saint but I set my sights on some kind of humanity which doesn't exist at the moment. That is on the Utopian scale; so to think that I might actually be just another appalling person, makes me wonder what kind of message I am trying to preach when I myself am committing the very crimes that I'm trying to tell people I don't want committed.

CLARE: I didn't say were you a difficult person, I said were you at times a difficult person?

MILLIGAN: I did say at times, but as much as you would be difficult and anybody else would be difficult.

CLARE: I don't know whether this is true or not, but you said that before your nervous breakdown you'd been quiet and gentle but afterwards you'd had to become tough to survive?

MILLIGAN: I did, that's so; true. Tony.

CLARE: And some people are at times deliberately tough to survive: In the business world, as you say, you've got to be tough.

MILLIGAN: I want to make an example. I spent an hour three nights ago trying to catch a moth at one in the morning and to put it out the window. I don't know where that puts me.

CLARE: That won't wash because I'm sure there are many examples you can give me of your decency, and at the moment I'm not pursuing your decency.

MILLIGAN: Yes, I suppose I'm all for this cross examination – I find out more about myself. I was just wondering where I was at then. I've admitted to all the things that suggest that I am difficult. You asked me a straightforward question – was I a difficult person – and I don't think I am a difficult person at home. You'd have to ask my children.
CLARE: What do you think they'd say?
MILLIGAN: I don't know. I don't know. I wish I could walk on water.

Spike Milligan does indeed find it difficult to admit that there are flaws in his character – he wishes he was omnipotent, perfect, like Christ walking on the waters – because to acknowledge flaws is to admit that he, the fierce, vitriolic opponent of man's inhumanity to man, can and does cause pain to others. His horror of pain is exquisite. Knowing what pain does to him, he cannot face the fact that he might, even inadvertently, cause it to others.

So does he perhaps retreat behind his illness, depression, seeking within it an excuse, an explanation, a justification even, for his intolerance, his insensitivity, his cruelty? How different is he when depressed from when he is not depressed? Is he as demanding, as irascible, as intolerant when well as when ill? I have interviewed him regularly in both states.

ALL-ENCOMPASSING GLOOM

When he is depressed, his pessimistic, misanthropic view of the world is unleavened by humour. It is uniformly grim. It oozes out of him and covers his listeners in a pall of mutual gloom. This is a feature of depression. The depressed individual can so powerfully communicate the awful wretchedness he feels that those around him begin to feel miserable too.

Teasing personality traits from illness can be difficult. Sometimes one can tell only after the person has recovered which of a person's feelings and attitudes are due to being depressed and which are due to basic personality traits. Many of the published interviews with Spike Milligan have been conducted when he has been depressed. He often comes across as a lugubrious, peevish man. But consider a classic description of the profound gloom of the depressive, provided in 1921 by Emil Kraepelin, the German psychiatrist who first described manic depression:

He feels solitary, indescribably unhappy, as 'a creature disinherited of fate'; he is sceptical about God, and with a certain dull submission, which shuts out every comfort and every gleam of light, he drags himself with difficulty from one day to another. Everything has become disagreeable to him; everything wearies him, company, music, travel, his professional work. Everywhere he sees only the dark side and difficulties; the people around him are not so good and unselfish as he had thought; one disappointment and disillusionment follows another. Life appears to him aimless, he thinks he is superfluous in the world, he cannot restrain himself any longer; the thought occurs to him to take his life without his knowing why. He has a feeling as if something had cracked in him, he fears that he may become crazy, insane, paralytic, the end is coming near.

The description, formulated around the time Spike Milligan was born, describes with unerring accuracy the comedian when he is depressed.

THE WELL MAN AND THE ILL MAN

At the end of 1991 I interviewed Spike Milligan again. Sitting in his lovely house overlooking Rye in Sussex on a glorious December day, I reminded him of our earlier meeting and his censorious attack on my unfettered procreation. He smiled benignly. He did not change his view. He did not modify his conviction that the world is overpopulated and that I had been irresponsible. But he made the points with gentleness, with tolerance, with humour. When ill, he can be the 'unforgiving Goon' that Lynn Barber described in her 1990 interview with him for *The Independent on Sunday*. Indeed, in that interview she made much of the fact that he gave the photographer a bad time for wasting the earth's resources of silver. When I saw him and he was once more well, he could not have been more courteous and helpful to the photographer who came to take a picture for this book.

Lynn Barber, understandably perhaps, doubted the existence of a 'well' Milligan who is kind and generous and an 'ill' Milligan 'who cannot be held responsible for his actions'. Described in such stark terms, perhaps not, but there are grounds for arguing that Milligan, when not depressed, is less abrasive, stubborn and single-minded. He is less unforgiving. He does see how it looks from the other side of the table.

It is true, however, that he has always held a somewhat pessimistic view of life and of human nature. In Chapter 5 of this book, I speculate on what it was that contributed to his intensely developed sense of loss, a loss that borders on betrayal. What is clear is that over and over again in his writings, and particularly in his autobiographical works, there reverberates a haunting longing for an earlier, simpler, more reliable world. One of his poems goes:

The new rose trembles with early beauty
The babe sees the beckoning carmine,
The tiny hand clutches the cruel stem,
The babe screams, the rose is silent, life is already telling lies.

When depressed and in torment, Spike's view of the falsity of life borders on the apocalyptic. It wraps him like a cloak and he cannot see any hope or point nor can he trust in anything, save his wife, his family and a very, very small circle of friends. His is a terrible vision fuelled by the peccadillos and perversities of his fellow men. His demand for understanding by others of him, of his illness, of his plunges into crucifying gloom is even more difficult for others to comprehend and tolerate, given that at such moments of misery his own tolerance is at a premium and his sensitivity to criticism or ordinary, mundane human clumsiness seems exquisite and self-righteous.

TEMPERED BY HUMOUR

When he is not depressed, the same tendencies are still there – the same expectation of high standards on the part of others and the same sensitivity to their failures – but they are buffered by his good humour. His bleak vision is softened by his childlike delight in absurdity. It is as if when depressed he is unable to take solace from the fact that, while man may indeed be an incorrigible, self-deluding, posturing piece of ordure, he is also, like the child, capable of lifting himself above such limitations to love, create and comprehend. Spike admires the innocence, openness, curiosity, humour of children. When well, he recognizes that such childhood elements, matured and somewhat altered, persist in the thoughts, feelings and behaviour of every adult. When he is well, this reassures him, gives him a reason why life might not be a pointless, Beckettian farce. When ill, it slips back into the recesses of his tortured mind and all he can see is futility.

THE UNFORGIVING GOON

But how different is he when well? Does he, for example, become a more forgiving Goon? Lynn Barber, following the interview with him in 1990 when he was clearly depressed, had dubbed him 'unforgiving', his downswings 'repellent, full of pessimism, vindictiveness and violent misanthropy'. This judgment was based partially on the fact that Milligan had pinned up a letter from Peter Sellers's widow in the downstairs lavatory of his Sussex home, where it would be visible to all. The letter, signed 'Lynne', was written in response to one from Spike asking if he could have access to some old experimental films he and Sellers had made together. The letter goes:

> Spike, I don't know how to tell you this but one day Peter destroyed everything that reminded him of you. I am very sorry. What more can I say?
> Lynne

Underneath, Spike has printed:

After writing six times to her – this is the emotional reply I got from Lynne Ungar – late Mrs David Frost, late Mrs Peter Sellers, late human being.

I raised Lynn Barber's criticism of his anger and vindictiveness with him 18 months later and suggested she had a point. Now that he felt better, what did he feel? His initial comments made me think he was speaking of Lynn Barber but it soon became apparent that, depression or no depression, he still felt pretty churned up by the other Lynne, the widow of his former Goon colleague.

MILLIGAN: Total heartlessness. No reason. I hardly knew her. I knew Peter well. We made quite a lot of 8mm films together which happened to end up in his possession. So I wrote to Lynne Fredericks (the former Mrs Sellers) and asked, 'Could I have some of these 8mm films I was in?' And she wrote back, 'Spike,' not 'Dear Spike,' 'for no reason Peter destroyed everything that reminded him of you. Lynne.' Icy cold. It did hurt. It hurts still.

As he told me this story he became clearly animated and distressed. The letter with his comments on it still hangs in his downstairs lavatory. He makes no apology for his action. He believes that Sellers remained his friend till he died. He doesn't accept that Sellers destroyed everything of their friendship and says that Sellers's son has since claimed that the films were not destroyed. Clearly, Spike can be an angry and unforgiving man, whether depressed or stable, particularly when affected by any suggestion that he is not loved. Lynne Fredericks's communication, with its unequivocal declaration of Sellers's hostility, cut deep. So how did he get on with Peter Sellers, who is sometimes described as having been a depressive himself?

MILLIGAN: Sellers did not get depressed to the degree that I did. He would get angry rather than depressed. He wouldn't express it to your face but did it in Machiavellian terms. He would get rid of a producer or a director he didn't like by circuitous means. He would go to the money backers and say, 'I don't like this particular producer. I'd like him to go.' He would never do it face to face. He was a moral coward.

CLARE: Would he get depressed in the sense of becoming withdrawn and uncommunicative?

MILLIGAN: No, no. We were very close together. I knew that whatever I wrote he would appreciate it to the maximum. He would say so – 'A very funny script, Spike, a very funny script.' It was very good for the ego. That did help to ease the mental pain.

CLARE: Would you ever get so low that even that would not help?

MILLIGAN: Strangely enough, I think I have a sufficient ego that even when I am very, very down and somebody would say 'This is a marvellous book' it would make the depression just that little bit lighter.

FELLOW GOONS

When Spike Milligan started out writing the material for *The Goon Show*, both Peter Sellers and Harry Secombe were establishing themselves as actors. While Spike struggled through the week putting together a script, for which he would be paid the princely sum of £25, his two colleagues were working five to six days a week, earning money, struggling to get their names in lights before turning up at the weekend to record the show. Was he jealous?

MILLIGAN: I am a jealous person, certainly, insanely jealous – when it comes to females. I had my first sweetheart and she was given a lift in a car full of people, sitting on a chap's lap. And I saw her and I stopped the car and I dragged her out and I beat this bloke up – just for the fact that she sat on his lap. I was 17 at the time. Raging jealousy. I have remained very possessive. I was then. Less so now.

CLARE: Did you think your talents were undervalued? Secombe and Sellers just performed yet did very well for themselves. You had to prepare and write the material to a deadline.

MILLIGAN: Yes, they were on the stage and earning. I was just writing, busy writing while they were acting through the week. I did wish that I wasn't such a prisoner and had an act of my own. I wasn't jealous though. Indeed, I felt 'good luck to them'. But the demands of a script a week, 26 weeks a year for seven years was too much. When I sold the scripts, which I had to do for money, they were massive. They reached the bloody ceiling.

CLARE: You weren't jealous of Sellers and his success?

MILLIGAN: No. I was very fond of him. He was likeable, amusing. We both enjoyed thinking up funny ideas. He had these different voices which were very, very amusing. He was a very entertaining man if he liked you. He could keep some people at arm's length and he was forever having terrible rows with film people. He never stopped doing that.

CLARE: Did you feel you got to know him behind the many voices?

MILLIGAN: Yes, I did. We were supposed to be meeting the week he died. Harry and I arranged this dinner and then he had this heart attack. I always think it was to avoid paying the bill!

CLARE: Some have suggested that Sellers behind all those voices was very uncertain as to who in fact he really was?

MILLIGAN: He may have been. He had a Jewish mother who married a very weak husband who used to be a pianist in the black-and-white silent movie days. Peter's mother was a rampaging Jewess who put her husband second and worshipped the ground that Peter walked on.

CLARE: He was an only child. Did she see him as extraordinarily talented?

MILLIGAN: She did. She even tried to get him out of the War by saying he had a weak heart. Ironic really, seeing he would die of it. When they kissed they were like lovers – rather nasty, not like mother and son.

CLARE: What did he make of you and your talent?

MILLIGAN: He really appreciated it. We were made for each other.

CLARE: Were they upset when the Goons stopped?

MILLIGAN: I don't know. I think we stopped at the right time.

CLARE: Do you hear anything of Harry Secombe?

MILLIGAN: Secombe seems totally enclosed in his Welshness. He never comes out. When you phone up there's always a Welsh voice on the phone, his father-in-law or somebody – very clannish. He must be a sanctimonious bastard. He does that TV God slot and he never goes to church, never says a prayer – [imitates ghastly Welsh singing] 'I love my God, I love him so.' He was always easy to know – a bit insecure, I suppose.

CLARE: Was it a big rupture when the Goons broke up?

MILLIGAN: Secombe wanted to go out on his own. So did Sellers. I didn't. I wanted us as a team to make some films. That never happened. Later I made them on my own and felt I had caught up with them.

CLARE: Would it have depressed you, the fact that their careers took off, whereas you, who had been the engine room of the series, encountered difficulties in getting work, at least initially?

MILLIGAN: Yes, it was difficult. But I wasn't jealous. I did break through with *The Bed Sitting Room* and with *Son of Oblomov. Oblomov* was a sell-out but I had enough after two years of it. I thought it might have gone to New York and been a success. These various struggles didn't help but they didn't cause the depression either. I have been depressed when everything was going well.

THE MANIC PHASE

Spike Milligan's illness has mainly been depressive in quality. Only once, at the very outset, was he seriously manic, although he has noted periods, very short periods, of intense energy, sleeplessness, a flood of ideas racing through his mind, and a feeling of being high. The precise features of mania are described in the next chapter, including the fact that even when ill many manic patients are capable of just about functioning, particularly in areas in which a certain amount of manic energy may be a blessing in disguise. In retrospect it does now appear that Spike Milligan was actually manic when he was writing scripts for his fellow Goons. Consider Milligan's own description of how he felt and behaved:

MILLIGAN: The best scripts I wrote were when I was ill. I've just recalled this – the ones that I wrote best were when I was ill – a mad desire to be better than anybody else at comedy, and if I couldn't do it in the given time of eight hours a day I used to work 12, 13 and 14. I did, I was determined. There was a time when I was positively manic. I was four feet above the ground at times, talking twice as fast as normal people. Working on this with great fervour to write this stuff and to hear them do it every Sunday. I couldn't wait for them to do it, to hear how it sounded, because it would be acclaimed when it went out. 'I've done it, I've done it' – and then I had to go and start all over again, that was the awful part of it.

CLARE: But it was a sensation of being high?

MILLIGAN: Yes, God it was – and when I look back at it, I think, 'Was that really me, was I ten feet off the ground all the time?' I was – I was terribly manic.

CLARE: Have you ever gone high since, ever been manic?

MILLIGAN: I once did write 10,000 words in one day, like Balzac! I was pressured inside. I couldn't sleep. I just wrote and wrote. I couldn't stop, couldn't control it. I did stop. In all, the state lasted about 48 hours. All I could think of was the book. I didn't think of time. I may have been manic once or twice since but I haven't noticed it.

CLARE: Did you note your mind generating ideas at great speed?

MILLIGAN: Oh, yes. Faster than I could get them down. I couldn't stop writing, actually. I didn't go to sleep, just kept writing. It had never happened to me before – not since the Goon scripts anyway.

CLARE: Do you feel high after a performance?

MILLIGAN: Not really, no. I have done a stage play when I was absolutely depressed, though! *The Bed Sitting Room*. I was absolutely, abysmally depressed. Yet somehow I managed to ad lib and everything. Isn't that strange? Inside I felt tortured but I kept going. I would just go straight home afterwards, terribly depressed.

FEELINGS OF VIOLENCE

One of the difficulties that bedevils psychiatric illness is its association in the public mind with violence. People fear emotional disturbance because they fear its unpredictability, its explosiveness. In fact, the overwhelming majority of psychologically stressed individuals are not violent and are probably more in danger of their own lives at the hands of the so-called normal than the normal are at the hands of them. But manic individuals can behave in a reckless and disinhibited way and, if crossed, can be irritable, abusive and even violent. In the *In the Psychiatrist's Chair* interview in 1982 I asked Spike whether he had ever been violent.

MILLIGAN: I wanted to be violent but somehow I felt inhibited. I thought that would be the last straw if I turned violent but I did feel violent.

CLARE: You wanted to be violent?

MILLIGAN: I felt like killing people.

CLARE: Wasn't there an episode involving Peter Sellers?

MILLIGAN: He didn't understand mental illness. He kept coming to the flat all the time and his phone had broken down and he wanted to use mine. And I couldn't stand the noise. I said, 'Tell him to stop it.' He said, 'Oh, tell him not to be silly.' So I got a potato knife from the kitchen. I had been wanting to get into hospital and I felt, 'Why won't they put me in hospital?' I thought, 'If I get a knife and try and kill him they'll put me somewhere' and I did. I went to attack him with a knife. I didn't mean to kill him, but I thought they will hospitalize me. They took me away to a hospital and put me under deep narcosis.

CLARE: What did Sellers make of that?

MILLIGAN: Nothing much! In many ways he was a very cold fish, Peter. He operated at an aesthetic level, but his normal, everyday social life didn't operate on a very deep basis.

CLARE: The people immediately around you didn't regard you as ill?

MILLIGAN: They knew I was ill. They were very wary of me. I was very brittle and about to explode at any time. I had terrible tantrums, chucking scripts out of the room. I smashed a room at Broadcasting House once, all the furniture, because Dennis Main Wilson [the Goons' producer] said something to me.

In the severest cases, individuals engage in a constant frenzy of activity, rushing about, cleaning, arguing, distracted and distractible, maintaining such behaviour for hours or even days with little sleep and less food, the entire state only terminating with exhaustion – what eventually occurred with Spike Milligan's first illness. In milder episodes, the exuberance, dynamism, flood of ideas and pulsing energy can combine to produce a creative state – raising the question as to whether there is some biological or even evolutionary purpose in mania. In Chapter 6, this issue of the relationship between manic depression and creativity is explored in some detail. For the moment, it is enough to note that Spike Milligan's most astonishing and creative spell of work, for which he will always be renowned, occurred when he himself felt out of control, and that when he is possessed by the crippling paralysis of depression he turns to poetry to express himself.

CONCLUSION

Spike Milligan's turbulent state has earned him the diagnosis of manic depression. In the next chapter the very concept is examined, while in subsequent chapters what is known of Spike's illness, together with possible causal and aggravating factors, is examined in the light of current theories concerning the nature of such a condition. No single case is typical of anything, and Spike's own account has a number of unusual features – not least his ability until relatively recently to keep performing even while in the very depths of depression. In trying to describe what it is like to be depressed, Spike realizes that many still won't understand. But it might become clearer if how depression and mania are currently defined and diagnosed were better understood, which is the topic of the following chapter.

2
WHAT IS DEPRESSION?

A T some time or another we all feel depressed. The death of someone we love, difficulty at work, a financial setback, an examination failure, frustration in some project or ambition – there is no lack of disappointments or disasters to cause any one of us to feel miserable, defeated, even despairing. People confess to feeling depressed when they watch the television news, with its seemingly endless account of terror, abuse, intimidation, brutality and rapacity.

The very fact that we all can and do feel depressed from time to time and get over it actually makes it more difficult for us to empathize with those who become severely incapacitated by depression. We become impatient with what seems to us to be a lack of will or backbone, a willingness to indulge and a refusal to fight. After all, since we all have been depressed we all think we know what it is like. So we think we know how to conquer it. It's just a matter of 'pulling yourself together', 'snapping out of it', 'not feeling sorry for yourself'. It is purely a matter of will-power. And those who remain persistently depressed? Well, they lack the stomach for a fight, they are weak-willed, they should pull up their socks.

After all, when we get depressed what do we do? We distract ourselves. We look on the bright side. We do things which we know from past experience will lift our mood, distract us from gloomy thoughts. We mix with friends, go to the movies, watch football. We go out and buy records or clothes, drink, eat, get our hair done. There are a hundred and one ways that people combat feeling gloomy and miserable, and for most people most of the time they work. But for some people for much of the time they do not. So what is it that turns depression, the everyday experience, into depression, the illness?

MOOD ALTERATIONS AND MOOD DISORDERS

Mood is best considered in terms of a continuum ranging from severe depression or melancholia at one extreme to extreme mania at the other,

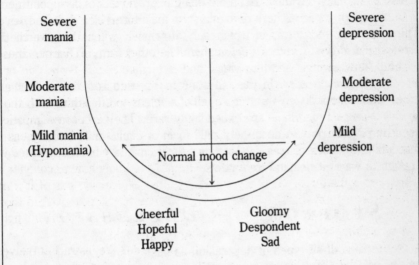

Figure 1. The continuum of possible moods, ranging from mania to severe depression.

Severe mania

Severe depression

Moderate mania

Moderate depression

Mild mania (Hypomania)

Mild depression

Normal mood change

Cheerful
Hopeful
Happy

Gloomy
Despondent
Sad

with so-called normal or stable mood at its centre. Most of us experience some mild alterations of mood throughout the average day – indeed, many feel mildly low in the small hours of the morning (particularly Monday morning!), or after a viral infection. Many more will notice fluctuations of mood after a long-distance flight, sleep deprivation or even an anaesthetic. Such disturbances of mood are usually mild, transient and responsive to efforts made by us to restore them to normal.

In contrast, depression as illness is not transient but persistent, not mild but profound; and, far from responding to our usual efforts to lift it, it remains incorrigible and malign. The very failure of efforts to lift it constitutes a further reason to feel hopeless and doomed. What can also be particularly dispiriting is that, try as the individual may, he or she is often unable to find any obvious reason for being depressed.

Contemporary researchers recognize two main forms of mood disorder. The more common form, in which only 'downswings' occur, is termed *depressive disorder* or *unipolar depression*. The other form is characterized by both 'downswings' and 'upswings' and is termed *manic depression* or *bipolar affective disorder*. In this, the one mood-state is followed by the other, either immediately or after a spell of stable mood. Upswings alone – so-called *unipolar mania* – are exceedingly rare. The term *hypomania* is used by psychiatrists to describe a mild form of mania, mild in the sense that while it causes distress and impairs function it is not usually severe enough to warrant hospital treatment.

SYMPTOMS OF DEPRESSION

A key feature of all types of depression as illness is a lowering of mood which, when particularly severe, is accompanied by a marked tearfulness or a profound desire to cry yet an inability to do so. There is a striking loss of zest – the sufferer is stricken by a debilitating lack of interest and drive. Nothing matters. As the depression worsens, other symptoms appear. The depressed individual becomes increasingly negative in thoughts and attitudes. The past looks miserable and unsatisfactory. The present lacks point and purpose. The future looms as a futile, empty and threatening vacuum.

Perhaps it is not surprising that many afflicted individuals conclude that the reason they feel so depressed is that they have committed some dreadful wrong, or that they are particularly defective, inadequate and unlovable people. Marked guilt and self-reproach develop. Slowly or suddenly, the depressed person may develop the conviction that he would be better off dead, better off for his own sake and/or for the sake of relatives and friends, for whom he believes he has become an unmitigated burden. It is the conviction that in turn can lead to suicide.

A number of physical symptoms also feature. These include a striking disturbance of sleep, often characterized by an inability to remain asleep, with frequent waking and considerable difficulty in returning to sleep. In a minority of depressed individuals, there may be a tendency to sleep excessively. Appetite is also altered. A majority of sufferers experience a notable loss of interest in food and, in consequence, a loss of weight – although here again a minority of sufferers develop an excessive appetite and put on a lot of weight. Other physical symptoms include agitation or noticeable slowing down (retardation) and a considerable loss of sexual drive and interest. Anxiety can also be present and many depressed individuals experience marked panic and restrict their social activities accordingly.

This cluster of symptoms, which together constitute the depressive syndrome, is increasingly referred to by psychiatrists as 'major depression' (although the term should not be taken to suggest that other forms of depression, less severe though they may be, are trivial). For classification purposes, it is now customary to identify as essential features of major depression the presence of the following criteria:

(1) Depressed mood or loss of interest, zest and pleasure

(2) At least four of the following:
- Feelings of guilt or worthlessness
- Loss of concentration
- Loss of energy and noticeable tiredness and fatigue
- Suicidal thoughts
- Loss or increase of appetite and weight
- Insomnia or excess sleeping
- Agitation or marked slowing down (retardation)

(3) A duration of at least two weeks

(4) No evidence of any physical or mental disorder causing the depression

There are various reasons why the general public finds it difficult to understand the notion of depression as a disease. I have already mentioned the fact that feeling depressed is an everyday feature of being alive. A second reason for puzzlement is the fact that the disorder depression is made up of a number of signs and symptoms, of which a depressed mood is but one – and sometimes not even the most obvious! Some sufferers insist that they are not depressed (nor dispirited, dejected, despondent or despairing – just some of the synonyms often used for depression) so much as tired, lethargic, unable to concentrate, slowed down, apathetic, or in mental pain. In this respect, it is interesting to note that the word 'depression', which in the late 19th century came to replace melancholia, is derived originally from the Latin 'de' (meaning down from), 'premere' (to press) and 'deprimere' (to press down). Spike Milligan's attempt to explain to me what being depressed feels like is peculiarly apposite:

> It's rather as though you are sitting with an eiderdown over you and you hear a doorbell ring and you think, 'I'll have to go and answer that.' And you struggle, but to little avail. You can perhaps just about go but it is a terrible effort because this wretched eiderdown just drags you back and down and smothers you.

DEPRESSION AND MANIA: A SLOWING DOWN AND A SPEEDING UP

One of the most useful ways to understand depression and mania is as a slowing down and a speeding up respectively, not merely of psychological functions but of physical functions too. In depression, the whole organism, physical and psychological, is slowed down. Given that existing becomes such a struggle against paralysis and inertia, the purpose of existence, perhaps not surprisingly, becomes difficult to identify. 'Life has all the pointlessness of electric light on a sunny day' is how Milligan describes it. In mania, by contrast, everything is speeded up. At its peak the person is in a wild state of overdrive, out of control – a state sometimes more apparent to others than to the affected individual.

The diagnosis of manic-depressive illness rests on a history of manic and depressive episodes, or their occurrence currently. For a diagnosis of mania to be made, it is now generally accepted that the following criteria have to be met:

(1) One or more distinct periods marked by a predominantly elevated, expansive or irritable mood. The mood must be a prominent part of the illness and relatively persistent, although it may alternate or intermingle with depressive mood.

(2) A duration of at least one week (or any duration if hospitalization is necessary) during which, for most of the time, at least three of the following symptoms have persisted (four if the mood is only irritable) and have been present to a significant degree:

- An increase in activity (either socially, at work or sexually) or physical restlessness
- Increased talkativeness or pressure to keep talking
- Flights of ideas, or a feeling that thoughts are racing
- An inflated self-esteem (there may be grandiosity which in turn may be delusional)
- A decreased need for sleep
- A distractibility, ie the attention is too easily drawn to unimportant or irrelevant stimuli

- Excessive involvement in activities that have a high potential for painful consequences, which is not recognized (eg buying sprees, sexual indiscretions, foolish business investments, reckless driving).

(3) There are no significant features suggestive of a schizophrenic or paranoid disorder.

MILLIGAN'S HISTORY OF MANIA AND DEPRESSION

On the basis of Spike Milligan's own testimony, the accounts provided in his medical case history and the accounts of those close to him – including his

FEATURES OF DEPRESSION

Psychological

questionnaire

Pervasive and unresponsive depression

Variation of daily mood, which is usually worse in the morning

Marked loss of self-esteem

Profound lack of energy (apathy)

Sad, miserable, regretful thoughts

Agitation and even panic attacks

Guilt about real or imagined failings

Thoughts about suicide and suicidal methods

Inabiilty to concentrate

Impaired memory for recent events

Loss of feelings, particularly affection and interest

Physical

Marked loss of appetite

Measurable loss of weight

Constipation

Impaired sleep with early-morning wakening

Loss of sexual drive

Intolerance of noise, bright lights

Slowed-down speech and movement

FEATURES OF MANIA AND HYPOMANIA

Psychological

Infectious mood – humorous, jocose, euphoric
Rapid flow of ideas
Exaggerated self-esteem
Grandiose ideas and delusions
Loss of judgment and marked impulsiveness
Loss of inhibitions, particularly sexual and social
Irritability and impatience
Marked distractibility
Excessive drinking, gambling, spending

Physical

Pressurized speech – fast, punning, rhyming
Marked physical over-activity and restlessness
Insomnia – inability or unwillingness to sleep
Excess appetite

wife Shelagh, his faithful manager Norma Farnes, and his sympathetic biographer Pauline Scudamore – there seems to be little doubt that over the years Milligan's mental condition has met the criteria for both manic and depressive disorders.

There have been distinct and persistent periods during which there has been a marked increase in activity, particularly activity related to his work as a performer and writer. He has become more talkative than usual, ideas have raced through his head and he has been unable to sleep. Spike has, fortunately, never been involved in activities with 'a high potential for painful consequences' (unless one includes some of the series he has done for the BBC!), neither has he used drugs or alcohol in such a way as to explain the emergence of manic symptoms.

Examining his history, there is evidence of at least two clear-cut episodes of mania, including the very first episode, which led to hospitalization in 1953.

More frequently, however, he has been depressed to an extent which meets the accepted criteria for a depressive illness. That is to say, he has had distinct periods of persistently low mood, characterized by feeling low, hopeless and irritable and accompanied by poor appetite, poor sleep, restlessness and agitation, a loss of interest and pleasure, marked fatigue and severe difficulties in concentration. There have, on many occasions, been recurrent thoughts of death and suicide. These episodes have typically lasted between three and six months, although in recent years the illnesses appear to have got longer. His most recent episode lasted for over 18 months.

THE PERSONALITY FACTOR

Psychiatric diagnostic classifications, in addition to defining diseases, also attempt to describe and categorize personalities. Whereas the symptoms and signs of illness are assumed to arise anew rather than to have been present from the time that the individual's personality was being formed, certain traits, attitudes, impulses and beliefs are regarded as part of the personality. This is because there is evidence that their presence in someone can be traced right back to adolescence (during which time the core elements of personality are laid down) and even before. Personality traits exist before symptoms and signs of any illness, and persist after such an illness lifts or is relieved. Because they are characteristic of the individual's current and long-term functioning, pathological personality traits are not limited to episodes of illness; they cause significant impairment in social or occupational functioning, and subjective distress.

Psychiatrists are interested in differing kinds of personality for the most part because some personality types are particularly prone to develop certain psychiatric illnesses. Spike Milligan's personality, by his own account and those of others who have known him through the years, is a complex and unusual one. In understanding him and his illness account has to be taken of his personality. This is true of anyone who suffers from depression, or indeed from any serious illness, physical or psychological.

Spike Milligan, at the best of times, takes a jaundiced, sceptical, harsh view of his fellow-men; at the worst of times this congeals into a misanthropic, pessimistic, disconsolate opinion. But depression does darken the sufferer's perception of the world. Those gloomy, doubting, futile feelings most of us entertain from time to time come to dominate our waking hours when depression becomes entrenched.

Depression also exacerbates certain personality attributes. Mild obsessional traits, such as a liking for punctuality, order, predictability, a sense of control, or a belief in high moral standards of behaviour and belief, can become transformed into crippling obsessional ruminations and doubts about sin, guilt and personal worthiness. They are relieved only by the performance of forceful, repetitive behaviours known as compulsions.

For instance, the over-religious depressive, tortured by worries over sin, seeks to purge himself or herself by indulging in repeated acts of self-punishment. Another example is the person whose normal temperament is a trifle dramatic, who craves excitement, and who has a tendency to be vain, demanding and inconsiderate. This individual will be prone to emotional outbursts and an intensification of these personality traits when ill, to such a degree as to make their illness even more difficult for relatives and friends to tolerate and understand.

It is these changes in personality or exaggerations of traits already present which occasionally lead others to insist that the depressed person has changed and changed utterly. There can be dark talk of a new personality or dire references to Jekyll and Hyde, and the existence of two personalities – one present when the person is well and another, a more disagreeable one, when ill.

In some instances, individuals become less assertive, less aggressive, less demanding when depressed. Some relatives acknowledge openly the dilemma whereby they find it easier to cope and live with the afflicted individual when he or she is ill than when well.

ATTITUDES TOWARDS TREATMENT

Personality traits do not merely colour an illness – they also affect such issues as acceptance of being ill and compliance with treatment. A tendency to be suspicious of authority figures, especially doctors, or of drugs, particularly those affecting the nervous system and mental function (the so-called psychotropic drugs), may be understandable. But when indulged in by an individual with severe depression, it can mean the difference between recovery and disintegration.

Likewise, a desire for simple answers to complex questions is understandable but is not always realistic, and in the case of depressive illness it is not realistic at all. There are no simple answers. Some people negotiate life quite successfully, insisting on issues being seen as black and white, on every question having an answer, on every problem being promptly solved. Some such individuals are to be found in the highest echelons of big business, the professions, politics. When they or someone close to them becomes depressed, they are distraught. None of their usual approaches to life's problems is now appropriate. The issue of depression is not black and white. There is, as the next chapters illustrate, no easy and unequivocal answer when it comes to the question of cause, treatment or prognosis. There can be no immediate solutions.

THE SILVER LINING

Like diabetes, cancer, stroke, heart attack, or any other serious illness, depression tests our basic strengths. It exposes our frailties and flaws and sounds out our attributes, our attitudes, our very beliefs. That is why those who have been depressed, like many who have had cancer or who have undergone a life-threatening operation, often say they have been transformed. They feel that they are now privy to a greater sense of self-knowledge; that, while they would never have asked to be depressed, it has given them an insight and an understanding of themselves and their relationships with others that has enriched their lives.

But not everyone feels that. Others regard their illness as, quite simply, an appalling ordeal that they would not wish on their worst enemy. And Spike Milligan is one of these. He is unshakeable in his conviction that nothing he has done with his life – none of the great achievements of his astonishingly prolific career as a poet, playwright, comic, performer, author, crusader – alters the fact that he was born with or developed an illness of such malign consequences that it would have been better had he not been born.

> I cannot reassure myself that it has been worthwhile. You don't need to feel this way to achieve, create, succeed. I do not hold with this romantic view of depression, that it has some purpose, that it is the downside of my achievements. As far as I am concerned it is without a redeeming feature and I would have willingly foregone my fame and achievements to have been rid of it. What is more, I have known as many and more sufferers from manic depression who have had no talent, no creative talent whatsoever – what do you say to them about the value of suffering this miserable disorder?

Such an uncompromising view is not uncommon among those who have previously been depressed and is commoner still among those who are depressed. Indeed such a view fuels suicidal impulses. It is a tribute to Milligan's powers of survival that he persists with his angry, animated, energetic insistence on living, and living exuberantly and creatively, in the face of such a terrible vision. I say that to him to his face, suggesting that such a decision to live in the face of a tormenting illness is itself inspirational, is itself a valuable consequence, a good outcome of an evil happening. He smiles wearily and remains unconvinced.

> I have little choice. I have to go on and when depressed I have to remind myself that it will pass, like all the others. But it has of itself no value – other than the poetry I tend to write when depressed. But I would forego that too if I had the choice.

COMMON PREOCCUPATIONS

Many depressed people, and Spike Milligan is one, worry that the illness may in some way be their fault, that they are to blame. Some search in their past for some peccadillo that they can identify as the cause of their wretchedness. One patient of mine became convinced that his depression was due to the fact that as a child, some 40 years before, he had stolen a couple of tin soldiers from Woolworths. Sometimes, the individual realizes that the guilt he or she experiences is indeed excessive, is disproportionate to any real or imagined sin or failure, but can do little to alter the feeling. In some distracted people it can become frankly delusional; that is to say, a fixed and false belief absolutely resistant to reason can develop. Then the individual is convinced that he has brought shame on the family, has committed some dreadful crime – perhaps one that is currently the topic of discussion in the newspapers – or that he has committed an unforgivable sin and is rightly damned.

Some sufferers become preoccupied with bodily complaints and wonder if some physical disease might not be the cause of their dreadful predicament. Some become convinced, despite all contrary evidence, that they have cancer, syphilis, Aids, that their bowels are blocked, their organs rotting or that they have some other physical affliction of a terminal nature.

Preoccupation with money is not uncommon either, with the depressed person exaggerating or worrying unnecessarily about minor financial difficulties. Delusions of poverty may develop, in which the individual becomes convinced that he is ruined, that his debts are unpayable, that all his possessions have to be sold. Initially, such beliefs may be expressed so persuasively and so plausibly that those not fully conversant with the individual's actual physical state or financial status may be convinced by the account.

HALLUCINATIONS AND DELUSIONS

Occasionally, the term 'psychosis' is applied to depression and manic depression, as in 'depressive psychosis' and 'manic-depressive psychosis'. In general it is used to describe conditions in which there is an inability to distinguish between subjective experience and reality, which shows up as hallucinations and/or delusions. Often, however, the adjective 'psychotic' is used, erroneously, as a synonym for 'serious' or 'severe'. Because of its aura of dangerousness, unpredictability and even criminality and because the conditions embraced by it have little in common, there is much to be said for discontinuing the use of the term psychosis altogether.

Some severely depressed or manic patients do, nevertheless, develop hallucinations and/or delusions. A hallucination is a sensory perception in the absence of an external stimulus to the sense organs. As there are five sense organs, it follows that there are five kinds of hallucination: auditory, visual, gustatory, tactile and olfactory. In depression, auditory hallucinations are commonest. The depressed person often hears a voice or voices talking to him, berating him with markedly critical comments.

Various delusions are described in severe depression. Commonly, sufferers become convinced that others are trying to harm them, damage their reputation or even kill them. Sometimes, the depressed person may believe that such persecution is understandable given his own guilt and evil. True depressive delusions involve guilt and worthlessness and may even become nihilistic; the individual believes that he is about to die, the world is doomed or, in extreme cases, he is already dead and rotting. Then again, the person may believe, in the face of all evidence to the contrary, that he is afflicted with a serious, even terminal disease. These are the so-called hypochondriacal delusions. Other delusions include religious delusions, whereby the depressed individual is convinced that he is possessed by the devil or is being punished by God for wrongdoing, and delusions of jealousy.

THE PAIN OF DEPRESSION

Whatever the form the depression takes, its overwhelming impact is highly distressing. In 1982, Dr John Horder, one-time President of the Royal College of General Practitioners and a highly respected GP in North London, gave an interview to the magazine *Medical News*. In it he reflected on the relative agony he has experienced when on separate occasions he has suffered from renal colic, a heart attack and an episode of severe depression.

> If I had to choose again, I would prefer to avoid the pain of depression. It is a surprisingly physical sensation, with a surprising resemblance to coronary pain, because it too is total. But it cannot be relieved quickly. It even threatens life. It is oneself and not part of one's machinery – a form of total paralysis of desire, hope, capacity to decide, to do, to think or to feel – except pain and misery.

When I asked Spike Milligan how depressed he had got during the 40 years he had experienced recurrent depressive episodes, he replied in similar fashion. 'I have got so low that I have asked to be hospitalized and for deep narcosis. I cannot stand being awake. The pain is too much. I have had thoughts of suicide.'

This 'pain' that those who have had depression often describe is one of the reasons that some sufferers are driven to self-destruction. But there are other reasons. Many depressed individuals become convinced that they constitute such a burden to those who are closest to them that all concerned would be better off if they ended their own lives. In a few tragic but much-reported cases, the depressed individual, unable to see anything in life other than pain, loss, destruction or corruption, concludes that not merely he but his loved ones would be better off dead. It is severe depressive illness that often lies behind the newspaper headlines telling a disbelieving and horrified world of an entire family killed by one or other parent who has then committed suicide.

THE SUICIDE RATE

Many depressed people kill themselves because they see nothing but futility and suffering. Many others become convinced that they suffer from an incurable and fatal disorder or that they are being harassed and persecuted. Psychiatrists speak of 'suicide potential' which they define quite simply as recurrent thoughts of death (not just fear of dying), recurrent suicidal ideas without a specific plan, or a suicide attempt or specific plan for committing suicide.

Between 25 per cent and 50 per cent of manic-depressive sufferers have attempted suicide at least once. A significant proportion of the 5000 people who kill themselves in England and Wales each year are believed to be depressed. One in seven people who suffer from major depressive disorder will die by suicide. Two in every five will at some time manifest suicidal behaviour – that is to say, they will collect pills or buy the means to do it (eg a rope, a knife), and take certain preliminary steps (putting their affairs in order, writing a suicide note). More than four in every five seriously depressed people will be troubled by intense suicidal thoughts at some time during their illness.

In one extensive two-year follow-up of over 1000 patients who had at some stage been hospitalized for the treatment of depression, 25 were found to have killed themselves (Black et al., 1989). In another study, in which 954 depressed patients were followed up for ten years, 68 had committed suicide in that time (Fawcett et al., 1990). Such findings confirm what every psychiatrist knows only too well: that suicide is a very real risk in every case of serious depressive illness.

Early estimates suggested that perhaps as many as 90 per cent of those who committed suicide were suffering from psychiatric illness. Today estimates are somewhat lower but it still seems likely that the great majority of those who take their own lives are seriously depressed at the time. About 1 per cent of deaths in England and Wales each year are due to suicide, a rate of eight suicides per 100,000 population. This rate increases with age, peaking for women in their 60s and for men in their 70s. The highest rates of suicide have been reported in Hungary (40 per 100,000) and the former East Germany (35 per 100,000), while the lowest reported are those of Spain (3.9 per 100,000) and Greece (2.8 per 100,000).

Such variations may well reflect differences in reporting as much as genuine differences in suicide frequency. In some countries, such as my native Ireland, suicide is still a crime, and under-reporting inevitably results. Irish coroners are constrained from returning a verdict of suicide by the Coroner's Act of 1962 which forbids them to attribute blame or exonerate in matters of civil or criminal liability. This state of affairs has led one commentator to observe sardonically, 'We can look forward to Eire having the lowest suicide rate in the world.' To get around the distortion due to criminalization, confidential police reports since 1967 are supplied to the Irish Central Statistics Office after inquests on deaths suspected of being unnatural. While this helps correct the suicide statistics, it is still believed that the official Irish rate may need to be multiplied by two or three to arrive at a true rate.

As it is, however, the Irish suicide rate, in common with rates throughout Western Europe, is rising. One Irish researcher, Professor Tom Fahy, has estimated that in the last ten years 'upwards of 20,000 Irish people have lost a loved one through suicide' (Fahy, 1991). Recorded suicides in the 1960s averaged 60 per year; by 1988 the annual number exceeded 300. The taboo against suicide, thought to be higher in Roman Catholic countries (although Hungary, a Catholic country, has a particularly high rate), is clearly losing its force.

SUICIDE AMONG THE YOUNG

While suicide has traditionally been associated with ageing, throughout Western Europe and North America the rate is rising among young people, particularly young males. In England and Wales suicide is now the third leading cause of death. In Ireland, the rate among those under 30 years of age has risen by over 1000 per cent in 30 years.

Some of these young people may well be seriously depressed – Russell Blacker and I found that rates of depression in young people attending one North London general practice were very much higher than we had been led to expect from the psychiatric literature. Many young people, however, may be killing themselves for reasons other than that of depression. There is evidence of much anger, frustration and a sense of isolation and purposelessness associated with young males who kill themselves, rather

FACTORS INCREASING THE RISK OF SUICIDE

Living alone

Immigrant status

Recent bereavement, separation or divorce

Recent loss of a job or retirement

Living in a socially disorganized area

Male sex

Older age

Family history of depression, suicide or alcohol abuse

Previous history of depression, suicide or alcohol abuse

Previous suicide attempt

Addiction to alcohol or drugs

Severe depression

Early dementia

Incapacitating, painful physical disease

than frank clinical depression. Other factors, including unemployment, drug and alcohol abuse, the breakdown of family and associated social structures, have all been identified as contributory factors in this rise.

WARNINGS AND THREATS

A distinction is often drawn between those who inflict harm on themselves (so-called 'parasuicides') and those who are determined and eventually succeed. They do differ in a number of important respects. Suicide, for example, although rising rapidly in the young, is still commoner in middle age, and rates are currently highest among men over 60 who are either widowed, divorced or single. Parasuicide, in contrast, is more likely in young women in the throes of relationship difficulties.

Yet there are similarities too. Both suicide and parasuicide are much more common among those who are unemployed and living in areas of multiple deprivation. Furthermore, 40 per cent of those who commit suicide have a history of parasuicide. (It is not, therefore, true that someone who repetitively engages in minor self-destructive behaviour – taking a few pills, scratching cuts on their wrists, half-heartedly tying ropes around their necks – will not therefore kill themselves. People who engage in repeated acts of self-harm often do end up dying at their own hand, either deliberately or accidentally.)

The majority of people who commit suicide contact their family doctor during the month prior to the act. Suicide rarely occurs out of the blue. Warnings are given, threats are made, notes are written. Yet suicide is almost invariably a horrendous tragedy, not merely for the individual whose life has been truncated but for those left behind, who remain bewildered, guilty, angry, ashamed and emotionally maimed. It is preventable in perhaps all but a small number dealing with a premeditated act, the thinking and planning of which can be detected and prevented if suspected early enough.

One crucial fact needs to be emphasized. There is a particular risk of suicide when the depressed individual is just beginning to recover. At such a time, some sufferers – who were too lethargic, indecisive, agitated or depressed when profoundly ill to elaborate a suicide plan and carry it out – as they recover (either with treatment or as part of a spontaneous recovery) so become a little more energetic and better able to act. Some depressed individuals even feign improvement in order to carry out a

SUICIDE AND PARASUICIDE

A comparison of risk factors

	Suicide	Parasuicide
Age	Rate increases with age and peaks at over 60	Rate highest in women under 30
Sex	Men more than women	Women – 2.5 times the risk of men
Marital status	Divorced, widowed, and single men	Divorced
Social position	Unemployment; no social class differences	Unemployment; lower social class
Precipitating 'life events'	Present	Present
Methods used	Planned and lethal	Unplanned and non-lethal
Previous psychiatric illness	Depression in two-thirds	No illness in two-thirds

From *The Nation's Health*, King's Fund, London, 1988

suicide plan undetected. Discharged too soon from hospital, for example, such individuals find themselves able to proceed with their intention just at the very time that hospital staff have relaxed and relatives are beginning to feel more hopeful.

SEEKING AN EXPLANATION

Suicide is a curious act. For the writer Albert Camus it was the one truly philosophical problem. For the poetess Anne Sexton, who was eventually to take her own life, it was 'the greatest act of courage I can think of'. While Alvarez argued that it is a natural reaction to an unnatural condition, Primo Levi – the concentration camp survivor, chemist and writer – noted that, in settings of the most unnatural and terrible tribulation, suicide is often unknown. The camps were such a setting; cases of suicide were rare.

Levi, in his compelling account *The Drowned and the Saved* (Levi, 1986), offers three explanations. First of all, he reminds his readers that 'suicide is an act of man and not of the animal; it is a meditated act, a non-instinctive, unnatural choice'. In the camps there were few opportunities to choose. The inmates lived like enslaved animals that occasionally allowed themselves to be killed but did not kill themselves.

In the second place, there were other things to think about. Levi quotes Svevo's remark in *The Confessions of Zeno* that 'When one is dying one is much too busy to think about death. All one's organism is devoted to breathing.' The usual exasperated expostulation in the face of a suicide – 'But he had so much to live for' – misses a crucial truth about suicide. Suicide is the decision of one who finds no purpose to live for within the very elements of living that provide others with life's point and purpose.

Third, argues Levi – and what he has to say relates especially to the position of the depressed – 'suicide is born from a feeling of guilt that no punishment has attenuated'. In the camps the very harshness of the conditions was itself perceived as punishment. There was no need to punish oneself by suicide for any true or presumed guilt since one was already expiating it by suffering every day. The feelings of guilt were relegated to the background. They did re-emerge after liberation.

Suicide, as Levi pointed out, 'allows for a nebula of explanations'. Shortly after the publication of *The Drowning and the Saved* he killed himself. He did so suddenly and with impulsive violence, hurling himself down the stairwell of the apartment building in Turin where he had been born and had spent much of his life. Many have speculated that his suicide related to the guilt and shame he felt at being one of the survivors of the holocaust, and to his conviction, expressed in much of his writing, that the best had perished in the gas chambers and that the worst had survived.

Perhaps this is the explanation – but perhaps not. Primo Levi was a chemist. Had he planned to destroy himself he could have opted for a less impulsive, less violent and more planned method. Then again, as Paul Bailey points out in his thoughtful introduction to *The Drowning and the Saved*, Levi had many other reasons to despair. He had undergone an operation for prostatic cancer. He was profoundly depressed, in particular by the condition of his beloved mother, and was being treated with antidepressant therapy by his doctor.

Levi's story illustrates the difficulty of providing an all-embracing and convincing account of the motivations behind suicide. Suicide rarely occurs as a result of factors purely biological or 'internal' to the individual; there is usually an interaction between the individual and his or her social circumstances. Suicide, like murder, simultaneously fascinates and appals. Once a sin, then a crime, it has now become a sickness and has spawned a new specialism – suicidology – for its analysis and explanation. Yet an adequate explanation still eludes us.

At the end of their extensive review of the subject, Robert Kastenbaum and Ruth Aisenberg (1974) suggest that only a handful of generalizations can with safety be made. Suicide, they argue, is but one subtype within the general category of self-murder. Causes of suicide can be divided into fundamental causes (sought within the psychology and biology of the individual), contributing causes (external situations and events) for individuals with suicidal tendencies, and precipitating causes triggering the act. A particular situation or event might either contribute to or precipitate a suicidal attempt, but the same objective circumstances will neither contribute to nor precipitate an attempt in a person who lacks a fundamental orientation towards suicide.

In truth, such a formulation about suicide fits depression too. Events and circumstances which provoke depression in one person do not necessarily do so in another. This fact puzzles the general public. It does more: it irritates. It causes ordinary people to be impatient with the depressed, the suicidal. Spike Milligan, recognizing our perplexity, puts the issue neatly:

> Only when you know what it is like to feel depressed, to feel you are dying inside, can you know what it is like to be suicidal, to think that the whole dreadful, terrible, nagging, awful pain of it all might be swept away by a simple, single act of self-destruction.

MANIA: HEIGHTENED EXCITATION

The initial picture presented by mania is the very opposite of depression. Whereas depression is characterized by low mood, poverty of speech, lack of interest and slowing down of activity, mania is marked by euphoria, pressure of talk, considerable over-activity and expansive, grandiose ideas. The manic individual is often jolly, displaying an infectious hilarity that moves the observer to smiles or laughter. But the euphoria is rarely sustained and tends to give way to irritability in the face of minor frustration, criticism or opposition. The mood is often rapidly changeable, and there can be fleeting moments of depression, even thoughts of suicide. A state of heightened excitation rather than truly euphoric mood might well be a better description of mania.

Manic patients often talk incessantly. In the milder cases it is usually possible to follow the direction of the individual's thoughts. In more severe forms of the illness it may be difficult because of a growing distractibility and dependence upon circumstances. In more severe cases again, so-called 'flight of ideas' occurs. The individual's thoughts leap from topic to topic with changes of direction determined by puns, rhymes or chance distractions from the environment – the sound of cars passing, steps in a corridor, a door banging, the colour of someone's tie. Although the central destination of the original conversation is often lost, the shifting direction of thought and the connection between successive topics can usually be understood by the observer.

Some manic individuals report subjectively that they experience thoughts racing through their minds, ideas generating at great speed and faster often than they can translate them into speech. Other manic individuals demonstrate a similar pressure by turning their thoughts into voluminous writings. In extreme forms of mania, a flight of ideas may degenerate into incoherent and unintelligible speech.

DELUSIONS OF GRANDEUR

Whereas the content of thought in depressive states is guilt-ridden, self-critical, remorseful and pessimistic, in mania it is expansive, self-confident and optimistic. The individual has never felt so well, is at the height of his powers and entertains limitless possibilities. Religion and wealth are common themes. So grandiose may the individual become that frank delusions may be expressed. He may insist that he has special abilities – can cure the sick, write better than Shakespeare, transform the basis of mathematical calculations. He may believe that he has an identity of special significance – as a member of a royal family, a statesman of international reputation, a reincarnation of Napoleon, a close relative of the Pope, a scientist who has made or is about to make an earth-shattering discovery. He may insist that he is a millionaire and, to the dismay of his family, act out such beliefs, spending money he doesn't have, running up large expenses and incurring serious debts. He may believe he has a serious mission – as a negotiator of the Northern Ireland problem, as an international spy, as a great spiritual leader with awesome healing powers.

In the early stages, it is rare that anyone save those closest to the manic individual notices very much amiss. The individual may be constitutionally a cheerful person, and a mild exaggeration of his normal ebullience may evoke no comment. Not until the full manic eposide is underway may anyone be particularly alarmed.

A very successful businessman caused little comment when, moving outside his normal expertise as a carpet manufacturer, he suddenly announced his intention of purchasing a disused airfield. His plan, as he told anyone who would listen, was to turn it into a massive open-air stadium where he would host mass audience pop concerts, flying in the performing bands from all over the world. Few took much notice save for his wife who began to worry that he was not sleeping, was irritable and overactive and seemed a changed man. On an impulse he flew to London and installed himself in an extremely expensive hotel where he proceeded to telephone wealthy American public figures seeking funding for his scheme. Costs including telephone bills mounted, but little was done until one evening he gatecrashed a debutante's ball and proceeded, uninvited, to play the drums. Hotel staff promptly concluded he was unwell and called a doctor. On examination, he was grossly excitable, irritable and grandiose.

The combination of over-activity, over-talkativeness, grandiosity and lack of inhibitions leads to extravagant behaviour, of which overspending is but one characteristic, albeit often the most noteworthy. Manic individuals throw lavish parties to which they invite comparative strangers, buy expensive clothes, cars and luxury items, and entertain elaborate schemes and ambitious ventures. Sexual drive is often increased and may lead to sexually provocative and indiscreet behaviour, incongruous liaisons and, in some instances, promiscuity. Excessive drinking during manic episodes is common too.

For most sufferers, mania plays havoc with their public and private lives, ruins their careers and severely taxes their families and friends. One of the most public examples is that of the late American poet, Robert Lowell, as chronicled in Ian Hamilton's superb biography. Hamilton describes how among Lowell's drafts for his celebrated poem 'Life Studies' there is a fragment in which Lowell tries to describe how his manic mental state seemed to him:

Seven years ago I had an attack of pathological enthusiasm. The night before I was locked up I ran about the streets of Bloomington, Indiana, crying out against devils and homosexuals. I believed I could stop cars and paralyze their forces by merely standing in the middle of the highway with my arms outspread. Each car carried a long rod above its tail-light and the rods were adorned with diabolic Indian or Voodoo signs. Bloomington stood for Joyce's hero and Christian regeneration. Indiana stood for the evil, unexorcised, aboriginal Indians. I suspected I was a reincarnation of the Holy Ghost, and had become homicidally hallucinated. To have known the glory, violence and banality of such an experience is corrupting . . . (Hamilton, 1983).

KEEPING UP APPEARANCES

Few of Lowell's friends realized how ill he was during such manic episodes and put his extraordinary behaviour down to fatigue, personal eccentricity, genius, drink or a mixture of all four. Spike Milligan has had similar experiences and again, to this day, there are those who insist that he has never truly been ill. 'He's an extraordinarily sane person,' Michael Bentine is quoted as saying of his fellow-Goon, adding, 'It's nonsense he's a nut. A nut isn't a shrewd businessman, a nut can't write a television series, a nut can't take up issues and see them through, and anyone must be nutty who thinks he is.'

Bentine's view of psychiatric illness is a common one, though rarely articulated so baldly. It is one reason why seriously disturbed and distracted people are identified so late, often too late. People expect them to be so disorganized, disintegrated and distracted as to be incapable of any kind of personal, social or occupational functioning. Eventually, of course, as in the cases of Robert Lowell and Spike Milligan, such a state of deterioration is reached. But before then, even while quite manic or depressed, many people can maintain a facade of function and persuade all save those closest to them that everything is just fine.

Expecting sufferers from manic-depressive illness to be 'nutty', ie chronically and flamboyantly psychotic, reflects a prevailing ignorance concerning the disorder. Manic depression is an illness with a good prognosis in many instances. It lacks the deteriorating and progressive course associated with other psychiatric disorders, such as schizophrenia, which would affect working and earning potential. The onset is generally sudden, without any prolonged period of deterioration. It begins usually, though not invariably, after adolescence and thus rarely interferes with opportunities for higher education. More importantly, individuals with manic depression frequently have a compensatory energy, drive and ambition.

Indeed, the literature on manic depression strongly suggests that it is associated with high social class and achievement. In one study of various categories of mood disorder, the epidemiologist Christopher Bagley found that in the group of patients suffering from bipolar manic depression, members of the professional and managerial classes were significantly over-represented. In Chapter 6, the popular idea of an association between manic depression and creativity is further explored.

CONCLUSION

It is useful and indeed reasonable to think of mood disorder falling on a continuum running from everyday human happiness and despondency through to severe mania at one end and profound depression and suicidal despair at the other. Mood disorders coexist with much physical ill-health and social deprivation. Given these facts, how can we tell if we are ill, if we are, for example, depressed to the point of illness, to the point of needing help? Researchers now believe that depression requiring intervention has the following characteristics:

- It has persisted for at least two weeks with little relief.
- It involves feeling low or without zest or interest for the greater proportion of every day in that two weeks.
- There is a pronounced lack of zest, a marked inability to derive enjoyment from anything or anybody.
- There is objective impairment of function, in work, family, marital, sexual or other personal relationships.
- Suicidal thoughts may be present, albeit often fleeting.
- All efforts on behalf of the affected person to lift the depression fail.

A number of self-rating questionnaires have been constructed to enable individuals to assess whether they are depressed and the extent to which it affects them. For example, the Hospital Anxiety and Depression (HAD) Scale is one that is particularly widely used, being simple to complete and score. By answering the questions the respondent can get a reasonably reliable idea of how depressed he or she is. The HAD Scale is shown in the box on page 54.

THE HOSPITAL ANXIETY AND DEPRESSION (HAD) SCALE

Circle the number next to the answer that best describes how you have been feeling over the past week. If you have difficulty deciding between two numbers, circle the higher one. It is important not to delay too long over selecting each answer - your immediate answer will almost certainly be more accurate. When you have completed the HAD Scale, add your scores for the odd- and the even-numbered questions separately. Odd-numbered questions measure anxiety whereas even-numbered questions measure depression. A guide to how depressed or anxious you are is:

- Below 8 on either set of questions = no depression or anxiety

(1) I feel tense or 'wound up'.

   0 Not at all
   1 From time to time,
     occasionally
   2 A lot of the time
   3 Most of the time

(2) I still enjoy the things I used to enjoy.

   0 Definitely as much
   1 Not quite as much
   2 Only a little
   3 Hardly at all

(3) I get a sort of frightened feeling as if something awful is about to happen.

   0 Not at all
   1 A little but it doesn't worry me
   2 Yes, but not too badly
   3 Very definitely and quite badly

(4) I can laugh and see the funny side of things.

   0 As much as I always could
   1 Not quite so much now
   2 Definitely not so much now
   3 Not at all

(5) Worrying thoughts go through my mind.

   0 Only occasionally
   1 From time to time but not too often
   2 A lot of the time
   3 A great deal of the time

(6) I feel cheerful.

   0 Most of the time
   1 Sometimes
   2 Not often
   3 Not at all

(7) I can sit at ease and feel relaxed.

   0 Definitely
   1 Usually
   2 Not often
   3 Not at all

(8) I feel as if I am slowed down.

   0 Not at all
   1 Sometimes
   2 Very often
   3 Nearly all.the time

(9) I get a sort of frightened feeling like 'butterflies' in the stomach.

   0 Not at all
   1 Occasionally
   2 Quite often
   3 Very often

(10) I have lost interest in my appearance.

   0 I take as much care as ever
   1 I may not take quite as much care
   2 I don't take as much care as I should
   3 Definitely

(11) I feel restless as if I have to be on the move.

   0 Not at all
   1 Not very much
   2 Quite a lot
   3 Very much indeed

(12) I look forward with enjoyment to things.

   0 As much as I ever did
   1 Rather less than I used to
   2 Definitely less than I used to
   3 Hardly at all

(13) I get sudden feelings of panic.

   0 Not at all
   1 Not very much
   2 Quite often
   3 Very often indeed

(14) I can enjoy a good book or radio or TV programme.

   0 Often
   1 Sometimes
   2 Not often
   3 Very seldom

- Between 8 and 10 on either set = borderline anxiety or depression
- Over 10 on either set   = a need for further assessment

It is important to remember that everyone feels low from time to time. It is the persistence of the low mood as well as its depth that is important. The occasional week can be difficult - a high score on the HAD Scale might reflect just such a week, so it is important to use a two-week period to determine whether a depression requires attention. It is also worth noting that whether the depression is 'understandable' or not (that is to say, whether there is an identifiable provoking stress) is irrelevant to the issue of getting help. It is the severity, the persistence over two weeks and the impact on everyday functioning, as well as the unresponsiveness of the low mood to your own attempts to lift it, that strongly suggest the need for professional help.

Which brings us back to the 'pull yourself together approach.' In the light of what has been said about the nature and severity of depressive mood swings, it should be obvious that such exhortations are more than useless. In June 1974, the Broadway producer Joshua Logan described his manic-depressive illness to a session of an American Psychiatric Association meeting in New York. Logan was one of the most talented producers, having a string of hits, including the musical *South Pacific*, to his name. In the course of his frank and revealing address, he had this to say about the 'come on and buck up' approach.

> It seemed to me that all friends of the average human being in depression only knew one cure-all, and that was a slap on the back and 'buck up'. It's just about the most futile thing that could happen to you when you're depressed. My friends never even hinted to me that I was really ill. They simply thought that I was low and was being particularly stubborn and difficult about things. If anyone had taken charge and insisted that I go to a mental hospital I probably would have gone straight off. Instead they simply said 'Please don't act that way. Please don't look at your life so pessimistically; it's not so bad as you think. You'll always get back to it. Just buck up.'

The point of this book is for fewer people to say 'buck up' and more people to know what to say and do when confronted by a depressed person or when depressed themselves. Given the prevalence of depression, all of us at some time in our lives will either be depressed ourselves or be close to someone who is.

3

How Common Is Depression?

*I*T has been estimated by the Mental Health Foundation in Britain, on the basis of surveys and studies, that some six million people suffer from psychiatric ill-health (mental illness) in the United Kingdom in the course of the average year. This figure represents one in ten of the population. The great majority of those affected, some 4.5 million people, are between 15 and 65, the age of the working population. A further 1.2 million are over 65, and approximately 300,000 are children.

DEGREES OF SEVERITY

What proportion of this overall pool of psychiatric ill-health is made up of depression? To attempt an answer requires a return to the pendular nature of mood disorder discussed in Chapter 2. The commonest forms of mood disorder are relatively mild. Severe depression is rarer, and established bipolar manic depression rarer still. The milder the psychiatric disorder, the more likely it is that its sufferer will never actually see a psychologist or psychiatrist. David Goldberg and Peter Huxley, summarizing a vast array of clinical and research data, conclude that only a small minority of psychiatrically distressed people will be seen by a mental health professional in any given year. Most consult their general practitioner, particularly for physical symptoms associated with depression.

The more seriously ill are much more likely to be seen by the specialized psychiatric services. Taking depression as an example, recent representative community studies suggest that about 6 per cent of men and 12 per cent of women each year suffer from depression and at least half of them experience long-term, chronic ill-health. As far back as 1947, Watts, a GP who was interested in psychiatric ill-health, pointed out that while much psychiatric ill-health seen by GPs was indeed mild, serious forms were commoner than was generally appreciated.

One of the first systematic studies, which was undertaken by Michael Shepherd and his colleagues in 1966 and which assessed 15,000 consecutive attendances at 46 London general practices, makes interesting and still relevant reading. 7 per cent of the men and 13 per cent of the women interviewed declared that they 'usually felt unhappy'. 2 per cent and 6 per cent respectively 'felt so unhappy that they wished they were dead'. 1.8 per cent of the men and 2.5 per cent of the women 'always felt miserable and blue', and 2.7 per cent and 4.4 per cent respectively 'felt that life was entirely hopeless'.

Subsequent studies have served to confirm Shepherd's findings. Considerable numbers of patients attending general practitioners do express depressive feelings. But if depression is common, how truly serious is it? A few years ago, a research colleague, Russell Blacker, and I, with the participation of some helpful North London general practitioners, decided to find out. Using questionnaires and standardized interviews, we screened over 2000 consecutive attenders at the group practice. The patients screened included young and old, men and women, single and married, unemployed and working.

Approximately one in every 20 consecutive attenders manifested a depressive illness of a severity similar to that seen by psychiatrists in specialized psychiatric settings. If we applied this finding to the nation as a whole, it would appear that approximately three million people suffering from significant depression visit doctors every year. Since we know that approximately half of sufferers go unrecognized, this figure brings us straight back to the Mental Health Foundation's own estimate of six million people a year in the UK suffering from mental illness.

The cost, emotional and financial, of such ill-health is staggering. A study by Croft-Jeffreys and Wilkinson in 1989 has calculated that psychiatric disorders presenting in general practice cost the British Exchequer £373 million at 1985 prices. The cost of providing specialized outpatient and inpatient psychiatric services for depression was estimated at £221 million. In contrast, the overall economic costs of high blood pressure were estimated by these same researchers as being £337 million annually.

SEX AND AGE DIFFERENCES

There are a number of consistent features of depression which emerge from studies of its prevalence. Women appear much more vulnerable than men. In the community, women have rates of depressive ill-health twice that of men, and in general practice the ratio rises as high as 3:1. Quite why there is this marked discrepancy is controversial, and the issue is discussed in more detail in Chapter 7.

It is commonly said by psychiatrists and others that depression is an illness that particularly affects the middle-aged and elderly, but this may be due in part to the fact that the middle-aged and elderly are more likely to be referred to psychiatrists. Spike Milligan was only 35 when he suffered his first episode of manic-depressive illness. Recent research undertaken in the United States, and the study by Blacker and myself, suggest that younger adults are not immune to depression and indeed appear increasingly prone to it. For example, an extensive survey of mental ill-health carried out under the auspices of the National Institute of Mental Health in the United States concluded that persons aged between 25 and 45 are at highest risk for depression whereas those over 65 have actually the lowest risk.

Nonetheless, depression in the elderly constitutes a major public health problem. When it occurs, it is very severe – 25 per cent of those who suffer a depressive illness over the age of 65 will commit suicide. (The comparable figure for severely depressed people in general is 13 per cent.) Depression is frequently missed in elderly patients and equally often is poorly treated. It is missed because it often shows up somewhat differently – with memory complaints, trouble concentrating, trouble sleeping, lethargy and weight loss. A depressed mood may not be so evident. There is a tendency for such symptoms to be attributed to 'getting old', to be dismissed as an understandable reaction to inevitable decay and therefore to be ignored. Severe depression in the elderly is frequently paired with a physical disorder, such as coronary heart disease, cancer or Parkinson's disease. (Depression may be present in up to 50 per cent of such patients.) But in many others, depression is the cause of all their symptoms. Given adequate treatment, such patients can be returned to an excellent level of physical and psychological health.

A particular problem is distinguishing depression from Alzheimer's disease, or dementia. Depression in the elderly is often accompanied by quite gross confusion, disorientation, memory loss and behavioural changes which may all strongly suggest dementia. Obviously, a correct diagnosis is vital, since depression is treatable and dementia is not. The use of tests such as brain scans, electroencephalography and psychological assessments can help make the distinction.

The occurrence of bipolar manic depressive illness in pre-adolescent children is controversial. Isolated cases have been reported but it does appear rare. For example, in 1970 child psychiatrist Michael Rutter and his colleagues found depressive disorders in only three of the girls and none of the boys among 2000 10- to 11-year-olds he studied, although depressive symptoms were common as part of another childhood disorder. Others, however, have argued that depression is common in childhood but appears in a 'masked' form. Children who are depressed can, it is argued, show a wide variety of symptoms, including abdominal pain, headache, loss of appetite and bedwetting. Depression in childhood is best treated by reducing stressful and unhappy circumstances such as family discord, sexual abuse or school bullying and by helping the child to talk about his or her feelings.

In contrast manic depressive illness is not uncommon in adolescents. A recent review (Jamison and Goodwin, 1991) has estimated that about 20 per cent of manic-depressive illnesses begin between the ages of 15 and 20 years. In general, the features are similar to manic-depressive illness appearing at a later stage.

Marital status, social supports, social stresses and life events are all important issues in depression and all affect its prevalence. When we come to discuss the possible causes of depression, in Chapter 5, these factors will be examined in more detail. At this stage, however, it is important to note that depression in the community and in general practice is common, is mainly mild to moderate in degree but can be severe.

LINK WITH ALCOHOL ABUSE

Complicating the issue of the prevalence of depression is its association with other psychiatric conditions, most notably alcohol and drug abuse. A significant relationship between alcohol abuse and mood disorder has been postulated since the time of the Greeks – indeed, Plato believed alcohol excess could cause mania. Today, researchers and clinicians struggle to clarify whether the link is because alcohol abuse causes depression or because depressed patients turn to drink.

It is clear that alcohol can cause depressive symptoms to appear in anyone. It is clear too that signs of temporary serious depression can follow prolonged excessive drinking. It is also clear that drinking increases in some instances of depression and mania. It is becoming clearer that some manic-depressive patients are alcoholics. In an attempt to clarify the link, Karl O'Sullivan, John Cooney, Maeve Daly and I studied over 300 male alcoholics at St Patrick's Hospital in Dublin. We were attempting to establish how many, following detoxification from alcohol, would show persistent mood changes and how many of these would have a history suggesting that the mood changes preceded the alcohol abuse. We concluded that about one in ten of our male alcoholics had a pre-existing mood disorder while one in four had mood changes secondary to the alcohol abuse. Many researchers in the United States, the UK and Europe have reported similar figures. Some suggest that the proportion of manic-depressives who go on to develop clear-cut alcohol dependence is even higher than our finding of one in ten.

Genetic findings do suggest that there is an underlying biological relationship between alcoholism and manic depression but there are contrary findings and researchers disagree. It has been argued that there is an increase in rates of manic depression in the female relatives and offspring of alcoholics, but again this is not a consistently robust finding. There is growing evidence, however – most notably from an extensive US study in which nearly 20,000 individuals were assessed for evidence of psychiatric ill-health – that, when alcohol abuse and mood disorder coexist, the likelihood is that depression precedes the alcohol abuse rather than the other way round.

DIFFICULTIES IN DIAGNOSIS

Given that mood disorders are common and can be severe, why do so many people – relatives, friends, general practitioners, hospital doctors – fail to detect them? Estimates vary but, conservatively, it does seem that as many as half the depressed patients consulting their family doctors are not diagnosed. American family physicians perform no better. The explanation may lie with the individual GP, with the patient, with some aspect of the consultation when they both meet, or with a mixture of these factors.

The general practitioner

Asked to identify someone to whom they would go if they suspected that they themselves might be depressed, 60 per cent of the respondents in the 1992 MORI poll on the subject of depression identified the GP. In any one year about 80 per cent of the people on the average GP's list consult him or her for some reason or another, and in two years over 90 per cent do – so it is clear that in the UK and Ireland, at any rate, the general practitioner is well placed to pick up and diagnose depression and to treat it, at least initially.

But general practitioners do differ from each other in the extent to which they report depression in their patients. Some GPs do not flinch from making psychiatric diagnosis; on the contrary they tend to be somewhat indiscriminate, thereby including some patients who are not depressed. Much more frequently, however, GPs are sparing with the diagnosis of depression. One reason is that they are anxious to avoid missing something physically wrong. Another factor is that GPs are keen to avoid 'labelling' the patient as psychiatric lest the patient think this is a euphemism for 'not being ill at all'. Yet another reason is that GPs restrict the diagnosis to depressions that do not appear related to environmental or personal stresses, but that arise from within. In such a situation, a severely ill depressed person might not receive the diagnosis of depression because the GP regarded the reaction as 'understandable' in view of some life event that could have caused it, such as the death of a relative or the loss of a job.

My colleague Russell Blacker, in his North London study, noted this tendency.

Psychiatrists, in contrast, make the diagnosis on the basis of persistence of symptoms and their severity, however much there might appear to be a 'legitimate' cause for the depression, on the grounds that such considerations are not relevant. After all, we treat an ulcer whether or not it is an 'understandable' reaction to alcohol or aspirin; we treat high blood pressure whether or not the patient works in a stressful situation.

The GP's preoccupation with the stigma of psychiatric disorder is an important issue. By the time the patient gets to the psychiatrist, the stigma issue has largely been set aside. The die is cast. A diagnosis of psychiatric disorder is but the final act. But the GP who avoids applying a psychiatric label until the last possible moment often feels that he or she is protecting the patient from stigmata associated with notions of moral weakness, culpability and madness.

A great deal of effort is being put into improving the ability of general practitioners to detect depression and to treat it. At the Department of Psychiatry at the University of South Manchester, David Goldberg and his colleagues have built up an impressive catalogue of good and bad professional approaches to diagnosing depression. Some GPs, they note, are just not 'psychologically minded'. Some are poor historians or fail to pick up the non-verbal cues of distress and unhappiness. Some avoid the issue because they are unclear what to do next. Goldberg's approach has been a positive one – not dwelling on GP failure but devising new, more sophisticated methods of training in the technique of the consultation, aimed at improving detection and treatment.

Physical symptoms of the depressed patient

Depressed individuals, particularly early in their illness, do not often visit their doctors declaring simply and helpfully, 'I am depressed.' Most – apart from feeling unwell, out of control, unable to cope – don't know what is going wrong. Like Spike Milligan at the onset of his first manic-depressive episode, they panic and struggle desperately and blindly. Many feel physically ill and complain of physical symptoms. They may worry that they have some physical disease. Some depressed patients who seek help from their doctor because they feel unwell do not mention psychological symptoms, and attribute their malaise to a physical problem. Others will admit to psychological symptoms but only when asked directly about them. Some depressed patients respond to treatment for depression with alleviation of their physical symptoms and complaints.

Patients who lay particular emphasis on the physical symptoms which commonly occur in depression and who play down or even deny the psychological symptoms are sometimes termed 'somatizers'. According to Zbigniew Lipowski, emeritus professor of psychiatry in Toronto and a psychiatrist who has studied somatization throughout his professional career, somatization involves three aspects: experiential, cognitive and behavioural. What the patient perceives, be it pain or some other bodily symptom, represents the experiential aspect. The way in which he or she interprets such perceptions – namely that they indicate the presence of a physical disease – and consequently decides to seek medical help for them, is the cognitive aspect. The patient's actions and communications, that is to say, the actual seeking of medical help and the reporting of physical symptoms, make up the behavioural aspect.

It is commonly assumed that so-called somatization is a form of response to psychosocial stress brought about by events and situations that have proved to be a considerable strain for the individual. However, a somatizing patient frequently fails to recognize and indeed may energetically deny a causal link between his or her physical symptoms and emotional distress. Indeed, they may blame the emotional distress entirely on the physical symptoms and on their concern about the symptoms' medical significance. When asked whether he or she is depressed, such a patient characteristically replies, 'Wouldn't you be depressed if you were as physically sick as I am?'

The GP who is not psychologically minded may unwittingly reinforce the patient's conviction that the underlying trouble is some hidden physical illness by embarking on a lengthy and unfruitful search for a physical cause without clarifying the patient's actual psychological state. Yet failure to diagnose depression in a person with physical complaints can have serious consequences. The person may commit suicide. He or she may develop a chronic depression as well as persistent somatization. The latter development can often result in chronic social and occupational disability and become a serious burden for the affected individual, their family, and society at large.

Common physical symptoms of depression include headache, backache, chest pain, indigestion, weight gain or loss, diffuse pains and aches, dizziness, palpitations and disturbed sexual function.

Psychological symptoms are also usually present but the GP may have to ask about them. Many patients are reluctant to complain of psychological symptoms lest their suffering be dismissed as 'imaginary' or 'all in the mind'. A diagnosis of depression may be seen as less serious or not really a diagnosis of illness compared with such vague but impressive physical diagnoses as 'flu', 'arthritis' and 'a virus'. Russell Blacker and I found that six psychological symptoms helped discriminate between psychiatrically ill patients and those with simple physical illness. These symptoms are:

- Insomnia
- Fatigue
- Loss of interest including motivation, drive and libido
- Morbid self-opinion
- Impairment of concentration
- Hopelessness and/or recurrent suicidal thoughts

While several of these symptoms are common, particularly insomnia and fatigue, this cluster of symptoms strongly suggests a depressive illness until proved otherwise. It is, of course, important to remember that depression can occur in the setting of serious physical illness. Many of the symptoms of depression – insomnia, fatigue, appetite loss, weight changes and loss of sexual interest and drive – can be caused by serious physical illness. The depressed patient needs to be appropriately screened for serious physical disease, without being given the impression that should such disease not be found then there is nothing actually wrong with him!

One reassuring finding is that GPs are less likely to miss severely depressed patients. Even here, though, there are problems. Those severely ill patients who go unrecognized tend to show less overt evidence of depression, tend to look less depressed and are much less likely to attribute their ill-health to depression. Here doctors may behave like lay people, taking what patients say at face value. Time and again, particularly when people muse over the death by suicide of one of their friends, the phrase 'he didn't seem depressed' hauntingly recurs.

The truth is that even seriously depressed people may not complain of depression but rather of a loss of energy or drive. They may seek the answer in a series of physical check-ups concentrating on such items as blood pressure, cholesterol, weight, diet, exercise, smoking and alcohol. The role of shame cannot be ignored either. Many people find it exceedingly difficult to admit to feeling depressed. Unless their doctor takes time and makes the effort to uncover what is actually going on, the patient may continue to lay the emphasis on one or more of the physical symptoms that anyway do commonly occur in depression.

Age and cultural factors

Are there any particular groups of depressed patients who are more likely to be missed? Sex does not appear a factor, depressed men being no more or less likely to be correctly detected than depressed women. Age, on the other hand, *is* a factor. GPs seem more accurate diagnosing depression in elderly sufferers, whereas they tend to miss it in the young. Students, for example, are more likely to have their psychiatric ill-health missed than any other group.

In some non-English-speaking cultures, individuals tend even more to display non-specific physical symptoms when they are depressed. This includes Mediterranean cultural groups, and many developing countries, including India, Colombia, the Philippines, Ethiopia and Kenya. In Kenya, the commonest symptoms exhibited by patients subsequently shown to be depressed are pain, tiredness, weakness, disturbed sleep, constipation, palpitations and diarrhoea.

There is a tendency to think of depression as a disease of affluence. The implication is that in cultures where survival is at a premium, where simply negotiating the basics of existence takes all one's time and energy, depression is not to be found. The corollary of such a view is the exhortation to the depressed person in Beckenham or Berwick-on-Tweed, in Dublin or Detroit, to be thankful for what they have. After all, they could as well be struggling physically to survive in parts of deprived Africa or Asia!

In fact, the prevalence of depressive illness in other cultures is at least as high as in Western society. Studies conducted in Saudi Arabia, India, Nigeria and Uganda, for instance, report prevalences every bit as high as those reported in London and in the Outer Hebrides (Burvill, 1990). The Ugandan study is particularly interesting. Two British researchers, John Orley and John Wing, using internationally standardized instruments, compared the prevalence of depression in two Ugandan villages with that of women in a southeast London surburb. They found that the prevalence of depression was considerably higher in the Ugandans than in the London women – a finding which may be related to the fact that in rural Africa depressive disorders remain untreated.

Symptoms of anxiety

One of the factors that certainly does contribute to difficulties diagnosing depression, and indeed treating it, is that depressed individuals often present with symptoms of intense *anxiety*. Now, anxiety states are common, particularly in the setting of general practice. There is currently much dispute over whether depression and anxiety are actually separate and distinct conditions requiring different treatment or whether they are in fact the same condition. Taken together, anxiety and depression make up the overwhelming proportion of all psychiatric ill-health presenting to doctors. In a World Health Organization study of psychiatric ill-health in four developing countries, anxiety and depression made up nearly 80 per cent of the psychiatric diagnoses. In another large transcultural study, Norman Sartorius and his colleagues showed the existence of a core of anxiety and depressive symptoms in cases of depression.

There is also an animated debate going on as to whether depression and so-called panic disorder are related. In panic disorder, the individual is suddenly struck by an intense fear and overwhelming anxiety. The heart pounds so hard and the breathing becomes so rapid and shallow that the person thinks he or she is about to suffocate and die. There often is associated sweating and chest pain and, not surprisingly, the individual may fear an imminent heart attack. Sometimes, these attacks are associated with agoraphobia – the term given to the fear of leaving one's home and going into other, usually crowded places.

The current evidence is that many panic and agoraphobic attacks are indeed associated with depression and can be relieved when the depression is treated. But because of the prominence of the symptoms of anxiety, many GPs treat depression with anxiety-relieving drugs, such as the tranquillizing drugs, which have little effort on depression. Such drugs are safer than antidepressants in cases of overdose, which may also explain why some GPs prefer to prescribe them to seriously depressed individuals. But the fact remains that they are not particularly effective as treatments for depression. Furthermore, they are not without their side-effects, of which addiction is probably the most serious. The problem for the GP is that, while it is important that he or she diagnose depression, it is not always easy to do so.

The consultation

One of the key features of consultations in British general practice is that they tend to be brief. Indeed, general practitioners can be classified according to whether they conduct fast consultations (an average of seven minutes or less per patient) or intermediate or slow consultations (nine minutes or more per patient)! Patients are certainly more likely to be satisfied if they have longer consultations and their relevant psychological and social problems are more likely to be dealt with. On the other hand, those doctors who do provide longer consultations do not necessarily manifest a greater ability to detect depression than those who do not.

It has been difficult too to show that GPs who appear to interview more competently and who manifest greater skills in managing the consultation are any better at detecting depression. But there are some pointers. For example, in a recently published study of consultations in which depression was recognized, the GP was more likely to have shown a high degree of empathy, to have tolerated and used silence effectively, to have listened attentively, to have made use of the patient's responses to take the consultation further, and to have taken note of the patient's non-verbal behaviour during the interview. Some of this may have been due to the patient, some to the doctor. After all, those patients who are more distressed are more likely to provide verbal, vocal and postural cues as to their true feelings during their consultations.

At the present time, the post-graduate training of general practitioners lays increasing emphasis on consultation skills, on eliciting the feelings of patients and on detecting common psychological problems, in particular depression. Given that the GP is effectively the gatekeeper of the specialized psychiatric services in countries with medical systems like that of the UK, it is crucial that he or she have the necessary skills of diagnostic detection if conditions are not to be missed and treatment prevented.

CONCLUSION

Depression is the most frequently occurring psychiatric disorder. It is particularly common in the general population and in patients consulting their general practitioners. Summarizing a voluminous literature, the prevalence of major, ie recognizable and serious, depression in the general population is 5 per cent, or one in 20. Three per cent of the general population are diagnosed by GPs as suffering from depression in a year, with an approximately equal number of sufferers going unrecognized. Rates for treatment by psychiatrists are very much lower – approximately three per 1000 – with only one per 1000 admitted to hospital for inpatient treatment in a year.

Over a lifetime, between one-third and one-half of the population can expect to suffer a depressive episode of sufficient severity as to impair function and require treatment. This makes depression one of the commonest of all medical conditions. The Mental Health Foundation points out that, when compared with other conditions which command much public attention and concern, mental illness (of which depression constitutes the major part) assumes a massive significance. For example, as we have seen, at the present time in the UK:

- one in 32,000 people suffer from Aids
- one in 50 people suffer from mental handicap
- one in 30 people suffer from cancer
- one in 10 people suffer from heart and respiratory disorders
- one in 10 people suffer from mental illness

That is to say, mental illness is as common as heart and respiratory disorders, is three times as common as cancer and three thousand times as common as Aids. The suffering involved in many forms of mental illness is on a par with that experienced with many of these other conditions and, as we have seen, it too kills.

4

THE CAUSES OF DEPRESSION

*D*URING the 25 years that I have worked in psychiatry and in the media I have received many letters from people asking me about mental illness in general and depression in particular. What, they want to know, causes depression? Is it physical? Is it due to stress? Bad diet? Unemployment? A virus? Is it passed on from one generation to another? Is it the result of disturbed hormones or is it an allergy? The simplicity of these questions is misleading. The issue of cause in psychiatric disorders in general, and depression in particular, is horrendously complicated.

The simple answer to the question 'What causes depression?' is 'We do not know'. One might add that if we did know we would almost certainly be more effective in treating it than we are at present. What we do know is that there is unlikely to be a single cause for depression, and thus far no single cause has been unearthed, none at any rate to compared with the tubercle bacillus in TB or the pneumococcus in pneumonia. We know much less about the way that depression affects and is affected by the physical functions of the body, much less for example than we know about the physiology and biochemistry of a disorder such as diabetes.

But slowly, very slowly, a core of understanding is being constructed as a consequence of painstaking and largely unsung research. Such efforts merit, and indeed are beginning to receive, greater public acknowledgement – which is good, for it provides seriously depressed people and their relatives with at least the reassurance that their plight is not forgotten and that efforts are being made to understand and ameliorate it.

Nonetheless, the failure to identify a simple cause for mood disorders such as depression and mania has led critics to ridicule what they see as an excessively medical approach and to endorse other explanations – existential, sociological, psychological, metaphorical. The extent to which there is support for such explanations is touched on in this chapter. For the sake of simplicity, the various possible causes will be grouped under three headings: physical, psychological and social.

PHYSICAL CAUSES

Depression, or melancholia to give it its older title, was recognized as a distinct disease as early as the fifth and fourth centuries BC. Hippocrates declared that 'fear or depression that is prolonged is melancholia'. Noting that it was associated with 'aversion to food, despondency, sleeplessness, irritability, restlessness', he taught that its cause lay in a disturbance in the equilibrium between the four humours (chief body fluids) which physicians of the time believed underpinned the individual's state of physical and psychological health. The four humours were each believed to be in the ascendent during one of the four seasons: blood in the spring, yellow bile in the summer, black bile in the autumn and phlegm in the winter. Melancholia was believed to occur as a consequence of an increase in the viscosity of black bile. Because it was believed that this was more likely to occur in the autumn, physicians of the time were of the view that melancholia was a disease of autumn. Such an idea has been revived recently.

Contemporary thinking has moved from the humours to a different set of physical or biological causes. Advances in the study of the role of genes in disease have inevitably led to speculation that some genetic disturbance might underpin mood disorders, given their long-recognized tendency to occur in families. For example, the 19th-century German psychiatrist, Emil Kraepelin, seen by many to be the father of current classifications of psychiatric disorders, argued that hereditary factors were evident in 80 per cent of the patients he saw in his hospital clinic in Munich. Somewhat more modest yet still significant hereditary rates are currently claimed.

Genetic causes

As noted in Chapter 1, researchers and clinicians have recently divided mood disorders into a bipolar type, which features episodes of manic and depressive illness, and a unipolar type, which features depressive episodes only. Most studies have found that relatives of patients suffering from unipolar depression have increased rates of unipolar depression compared with the general population. Relatives of sufferers of bipolar manic depression have increased rates of both unipolar and bipolar illness. McGuffin and Katz (1989) have estimated that the risk of the average person suffering from mood disorder over a lifetime (the so-called lifetime risk) is about 1 per cent for bipolar manic depression and 3 per cent for unipolar depression. However, this lifetime risk for first-degree relatives of individuals suffering from unipolar depression rises to 10 per cent, and for relatives of individuals suffering from bipolar manic depression it rises still further to 19 per cent.

The fact that the relative of a sufferer from depression has himself or herself an increased risk of suffering from the same condition could be due to a shared gene. It could, however, also be due to a shared environment. To clarify the possible genetic role in the illness, it is necessary to separate genetic and environmental effects. Before examining that issue, however, it might be helpful to remind ourselves about what exactly genes are.

The human body is made up of three million, million cells, each of which contains all the instructions needed to build the body. Each cell has a nucleus, or centre, containing 23 pairs of sausage-shaped chromosomes. Each chromosome contains a chemical thread called DNA (deoxyribonucleic acid), which carries the coded instructions, or genes, that give the cell its characteristic function. The structure of DNA is a double helix; if stretched out it would look rather like a step ladder. Along its length it carries the genetic code, which is written in varying combinations of four chemical proteins: adenine, guanine, thymine and cytosine. Each gene contains thousands of these proteins in various combinations. Finding a single gene thought to cause this or that disorder has been likened to looking for an ant on Mount Everest.

Before embarking on any such search, however, it is necessary to try to establish that there is indeed a persuasive case for a genetic cause in the first place. Two classic methods have been employed: twin studies and adoption studies.

Twin studies

Twin studies rely on the fact that so-called identical twins have exactly the same genes, whereas non-identical twins share on average about 50 per cent of their genes. Thus a significantly higher 'concordance' rate (the probability of the second twin developing the same disorder as the affected first twin) in identical twins than in non-identical twins strongly suggests a genetic influence. A research group working on the sophisticated Danish twin register reported concordance rates of 74 per cent among bipolar identical twins and 43 per cent among unipolar non-identical twins. This suggests that there is a more powerful genetic factor operating in bipolar manic depression than in the unipolar form. In an earlier review of seven different research studies, the British researcher, John Price (1968), concluded that the concordance rates of manic depression were 68 per cent for identical twins reared together, 67 per cent for identical twins reared apart and 23 per cent for non-identical twins. However, although studying twins who were reared apart does help separate the influence of genes from the influence of environment, it is not without its shortcomings. Adoption studies are increasingly employed for this purpose.

Adoption studies

The underlying rationale of adoption studies can best be grasped by reference to a particular study. Eight individuals, each born to a parent with manic depression and then adopted by a healthy couple, were examined. Three of the eight (37 per cent) developed the illness, as against only 8 (7 per cent) of 118 adoptees whose biological parents either suffered from a different psychiatric disorder or were psychiatrically healthy. In another study of 29 manic-depressive adults who had been adopted as infants, 31 per cent of their biological parents were found to have the illness compared with only 12 per cent of the adoptive parents.

When similar methods of study have been applied to individuals suffering from the less severe forms of depression, concordance rates between identical and non-identical twins and between biological and adoptive relatives of affected individuals converge, suggesting that genetic factors are less important.

Genetic transmission

There are conflicting theories about how the gene or genes for manic depression are actually transmitted. Is there just one gene responsible (the single gene hypothesis) or are a number of different genes involved (the polygenic hypothesis)? There might be one important or major gene working in concert with one or more less influential genes (the mixed model of genetic causation). None of these models has been unequivocally established as the mode of genetic transmission in manic depression.

Linkage

Attempts to find genetic markers have not yet been particularly successful either. One approach utilizes the phenomenon of linkage. Linkage refers to the tendency of genetic variations at different places on chromosomes to be inherited together. Two genes that are close to each other on a chromosome are more likely to be inherited together than two that are further apart. Thus genetic variations whose gene locations are known, such as colour blindness, can serve as linked markers for other genes by 'tagging' their presence and approximate it is close to the gene that controls an enzyme involved in the synthesis of monoamines, substances which have been implicated in the causation of manic depression (see pages 73–4). Detecting the genes responsible for manic depression and the places, or loci, on the chromosome or chromosomes where they reside is clearly a mammoth task. It is not helped by the diagnostic problems which still surround the entity manic depression nor by the need to study very large location. There have been linkages reported between manic depressive illness and colour blindness and between manic depression and certain blood groups but none has been confirmed.

The colour blindness linkage is particularly interesting for another reason. There are, as we noted at the outset, 46 chromosomes in each cell of the body, of which two are the sex chromosomes – X and Y in the male and XX in the female. Defective colour vision is a genetically inherited condition, usually inherited as an X-linked condition, ie the abnormal gene responsible for the disease is carried on the X chromosome. For a woman to be affected she has to have the responsible gene on both her X chromosomes. The gene present on one alone leaves her asymptomatic but a carrier. The gene is accordingly deemed a recessive gene. Males, however, have only one X chromosome, and if the gene for defective colour vision is present on it, the man will be colour blind. About one in 12 men are colour blind, compared with less than one woman in every 200. In 1969 the first reports of linkage between colour blindness and manic depression appeared; the finding was subsequently replicated in two major investigations of the pedigree of manic-depressive patients in the following 20 years. However, it has not been replicated in a number of other studies involving sizeable pedigrees.

More recently, newer techniques of molecular genetics have been used to look for linkages between identifiable genes and manic-depressive disorder in the members of large families. In 1987 there was considerable excitement when a study was reported of a family pedigree in the Old Order Amish community in Pennsylvania which appeared to indicate that manic depression is linked to two marker genes on the short arm of chromosome 11. In the words of a respected American researcher, Elliott Gershon, 'The methodology appeared impeccable and the statistics were very convincing.' The original research group, however, subjected the material to further analysis, added some individuals who had been inadvertently left out, included new clinical information on individuals who had become ill since the earlier report and added two newly investigated and somewhat remote extensions of the pedigree. The statistical analysis now proved negative.

And so the issue of chromosome 11 remains an open one and the search for the location of the gene or genes involved in manic depression continues. The failure to find the genes or at least their location may in part be due to failure to study a sufficient number of pedigrees. The researchers remain hopeful. Quoting Gershon again,

> Mulitple investigators, using presently extant diagnostic methods and the rapidly evolving technologies of genotyping, will eventually study enough pedigrees to separate out the reproducible from the non-reproducible linkages. At present the reported linkages in major psychiatric disorders must be considered cautiously but this will not always be the case.

What does seem clear is that the clustering of manic depression in families does have a genetic basis to it and is not due simply to shared environmental effects.

Biochemical causes

If a gene or genes are operating in severe depression, how might they exercise their effects? At the present time, most interest focuses on three main areas: the role of neurotransmitters in the brain, changes in water and electrolytes, and hormones.

Neurotransmitters

Neurotransmitters are chemical substances released in minute amounts at the endings of nerve fibres in response to the arrival of a nerve impulse. The functioning of the brain depends on impulses, or messages, being transferred from one neurone (nerve cell) to another. Each neurone consists of a cell body out of which sprout short branches known as dendrites and an elongated fibre known as the axon. Information in the form of electrical pulses passes from one neurone to another. In fact, the situation is very much more complicated, in that each neurone may pass information on to several others and may itself receive input from hundreds, even thousands of different neurones.

When a neurone is stimulated, or excited, an electrical pulse, produced by the movements of various chemicals (mainly sodium and potassium) in and out of the neurone, passes down the axon. It encounters a gap, between the end of the axon and the dendrites or cell body of the next neurone – the gap is called a synapse.

When the electrical pulse reaches the synapse, the neurotransmitter – a monoamine such as noradrenalin – is released into the synaptic cleft. (Neurotransmitters are normally stored in small vesicles at the end of the axon.) It passes to the other side where it activates the next neurone, resulting in chemical changes which lead to new pulses of electricity passing over the cell body and down the axon of the second neurone. The neurotransmitter produces its effects by fastening on to receptors on the outside of the receiving neurone. Research has shown that there are many different transmitter chemicals and that each of them binds with only certain types of receptor.

Once a receptor has been released and has completed its job of stimulating receptors on the other side of the synapse, it has to be removed or broken down. If it is not, it will go on stimulating the second cell until the latter becomes exhausted. Enzymes help break down the receptor into inactive substances, which are then usually excreted from the body. Alternatively, the neurotransmitter is reabsorbed into the axon from which it was originally released and stored once more in the vesicles until required again.

One more complication is that not all neurotransmitters act to pass information from one neurone to the next. There are some that do quite the opposite – on being released into the synaptic cleft they actually inhibit the second neurone, making it less responsive to stimulation. The combination of stimulation and inhibition by neurotransmitters provides the brain with a subtle and complex mechanism of organizing the flow of nerve impulses within it.

The so-called amine hypothesis of manic depression emerged during the late 1950s. Around that time the drug reserpine was introduced into clinical practice as a treatment for high blood pressure. Within a short time it was discovered that between 6 and 15 per cent of individuals treated with the drug became severely depressed. It was also noted that reserpine prevented storage of amines by the nervous system. Two British researchers, Michael Pare and Merton Sandler, suggested that depression might result from a combination of lack of amines in the brain and decreased amine activity. Two other workers, Joseph Schildkraut and Seymour Kety, in the United States, noting the way that the brain stimulant amphetamine boosted mood and increased the sensitivity of neurones to amines, suggested that reduced brain levels of the monoamine noradrenaline resulted in reduced noradrenaline effects and activity, which in turn led to depression. Mania was thought to develop when an excess of amine and amine activity occurred.

A related line of enquiry emerged from another observation. The prevention of the breakdown of amines through the use of an enzyme, monoamine oxidase inhibitor or MAOI (thereby increasing amine levels in the brain), together with the addition of the amino acid tryptophan (a precursor of one of the crucial amines involved, serotonin), raised the mood of a group of chronic psychotic patients. When tryptophan was added to MAOI in the treatment of depression, recovery was accelerated. This suggested that reduced serotonin levels and reduced serotonin function could be involved in depression.

The monamines serotonin, noradrenaline and dopamine have been particularly implicated and studied in manic depression. Three approaches to clarifying the role of these neurotransmitters have been explored. The first involves examining the metabolism of the neurotransmitters themselves. The second considers the effects of giving substances which enhance or block the function of the neurotransmitter in question. The third looks at the way in which antidepressant and antimanic drugs affect these neurotransmitters' systems. The research is complicated and continuing. Results are promising but occasionally contradictory. The situation at the present time can be summarized as follows:

(1) Drugs used in the treatment of depression increase the level of

available monoamines in the brain while drugs used in the treatment of mania reduce the level.

(2) Drugs which increase the level of such monoamines in the brain produce overactivity and alertness in experimental animals.

(3) Drugs which reduce the level of such monoamines in the brain produce inactivity and sedation in experimental animals.

(4) Drugs that reduce brain monoamines cause depression in man.

The classical amine theory of mood disorders states that depression is associated with a deficiency in one or more of the neurotransmitter systems at critical synapses in the central nervous system while, conversely, mania is associated with an excess of such amines. To establish whether this is, in fact, the situation, research has involved the following: the study of the levels of such amines and their metabolites in various fluids and tissues obtained from depressed and manic subjects; the study of the activity of enzymes that control the formation and the breakdown of such amine transmitters; the study of the relationship between the effects of various drugs in animals and their respective behavioural effects in man; and the effects of various tests of amine function using hormone and other pharmacological probes.

The problem is that while it is indeed tempting to think of depression in terms of too little neurotransmission, and mania as too much, the supportive evidence is elusive and largely circumstantial. We do not yet understand the biochemical basis of depression and mania. Neither do we understand the way that effective drugs work. The authors of the *Oxford Textbook of Psychiatry* warn:

> In any case, it is dangerous to argue from the effects of drugs to the biochemical basis of disease. Anticholinergic drugs relieve the symptoms of Parkinsonism but the underlying fault is a deficiency of dopaminergic function not an excess of cholinergic function. This example is a reminder that transmitter systems interact in the nervous system, and that the monoamine hypotheses of depressive disorder are based on considerable oversimplification of the events at synapses in the central nervous system.
>
> (Gelder, Gath and Mayou, 1989)

Nevertheless, the amine hypothesis has provided the basis for much of the development of potent antidepressant drugs (see Chapter 8) and as a working hypothesis probably possesses more advantages than disadvantages at the present time.

Water and electrolytes

To those who visualize depression as occurring when the battery of the brain goes flat, the suggestion that alterations in water and electrolytes and an interference in the distribution of electrical charge across the membrane of the nerve cell might lie at the heart of disturbances in mood may appear oddly appropriate. The body's 'residual sodium' (roughly equivalent to the sodium contained within cells) has been reported to be increased in both depression and mania. There have also been reports of alterations in the active transport in and out of cells of sodium and potassium during recovery from depression and mania. Research continues, stimulated by the fact that lithium, a salt which is used to stabilize manic and depressive swings of mood, affects sodium and potassium metabolism in body cells.

Hormones

There are several reasons that hormones have been a target of interest for researchers seeking the cause of mood disorders. First, there is the fact that some hormonal disorders are followed by depression more often than would be expected by chance. For example, myxoedema, which occurs as a result of a deficiency of thyroid hormone, is commonly associated with depression. Cushing's syndrome, characterized by a marked excess of the adrenal cortex hormone, cortisol, is another hormone disorder in which depression frequently occurs.

Second, hormonal abnormalities are frequently found in depression, which suggests that there may be a disorder of the centres that control the hormone or endocrine system (found in the hypothalamus of the brain). Third, those hypothalamic centres are themselves partly controlled by monoamine systems – thus endocrine changes seen in depression might well reflect the very abnormalities in monoamine systems believed by many to hold the key to our understanding of that depression.

Much of the research effort has focused on an important axis linking two centres in the brain, the hypothalamus and the anterior pituitary gland, with a number of major endocrine glands, particularly the thyroid and the adrenal glands. Disorders of thyroid function are frequently accompanied by marked alterations in mood. Manic-depressive patients often manifest disturbances in the hypothalamic-pituitary-thyroid axis (HPT). Thyroid hormones can alter the clinical course of some depressions, they appear to strengthen the actions of some antidepressants and they can even precipitate mania. Finally, both lithium and carbamazepine, drugs used to stabilize recurrent manic depression, have been shown to alter HPT function.

Even more interest is currently focused on the relationship between the hypothalamus, the pituitary gland and the adrenal cortex (the part of the adrenal gland which secretes the hormone cortisol). An early endocrine finding was that cortisol is increased in over 50 per cent of significantly depressed individuals. Even more interesting is the discovery that the normal diurnal pattern of secretion of cortisol is altered in depression. Normally, cortisol is secreted in highest amounts during the small hours of the morning and falls off during the late morning, afternoon and evening. In individuals who are seriously depressed cortisol secretion is abnormal, in that its level remains high throughout the afternoon and evening.

In some depressed patients it is difficult to suppress this secretion. Normally, suppression is achieved by giving the individual the powerful synthetic steroid dexamethasone at about midnight. In up to 40 per cent of depressed patients (some researchers report even higher percentages) dexamethasone-induced suppression does not occur. This has led some psychiatrists to claim that the 'dexamethasone suppression test', the DST, is the first laboratory test of depression to be devised.

There are, sadly, some snags. The finding is not specific to depression but is also found in other conditions, including mania, chronic schizophrenia, anorexia nervosa and dementia. Nor is it especially sensitive. Some very depressed patients do show suppression of cortisol with dexamethasone. In addition, not all depressed individuals hypersecrete cortisol. Nevertheless, the development of the DST is something of a landmark in psychiatric research. On its own, its use and value appear limited. But together with other tests of the hypothalamic-pituitary axis, it offers assistance to clinicians considering a diagnosis of depression.

Researchers are currently working hard to establish the precise relationships between the hypothalamus, the pituitary, the target endocrine organs, the monoamine neurotransmitter systems and the body's 24-hour circadian rhythms. Disturbances in each of these areas are found in mood disorders. Originally, it was believed that monoamine abnormalities were the cause of depression, but increasingly these are seen as secondary changes and the primary cause is being sought elsewhere. The hypothalamic-pituitary-adrenal axis is a particularly tempting target. It is crucially involved in the body's responses to stress. Stress causes corticotrophin-releasing hormone (CRH) to be released from a nucleus in the hypothalamus; this in turn causes the release from the pituitary gland of the hormone ACTH (adrenocortico-tropin). ACTH causes a variety of steroids to be released from the adrenal gland, including cortisol. A wide variety of physical and psychological stresses evoke this response, which is essential to survival. Clarification of the precise nature of the alterations in this system that occur during manic depression may well lead to the identification of the basic abnormality in brain function believed to hold the key to manic depression.

Seasonal variation

The early Greek physicians, Hippocrates and Arateus of Cappadocia, both noted a relationship between the occurrence of disorders of mood and the changes of the season. Many centuries later, in 1838, Esquirol argued that there was an increased frequency of insanity in the summer months, while Emile Durkheim, the famous French sociologist, described in 1872 a seasonal fluctuation of suicides. In 1968, Jules Angst analysed data derived from Basle, Berlin, Lübeck and Zurich, and found that psychiatric hospital admissions peaked in late spring and early autumn.

Such findings have since been replicated in a variety of countries in both the northern and southern hemispheres. Seasonal variation has been reported in mania too. In the British Isles, there is an obvious peak in June-July, a peak attributed by some to the temperature rise, the amount of sunshine, the relative humidity and the ionization of the air. But since these meteorological changes all correlate with each other, the significance of each is far from clear. Tony Carney and his colleagues at University College, Galway showed a seasonal variation over a five-year period for the prevalance of mania in adult admissions, with an admission peak in August-September for both males and females.

The seasonal variation in depression applies not merely to hospital attendances and admissions but to GP attendances too. Nor does it seem confined, as once was thought, to bipolar manic-depressive illness. In our study of over 2000 patients attending a North London group practice, Russell Blacker and I found a seasonal peak in attendances of depressed patients. Interestingly, though, this occurred in January-February, a little earlier than that reported for severe depression seen at hospital clinics, namely March-April. Even more interesting was the fact that while the seasonal variation was obvious for cases of major depression being seen by the GPs, it disappeared when all forms of depression, including minor and short-lived forms, were taken into account.

It appears that only a minority of manic-depressive patients have illnesses which classically recur at the same time every year. An American research group (Rosenthal et al., 1984) reported that about one-quarter of the patients being seen at their clinic for bipolar manic depressive disorder regularly became depressed in the autumn or winter, with an elevation of mood – sometimes to the point of mild mania – the following late spring or early summer. They gave the name seasonal affective disorder (SAD) to this condition. Certain symptoms, they claimed, occur more frequently in seasonal affective disorder than in mood disorders that do not show a seasonal pattern. These symptoms are increased sleep (hypersomnia) and increased appetite, with a particular craving for carbohydrate, in contrast to the diminished sleep and loss of appetite more frequently complained of in the more usual forms of mood disorder.

Several sufferers of SAD related their seasonal depression to day-length, and some found that holidaying in the sun improved their depression. While depressive symptoms could occur at other times of the year, they tended to be less severe and more short-lived than in the winter and more likely to follow a stressful life event such as bereavement or family problems.

In the United States, a newspaper-based survey revealed that the prevalence of SAD was highly correlated with latitude. The shorter the length of the day, the greater the cloudiness, and the lower the temperature in winter months, the greater the number of self-reports of seasonal depression. Longitude was not found to be important. A Norwegian research group found that SAD was reported more frequently in the northern part of the country, being highest in those areas within the Arctic Circle.

More recent research suggests that the episode length of a seasonal depression varies with latitude. Two Illinois researchers, Henry Lahmeyer and Jamie Lillie, reviewing the findings, conclude that episode length in Maryland averages five months, in Chicago six months, and in London 5.7 months, the length paralleling the difference in the length of winter in these locations. According to Laymeyer and Lillie, there is a distinct sequence of symptoms in seasonal affective disorder.

> Frequently, decreased energy is the first symptom noted in the fall [autumn] and is followed by hypersomnia, increased appetite, weight gain and anhedonia. Usually these symptoms are followed by depressed mood, and then typical symptoms of depression such as difficulty in concentrating, self-reproach, somatic symptoms and insomnia occur over the next four to six weeks.

Silverstone and Romans-Clarkson, in a useful review, note that while longitude itself does not appear to be related to the incidence of mood disorders, the sudden shifts of time that occur when travelling by air eastwards to westwards may well be. Examination of psychiatrically ill patients arriving at London Airport revealed a significant increase in depressive syndromes among patients flying east to west when compared with those travelling from west to east. Conversely, manic symptoms were seen more frequently in patients who had flown from west to east. In keeping with these findings are the reported effects of changes associated with the starting and ending of daylight-saving time in the United States. It has been suggested that alterations in sleep pattern produce such changes (Wehr et al., 1987).

The average reader may wonder what all the fuss is about. After all, winter is a somewhat depressing time, and in summer or in periods of excellent weather many people describe feeling a considerable lift in spirits. Surely what is being described by these researchers is an exaggeration of a widely distributed phenomenon, rather than one that is qualitatively different? And that indeed does appear to be the case. Population studies do suggest that, in the northern hemisphere at least, many people who do not become clinically depressed report experiencing one or more symptoms of seasonal depression such as increase in sleep, weight and eating, and some downswing in mood. Given that all animals living in northern climates manifest seasonal changes in behaviour and physiology, we should not be surprised that human beings do too. Nevertheless, a better understanding of the numerically small but interesting group of people showing markedly exaggerated seasonal patterns could help unravel the biology of mood in general and contribute to the development of better methods of treating severe mood disturbance.

But how might seasonal changes bring about alterations in mood? Interest has focused on the hormone melatonin, which is produced in the pineal gland in the brain. Its production and secretion into the bloodstream are closely related to exposure to light. Melatonin is normally only released at night; bright light suppresses its release. It is intriguing to note that manic-depressive sufferers appear to be particularly sensitive to this effect. Melatonin is believed to induce sleep, and a number of treatment approaches have concentrated on the possibility that exposing depressed patients to artificial bright light might help alleviate seasonal affective disorder. The results of such an approach are discussed in Chapter 8.

Disturbed circadian rhythms

A number of biological rhythms in animals and man have a special role in matching rhythmic patterns in the physical environment. Human beings have to adapt to a light-dark, sleep-wake cycle. Various 24-hour bodily rhythms, called circadian rhythms, match these environmental rhythms – most notably hormonal rhythms, sleep rhythms, libido, temperature and appetite. It has been found that in the absence of external time cues, such as changing sunlight through the day, the circadian rhythm of man is longer than 24 hours. This slightly slower-running inner clock is regulated each day to a period of 24 hours by external time cues. Daylight appears to be a very important time cue, not merely for animals but for man too. It appears that the brightness of the light should not fall below a given threshold. Such biologically active light needs to have an illumination intensity of at least 2000 lux. For comparison, on a sunny day, the light intensity is as high as 100,000, whereas artificial lighting in the home has an intensity of about 300-500 lux. Living under artificial light conditions constantly can have consequences for human circadian systems and human well-being.

What is of particular interest at the present time is the fact that in depression a number of circadian rhythms appear to be disturbed. For example, as already mentioned, cortisol secretion – normally at its highest in the small hours of the morning before falling steadily – is considerably increased in depressed patients, and, while it does fall through the day, never reaches the low levels that occur normally. Somewhat similar findings occur with hormones such as melatonin.

Something similar occurs with sleep. In depressed individuals, the amplitude of sleep is decreased. There is a disturbance in the sleep-waking cycle, with early-morning waking (around 3-4 am) a common complaint.

There is also a marked intensification of mood variation within the 24-hour period. Depressed patients classically complain of severe depression in the early morning and some degree of improvement as the day proceeds – so-called diurnal variation of mood.

David Healy and J M G Williams, two Cambridge researchers, have summarized the evidence in favour of the view that at the heart of depression is a disturbance in the biological clock that regulates these various biological rhythms. This clock appears to be located in the suprechiasmatic nucleus of the brain, a centre which is densely linked with centres regulating appetite, sleep, temperature, sexuality and mood. Healy and Williams argue that one merit of any hypothesis invoking circadian rhythm dysfunction 'lies in its ability to account plausibly for clinical features of the illness, in contrast to hypotheses of single neurotransmitter defects'.

They point out that whereas monoamines clearly have a role in the regulation of sleep, appetite, libido and hormone output, simple deficiencies of noradrenaline or serotonin do not lead to prolonged disturbances of these functions, presumably because abnormalities of one neurotransmitter system appear to elicit compensatory functioning of others. Nor can the various disturbances in sleep pattern, rhythmicity and organization or the variation in appetite disturbances seen in depression – varying from marked anorexia to overeating – be easily attributed to one disturbed neurotransmitter. A disruption in circadian rhythm function, in contrast, does explain many of these changes. It may also explain a puzzling fact emerging from treatment, namely the fact that antidepressants, as we shall see, are not specific to one neurotransmitter system. But antidepressants do have effects on circadian rhythms, enhancing their amplitude and shifting their phases.

One other point in relation to circadian rhythms merits a mention. It has been suggested that disturbing the biological clock that regulates bodily rhythms can cause 'pain'. In addition to peripheral components of pain – the nerve endings in the skin, muscle, bone, etc, the nerves bearing painful sensations to the spinal cord, the cord transmitting these impulses to the brain – it is clear that the brain itself is crucially involved in integrating these various impulses and making pain perceptible. There does not appear to be a specific pain centre in the brain. Rather, the whole brain appears to be involved. Disturb the biological clock, the hypothesis goes, and you disturb the brain and cause pain. Intriguingly, depressed patients commonly complain of 'pain', while finding it devilishly difficult to locate. Antidepressants have been found to have analgesic properties although there is no evidence that they possess an anti-inflammatory effect or relieve pain associated with peripheral injuries. What antidepressants appear to relieve is centrally perceived pain and, again, it is argued, this is by way of their effect on the biological clock.

PHYSICAL DISEASE

As already mentioned in Chapter 3, many people when they become depressed worry that they may be suffering from an underlying physical disease. Given that symptoms such as weight and appetite loss, sleep disturbance, pain and a generalized sense of illness not uncommonly occur in a variety of physical diseases, the possibility that depression is itself a symptom of physical disease cannot be ruled out in every case. Earlier, the association between mood disorders and endocrine disorders such as Cushing's syndrome and thyroid disease was mentioned. Some cancers, most notably those affecting stomach and bowel, can initially be accompanied by depression. To complicate matters still more, some treatments for physical disease, such as drugs for hypertension, epilepsy and allergies, and drug and radiation treatment for cancer, can themselves provoke depressed reactions. Mania too can have physical causes (see box on this page). A fuller discussion of drugs as a cause of depression is on

SOME PHYSICAL CAUSES OF MANIA AND HYPOMANIA

Drugs

Decongestants
Bronchodilators
L-Dopa
Steroids
Hallucinogens
Antabuse
Alcohol
Barbiturates
Anticonvulsants
Benzodiazepine tranquillizers

Metabolic disturbances

Postoperative states
Haemodialysis
Vitamin B12 deficiency
Addison's disease
Cushing's disease
Hyperthyroid

Neurological conditions

Disseminated sclerosis
Epilepsy
Stroke

Infection

Influenza
Neurosyphilis
Herpes simplex
Aids

Other conditions

Brain tumour
Post-traumatic confusion
Post ECT
Delirium

Physical causes of depression

Cancer – particularly of lung, stomach, pancreas, brain

Hypothyroidism

Hyperparathyroidism

Steroids

Vitamin deficiencies – B12 and Folate

Mineral deficiencies – potassium, calcium, sodium, zinc

Post-infection – influenza, herpes, glandular fever

Liver disease – cirrhosis, hepatitis

Strokes, head injury

Porphyria

page 89).

Indeed, it is hardly surprising that many people who suffer chronic, incapacitating, disfiguring and/or disabling conditions – conditions that deplete people's emotional resources and seriously limit their autonomy and freedom – become depressed. Depression can complicate any chronic disorder like rheumatoid arthritis, stroke, epilepsy, diabetes, disseminated sclerosis, or Parkinson's disease. In the London general practice study to which I have already referred, Russell Blacker found that approximately one in four of the significantly depressed patients attending their GP had a significant co-existing physical illness believed to be playing a causal role in the depression.

There are other difficulties. Many patients who suffer from depression find it difficult to accept that this is what they are suffering from. They continue to believe and insist that underlying their ill-health is a physical disease. Given that many still regard physical disease as 'real' disease and psychiatric disease as 'imaginary', it is hardly surprising that some depressed individuals persist for months in the search for a physical disease, even if the disease being sought has a worse outcome than depression itself!

Over the years, conditions such as premenstrual tension (PMT), myalgic encephalopathy (ME), vague viral disorders and slipped disc have been suggested as explanations for the occurrence of depressive symptoms in various people. The fact that these conditions are defined in such a way as to include some of the commoner and definitive symptoms of depression explains the overlap. The fact too that many of these physical diagnoses, in common with depression, lack a clinching diagnostic biological test means that it is very difficult to rule out the possibility that they might be present.

This whole area is well illustrated by the condition known variously as myalgic encephalopathy (ME), chronic fatigue syndrome and post-viral fatigue syndrome.

Chronic fatigue

The features of ME include a profound and debilitating mental and physical fatigue and a variety of other symptoms, particularly neuromuscular, cardiovascular and gastrointestinal. Many argue that the condition is due to a virus and it is even suggested that it was first identified in an outbreak at London's Royal Free Hospital in 1955 (hence another name for the condition – Royal Free Disease).

In a scholarly review article, however, Rachel Jenkins suggests that the first recorded epidemic occurred among doctors and nurses at several general hospitals in Los Angeles in 1934 (Jenkins, 1991). At the time the condition was thought to be an atypical form of poliomyelitis. Features included muscle weakness, cramps, pain in the back and extremities which was often excruciating and persistent, tenderness of muscles and alterations in sensation together with feelings of heat and cold. A psychological explanation was suspected for some of the cases but the striking uniformity of the clinical picture and the debility and severity of the condition led most observers to believe that some organic element was present.

In the half century since then, there have been many other reports of epidemics of fatigue and also individual case reports. In the late 1930s there were epidemics in Switzerland: in the winter of 1948-9 an extensive epidemic broke out in Akureyi, a town in northern Iceland, and in Adelaide, Australia; while in the 1950s and '60s there were epidemics and outbreaks in Denmark, the United States and Coventry, England. In the summer of 1955 the Royal Free Hospital Group in London suffered a massive epidemic, with over 300 of its 3500 staff affected. The clinical picture consisted of an onset marked by sore throat, headache, stiff neck, blurred vision, low-grade fever and swelling of the lymph glands in the neck. After a few days, dizziness, double vision, pins-and-needles in the arms and legs, muscle tenderness, apathy and depression occurred. The nervous system was affected with varying degrees of paralysis and weakness. In general, laboratory and other tests were unhelpful although there were in many cases abnormalities in muscle function detected by electromyography. No infectious agent was ever identified.

In 1970, two psychiatrists, McEvedy and Beard, suggested that the epidemic at the Royal Free had been hysteria. They were particularly struck by several features: the majority of the patients were female (!); the intensity of the reaction seemed out of all proportion to the fever; many of the symptoms (particularly the sensory symptoms in the arms and legs) could have been produced by hysterical overbreathing; and there were no abnormal findings in special investigations.

Whether it was a hysterical epidemic or an organic syndrome of unknown origin, the condition refused to go away. Indeed, it proliferated, and to such an extent that in November 1990 *Newsweek* declared the chronic fatigue syndrome to be 'a major public health concern'. Though precise numbers are hard to find, it is estimated that, in the United States alone, between two and five million Americans have been affected. Four national patient organizations have been formed there. The Center for Disease Control in Atlanta, the US federal agency responsible for monitoring infectious diseases, reported calls about the condition running at between 1000 and 2000 a month through 1990. Similar developments have occurred in Britain, and a powerful sufferers' lobby has formed under the influential guiding hand of yachtswoman and ME sufferer, Clare Francis.

The chronic fatigue syndrome puzzles muscle experts, immunologists, biochemists, molecular biologists, neurologists and infectious-disease experts – to name but some of the specialists who have subjected it to analysis. Muscle experts are struck by the muscle tenderness and complaint of muscle weakness but in general have been unable to identify any consistent abnormality in muscle itself. Immunologists, impressed by the strong suggestion of viral involvement, have chased a variety of viruses, including polioviruses, coxsackie viruses and various viruses associated with other forms of fatigue; but again consistent findings have proved elusive. Research has been hampered by the lack of an agreed definition of the syndrome, the varying samples of patients studied, the way such groups have been compared with non-affected groups, and the measurements used in assessments of the various forms of disability involved.

The debate has also involved psychiatrists. The reason for this is that in addition to the fatigue, the diffuse and often poorly described pain and the suggestion of overbreathing, many patients suffer mood swings and panic attacks. The patients, by and large, resent psychiatric involvement. They insist that anyone who has suffered intermittently over many years from chronic fatigue would have to be mentally unusual if he or she never got depressed – a fair point, it has to be said. Psychiatrists counter by suggesting that at least some of the cases of chronic fatigue syndrome are actual cases of atypical depression.

In March 1990, some 20 researchers and clinicians spent a day at Green College, Oxford, struggling to establish guidelines for the future study of the chronic fatigue syndrome, ME and related disorders. The term 'viral' was dropped at the outset. Some disputed that viruses are involved at all, despite the fact that fatigue commonly accompanies and follows infection with influenza and other viruses (as indeed does depression). Given the plethora of symptoms reported in ME and fatigue syndrome, a precise definition of the conditions proved elusive. There was also the issue of depression. Some experts wanted patients who manifested depressive symptoms to be removed from consideration as ME sufferers. Others felt that, were that to be done, precious few patients would remain to be studied! Eventually, agreement was reached on the definitions, which are shown in the box on this page.

Other criteria have been suggested and indeed are in use but no classification has proved entirely satisfactory. The problem is compounded by a lack of agreement concerning treatment. One group of clinicians strongly recommend a protracted period of bedrest followed by a graduated return to function. Others are sharply critical of such an approach, pointing out that too much rest can compound the muscle weakness, lead to wasting, and exacerbate other symptoms including dizziness and fatigue. To complicate the picture even more, there is some evidence that antidepressants can help relieve the symptoms, although whether this is by way of their effect on mood or on some other physical system or function remains unclear.

The taint of psychiatry

Of particular interest to the discussion of depression, however, is the controversy that psychiatric involvement has provoked. Some sufferers from ME, for example, have attacked the notion of psychiatrists being

FATIGUE: CLARIFYING THE ISSUE

Criteria for chronic fatigue syndrome

- A syndrome characterized by fatigue as the principal symptom.
- A syndrome of definite onset (that is, not life-long).
- The fatigue is severely disabling and affects physical and mental functioning.
- Other symptoms may be present, particularly myalgia, mood disturbances and sleep disturbance.
- A minimum of six months of fatigue present for more than 50 per cent of the time.

Criteria for post-infectious disease syndrome

- Chronic fatigue syndrome but with definite evidence (patient's reports are unlikely to be sufficiently reliable) of infection at onset or presentation.
- Present for more than six months after onset of infection or after resolution of clinical signs associated with acute infection.
- The infection has been corroborated by clinical signs or laboratory evidence.

involved in discussions about the condition. The very taint of psychiatry, they argue, is enough to suggest that ME does not exist and that sufferers are hysterical. One psychiatric researcher in this area, Simon Wessely, points out that arguments over the status of ME most revealingly indicate how persistent is the idea that dubbing a condition 'psychiatric' is tantamount to declaring it a non-disease. The suggestion that a patient see a psychiatrist is likewise regarded by many as a declaration to the effect that the referring doctor believes that the symptoms are 'all in the mind' or 'faked' and that in reality 'there is nothing wrong with the patient'.

It is now a century after Freud, nearly half a century after the discovery of the antidepressant and antipsychotic drugs, 30 years after the process of running down the large mental hospitals commenced in Europe and North America and thousands of psychiatric patients began to be reintegrated within the community. Yet many patients and many members of the general public still believe in their hearts that psychiatric illnesses are not real illnesses at all but value judgements, statements about moral weakness, euphemisms for malingering behaviour or culpable evasions of responsibility. It is not only a question of the lay public. Many doctors hold similar views, if Simon Wessely is to be believed:

> Doctors either indicate their disbelief in the reality of suffering or, just as deleterious in the long-term, react to such unhelpful views by totally denying the possibility of psychological distress. Such attitudes have led to anxiety, annoyance, and ultimately a polarization of attitudes between doctors and also between doctors and patients.
>
> (Wessely et al., 1991)

Neurasthenia and ME

It may not help that a number of critics of the physical basis for the chronic fatigue syndrome draw parallels with the 19th century diagnosis of neurasthenia. Peter White (1989), a British researcher, has even suggested that the fatigue syndrome is 'Neurasthenia Revived'. It was the American neurologist George Beard who introduced the term in an essay that he published in 1869. He argued that it was a disease characterized by profound mental and physical fatigue; that it was entirely organic, commoner in the professional and educated classes, and produced by largely environmental factors; and that the treatment was rest. Beard compared the lack of physical and mental energy to a discharged electrical battery. Some years later, two American physicians attempted a more comprehensive if no more specific description. Neurasthenia was seen as:

> a disease of the nervous system, without organic lesion, which may attack any or all parts of the system, and is characterized by enfeeblement of the nervous force, which may have all degrees of severity, from slight loosening of these forces down to profound and general prostration.

Beard was unable to be precise about the organic basis of neurasthenia, but early descriptions emphasized the neurological features. Today, precision is likewise lacking in relation to ME but most protagonists of the organic view believe that there is some disturbance in muscle function in afflicted patients. Mental fatigue and physical fatigue too are common to both neurasthenia and ME, while Wessely points out the similarity between the list of physical symptoms that 19th century physicians ascribed to neurasthenia and 20th century physicians ascribe to ME (Wessely, 1990).

Why did Beard identify neurasthenia as a disease of the upper social classes? It is rather like many of today's physicians, psychologists and psychiatrists, who go on about stress as though it were the preserve of managerial, business and industrial leaders. Beard blamed 'civilization', just as today's theorists blame capitalist competition, the pressure of the market or the demands of constant change. The high prevalence rate of neurasthenia in America was attributed to a number of factors,

> the chief of which are dryness of the air, extremes of heat and cold, civil and religious liberty, and the great mental activity made necessary and possible in a new and productive country under such climatic conditions.
>
> (Beard, 1881)

All manner of features of modern technological progress were blamed: clock-induced punctuality, the printing press, electric light, tobacco, alcohol and 'other familiar excitants'. The fact that neurasthenia was diagnosed more frequently in women than in men (which is true of chronic fatigue syndrome today) was attributed to women's attempt to leave their domestic responsibilities and compete with men.

Just like today's chronic fatigue sufferer, the 19th and early 20th century neurasthenic received multiple forms of therapy. Abraham Myerson, the professor of neurology at Tufts Medical College, outlined the response to the average sufferer of the time:

> Every practising physician, every hospital clinic, finds her a problem, evolving pity, concern, exasperation and despair. She goes from specialist to specialist – orthopaedic surgeon, gynecologist, X-ray man, neurologist. By the time she has completed a course of treatment she has tasted all the drugs in the pharmacopeia, wears plates on her feet, spectacles on her nose, has had her teeth tinkered with, and her insides straightened; has had a course in hydrotherapeutics, electrotherapeutics, osteopathy and Christian Science!
>
> (Myerson, 1927)

The fact that 19th century neurasthenia and 20th century chronic fatigue syndrome look uncommonly similar, and that neurasthenia fell out of fashion when no organic cause could be found, does not mean that chronic fatigue syndrome will suffer the same fate. After all, many neurasthenics may well have had what contemporary physicians would diagnose as fatigue state or ME.

Links between chronic fatigue and depression

But what is the argument really about? If we say, for example, that chronic fatigue state is a variant of depression, are we saying it does not exist, or should not be treated as a legitimate disease, or cannot have organic factors operating, or is not appropriately treated by physical means? How can that be so, given that much contemporary research strives to establish that depression not merely exists and is a legitimate disease but has a physical element to it, even if the precise nature of that element remains to be established? What do those who most object to categorizing ME or chronic fatigue syndrome as a psychiatric disorder think of depression, which *is* a psychiatric disorder? If to be categorized as psychiatric is indeed to be dubbed hysterical, neurotic, morally weak or blameworthy, where does that leave people like Spike Milligan who suffer from depression?

Phenomenologically speaking, it makes as much sense to call myalgic encephalopathy a psychiatric disorder as it does to classify manic depression as one. Neither has a physical basis that can be demonstrated. Both are categorized as diseases on the grounds that they consist of a cluster of symptoms and signs which reliably, repeatedly and consistently cluster together in syndrome form. Both are accompanied by a variety of psychological symptoms and associated physical ones.

It is quite possible that some sufferers from what is now called ME do indeed suffer from depression; it is also perfectly possible that some sufferers from what is now termed depression suffer from ME. It does not help for polemicists to recoil from any suggestion that psychological factors may be operating in the one disease any more than it helps if they recoil from the suggestion that physical factors may be operating in the other. Yet this is where medicine finds itself at the end of the 20th century. There is a hard core of people who insist that manic depression must be an entirely psychological condition because it lacks an unequivocal biological basis. There is an equally hard core of critics who insist that chronic fatigue syndrome or ME must be a physical disease, yet it too lacks an unequivocal physical basis!

The reason quite simply that sufferers from ME, premenstrual tension, epilepsy or whatever do not wish to be classed as suffering from a psychiatric disorder is that psychiatric disorders are still seen by many people, professional and lay, as not real diseases. Tagged psychiatric, the patient fears being left untreated or given inappropriate treatment. Far from being a confirmation of a disorder needing prompt and appropriate action, a psychiatric diagnosis is widely regarded as a denial of disease and the stigmatization of the sufferer as a fake.

For most people what gives a disease legitimacy, what eliminates the possibility that it is pretence or malingering, is the demonstration of a physical abnormality, an abnormal blood test, a deviant enzyme, a discrepant X-ray, a faulty neurotransmitter. The day that a biological abnormality is found in manic depression and consistently replicated by researcher after researcher will be the day that sufferers from the disorder take their place among the so-called 'genuine ill'. Until then, there will remain a question mark in the minds of many as to quite precisely what this psychiatric disorder actually is.

Drugs

It was the fact that the drug reserpine, which was used to treat hypertension, caused some patients to become depressed that led research workers to speculate that neurotransmitter disturbances might lie at the heart of the depressive illness. But reserpine is by no means the only drug that can cause depression. There are many other such depression-inducing drugs. Steroids, used in the treatment of conditions such as arthritis, skin disorders and infection, can lead to depression, as can drugs used in the treatment of cancer. Many women taking the contraceptive pill, particularly the older, heavy-dose form, noted a lowering of mood, and some became clinically depressed. In addition to reserpine, other drugs used in the treatment of high blood pressure, such as methyldopa and clonidine, have caused depressive symptoms. Some drugs used to treat Parkinson's disease, most notably levodopa and amantadine hydrochloride, can depress mood.

Mania too can be caused by drugs, particularly stimulant drugs such as amphetamines, cocaine, and thyroid extract. Given that many antidepressants bring about increases in amine neurotransmission, at least in the short-term, and such increases are found in mania, it is hardly surprising that treatment with antidepressants can itself result in mania. The US researcher William Bunney reported in 1978 that as many as 10 per cent of depressed patients treated with antidepressants became manic shortly after starting treatment. Bipolar manic-depressives appear to be more sensitive in this respect than unipolar depressives, with some studies reporting up to 60 per cent becoming manic. Although there is little evidence that the introduction of antidepressant drugs in the 1950s has increased the overall prevalence of mania, in general it does seem that some bipolar patients are susceptible to the mania-inducing potential of antidepressant drugs.

Sleep

By convention, human sleep is divided into two major phases that alternate throughout the night; they are defined by whether rapid eye movements occur (REM sleep) or do not occur (non-REM sleep). Normally, adults on falling asleep go into non-REM sleep, a period of rest and energy-conservation during which the brain cools down literally while breathing, pulse, blood pressure and some other bodily processes slow down. The eyes are still or move very slowly and the muscles are flaccid. This opening phase of sleep is made up of four stages of progressively deeper sleep. On electroencephalographic (EEG) recordings, the frequency of electrical activity decreases steadily from stage 1 to stage 4 while the amplitude, the energy discharged at each impulse, increases.

In REM sleep, the eyes move rapidly and there is a loss of muscle tone. This sleep period is marked by intense brain activity when dreaming occurs and brain metabolism increases. The pulse and blood pressure rise and fall, and respiration becomes shallow and irregular. The EEG shows a sawtooth pattern, low in amplitude and variable in frequency, similar to that seen in phase 1, between wakefulness and sleep.

Humans appear to need both these main phases of sleep. Being deprived of REM sleep for a prolonged period leads to visual, and to a lesser degree auditory, hallucinations, anxiety and irritability. When sleep is permitted, there is a rebound of REM sleep as if to make up for the deprivation.

In severe depression, there are a number of sleep abnormalities. For example, the period between the onset of sleep and the onset of REM sleep is shortened. REM sleep is distributed differently through the night. Instead of occurring every 90 minutes or so, it occurs more frequently during the first few hours of sleep. In addition, the frequency of eye movements during REM sleep in depression is increased, a feature referred to as increased REM density.

These and related sleep disturbances are currently much studied, but they appear to reflect abnormal functioning in sleep-related processes, such as the regulation of circadian rhythms mentioned above, rather than to have true causal significance.

Paradoxically, many depressed patients improve when exposed to sleep deprivation, although they usually relapse after sleeping again. The therapeutic effect does not appear to depend on loss of sleep *per se*, but rather on not being asleep in the second half of the night. In one study, researchers compared an equivalent amount of sleep loss (four hours) distributed either in the first half or the second half of the night. Improvement was associated only with being awake in the second half. Advancing the period of sleep by about six hours has been shown to produce antidepressant effects, an improvement which can last up to two weeks. (This finding may reflect the time it takes the circadian clock to fully reset itself.) These changes, which are not easy to understand, are used by some to support the view that at the heart of the disturbance in depression is a disturbance in the biological clock regulating sleep.

PSYCHOLOGICAL CAUSES

One of the most influential theories of psychological causation derives from Sigmund Freud. Indeed, two American psychotherapists, Silvano Arieti and Jules Bemporad, believe that Freud's short essay, 'Mourning and Melancholia', published in 1917, 'changed the course of psychoanalysis'. The essay is unusual in that it was the first time Freud discussed the possible causal mechanisms underlying a condition and did not postulate that thwarted sexuality might play a role! The essay is short, barely 20 pages long, yet its effect has been remarkable. It continues to influence theories on depression nearly a century later.

Melancholia and mourning

At the core of the essay is a comparison between melancholia and the process of mourning. Both share a painful sense of despair over loss, a significant lack of interest in the outside world, a loss of the capacity to love and a marked reduction in activity. Freud, however, noted that only in melancholia is there a reduction in self-regard to the extent that the afflicted individual expresses self-reproach and an irrational expectation of punishment. More noteworthy, though, is the fact that the severely depressed person is vague concerning quite precisely what has been lost. Nor are they clear as to what has given rise to the sadness.

Freud decided that the loss in melancholia is internal and unconscious. 'In grief', he stated, 'the world has become poor and empty; in melancholia it is the ego itself.' But what leads to this inner sense of loss? Freud suggested that the self-reproach that is so often a feature of severe depression is not directed at the self at all but at some person whom the patient loves, has loved or ought to have loved. That is to say, the self-reproach is actually shifted from a loved object and redirected on to the self.

But why does the patient shift the reproach? Freud suggested that the cause of the shift lay in childhood. The future depressive, he speculated, forms an intense emotional relationship that is then undermined because of some disappointment or failure involving the loved person. Two things then happen. The emotion originally invested in the loved object is turned against that portion of the loved object that has become absorbed within the patient. Here is how Freud himself describes it:

> If one listens patiently to a melancholic's many and various self-accusations, one cannot in the end avoid the impression that often the most violent of them are hardly at all applicable to the patient himself, but that with insignificant modifications they do fit someone else, someone whom the patient loves or has

loved or should love . . . The woman who loudly pities her husband for being tied to such an incapable wife as herself is really accusing her husband of being incapable, in whatever sense she may mean this. There is no need to be greatly surprised that a few genuine self-reproaches are scattered among those that have been transposed back. These are allowed to obtrude themselves since they help to mask the others and make recognition of the true state of affairs impossible.

In subsequent writings Freud constructed his model of the super-ego, the conscience of the self or ego, to account for the severity of the underlying guilt. But Freud acknowledged problems in this analysis. For one thing, melancholia passes off after a certain length of time. Why should that be? Perhaps, suggested Freud, it is a little like what happens in mourning. Gradually, the affected individual comes to terms with the loss. Why are there particular biological-type symptoms such as diurnal variation of mood, the specific form of sleep disturbance and the marked appetite and weight changes? Freud conceded:

> These considerations bring up the question whether a loss in the ego irrespectively of the object – a purely narcissistic blow to the ego – may not suffice to produce the picture of melancholia and whether an impoverishment of ego-libido directly due to toxins may not be able to produce certain forms of the disease.

Towards the end of his paper, Freud briefly considered mania and suggested that it might occur as a consequence of the individual's ego overcoming the melancholia and experiencing a substantial release of energy.

Other psychoanalytic views

Freud remained doubtful that an illness like manic depression would be responsive to psychotherapeutic endeavours. Others, however, were much more optimistic. Karl Abraham regarded the illness as the consequence of a withdrawal of love during infancy, which led to an excessively dependent relationship with key persons in later life. For Abraham, a repetition of the primary or infantile disappointment in later life became 'the exciting cause of the onset of a melancholic depression'.

Melanie Klein in 1934 presented a definitive paper, 'A contribution to the psychogenesis of manic-depressive states', in which she outlined her theory of the depressive position and the manic defences mobilized in the attempt to relieve the guilt aroused by the destructive fantasies of the melancholic. Klein had conceived of a series of basic 'positions' or phases in normal psychological development through which the child passed.

The so-called 'depressive position' was negotiated by the average infant in the latter half of the first year. Klein argued that this phase is associated with anger, guilt, anxiety and sadness. These reflect the infant's frustration in the face of his lack of control of the resources represented by the mother/love object, his guilt about his own dangerous and intolerant demands and his grief at the impending loss of such dependence. Depending on the circumstances in operation during this critical phase, the infant could negotiate it safely or could become fixated and experience recurrences of the feelings of the phase in the form of depressive episodes in later adult life.

The normally developing child learns that the mother he hated (the frustrating, 'bad object' mother) and the mother he loved (the gratifying, 'good object' mother) are one and the same, negotiates the depressive phase and resolves the issues. If, however, for one reason or another, the anger and frustration considerably exceed the love towards the mother/ love object, the child is likely to fail to integrate the 'bad' and 'good' mother/ love objects and thus fail to develop what Klein termed a 'good internal object'. Successful resolution depends on the extent to which the child comes to feel loved and valued. Without this, the normal ambivalence towards the mother is not resolved, self-esteem is not developed and the risk of falling prey to anxieties and depressions in later life is enhanced. Linking melancholia with mourning, like Freud, Melanie Klein summed up thus:

> The fundamental difference between normal mourning on the one hand and abnormal mourning and manic-depressive states on the other, is this: the manic-depressive and the person who fails in the work of mourning, though their defences may differ widely from each other, have this in common, that they have been unable to establish their internal 'good' objects and to feel secure in their inner world. They have never really overcome the infantile depressive position.
> (Klein, 1948)

The views of Freud, Abraham, and Klein have been developed and modified by several generations of psychoanalysts and elaborated into quite complex theoretical formulations. While there is considerable controversy concerning the scientific status of the formulations, there is much less argument regarding the central contention. This is that at the heart of depression is the notion of loss and the related suggestion that situations which involve loss serve to precipitate depression in predisposed individuals.

A disturbance of cognition

But there are psychological theories of causation other than those of the psychoanalysts. A particularly influential theorist and practitioner at the present time is Aaron Beck, who argues that depression is not so much a disturbance of emotion as cognition. That is to say, it is the negative views that a person holds towards himself and the world which make him feel depressed - not the other way around. Depressed thoughts lead to depressed feelings, says Beck, in contrast to most other theorists who argue that it is depressed feelings that cause depressed thoughts.

Beck, a clinical psychiatrist at the University of Philadelphia, had become disillusioned with the results of psychoanalytic psychotherapy for depressed patients. He was struck by the fact that it is characteristic of depressed people, and not of those who are not depressed, that they evaluate themselves negatively, consider themselves deprived, exaggerate problems and difficulties, and wish to escape or even die. He saw these themes as deriving not from underlying unconscious conflicts, nor from biochemical abnormalities, but from a set of basic cognitive patterns that are activated in depression. He identified what he termed a 'primary triad' in depression: (1) construing experiences in a negative way; (2) viewing oneself in a negative way; (3) viewing the future in a negative way.

These three cognitive patterns, Beck argues, lead to the depressed mood, the loss of drive, the suicidal feelings and the increased dependency that are features of depression.

But how does the individual develop these cognitive patterns? Like the psychoanalysts, Beck returns to early childhood. During infancy and childhood, the depression-prone individual acquires certain negative attitudes towards himself, the outside world and the future. He is thus exquisitely sensitive to subsequent stresses, such as being deprived, thwarted, rejected or unloved. To such stresses, this vulnerable individual responds with ideas of self-blame, pessimism, guilt and sadness. Beck went on to construct a treatment approach – cognitive therapy – which he and those who practise it argue corrects the faulty cognitions and erodes the depressive posture.

Learned helplessness

A third psychological approach to depression is the concept of 'learned helplessness' formulated by Seligman. The theory declares that organisms exposed to uncontrollable events learn that responding is futile. Having learned this, the individual no longer has any incentive to respond and therefore suffers a profound interference in motivation. In addition, he fails to discover what events in his environment may actually be controllable and so experiences considerable cognitive distortions. In contrast, as Seligman points out,

> The fear of an organism faced with trauma is reduced if it learns that responding controls trauma; fear persists if the organism remains uncertain about whether the trauma is uncontrollable; if the organism learns that trauma is uncontrollable, fear gives way to depression.

Seligman derived his theory from observing animals exposed to electric shocks, but he proceeded to apply it to human beings, arguing that, to the degree that uncontrollable events occur in life, depression will occur and self-confidence will be undermined. In contrast, the degree to which controllable events occur will contribute to a sense of mastery and achievement, and resistance to depression will result.

The notion of loss

There is no shortage of psychological theories at the present time. Indeed, the variety of such theories is 'seemingly endless'. At the heart of the majority is the notion of loss – where the biologist identifies a loss of physical function as the causal agent, be it neurotransmitter or sodium balance, the psychoanalyst or psychologist selects loss of love, of nurturing, of security. But the human individual, biologically and psychologically, does not exist in a cultural vacuum – there is much interest too in possible social factors operating to cause or precipitate depression.

SOCIAL CAUSES

One of the most popular questions concerning the cause of any psychiatric illness relates to the issue of 'stress'. Does stress cause depression? In truth, the medical profession dislikes the term stress. It is all-embracing, imprecise, vague. It is difficult to know whether it is best used to describe the cause of someone's trouble, the trouble itself or the impact of the trouble on the troubled! Nor is it clear whether stress is abnormal and therefore something to be avoided and prevented, or normal and therefore something to be encouraged and cultivated.

Such has been the confusion that Lawrence Hinkle, one of the pioneers of modern stress research, went so far as to suggest in a paper in 1972, entitled 'The Concept of Stress in the Biological and Social Sciences', that the term be dropped altogether, since it appeared to have no scientifically meaningful definition. Yet, some 15 years later, in a subsequent paper entitled 'Stress and Disease: The Concept After 50 Years', he admitted defeat.

Despite there still being no generally agreed definition of stress such that its presence or absence could be unequivocally agreed and its elements consistently measured, the term persists. Scientists themselves may disparage it, but they continue to use it – the 1990 edition of the *Cumulated Index Medicus* listed nearly 1200 scientific articles relating to 'stress' or its effects, 'stress disorders' and 'psychological stress'.

What is meant by stress

Nonetheless, it is helpful to spell out precisely what we do mean by stress. The *Oxford Companion to Medicine* defines it as 'the totality of the physiological reaction to an adverse or theatening stimulus, or the stimulus itself'.

The *Companion* goes on to point out that such stimuli include all forms of physical, mental and emotional trauma, 'indeed any event which threatens the body's "homeostasis" [balance]'. Such a definition incorporates the biological alterations which occur when the body is exposed to stressful stimuli – changes in a variety of hormones including cortisol, growth hormone, the hormones regulating thyroid secretion and the endorphins. These stress-related changes have been found to occur in a variety of 'stressed' individuals, including naïve parachutists contemplating their first jump, patients exposed to a wide range of medical and surgical procedures, parents helplessly watching a child die of leukaemia, and students in the midst of examinations.

The definition likewise incorporates those stressful stimuli which for that reason are termed 'stressors'. In recent years, much interest has focused on what have come to be called 'life events' as potential psychosocial 'stressors'. This is in the light of findings suggesting an increase in the incidence of adverse social factors just prior to the onset of diseases such as TB and coronary heart disease, and a decrease in life expectancy following such life events as bereavement and retirement.

A somewhat simpler and more readily comprehensible definition of stress declares that it is what occurs when there is an imbalance between resources and demand. Too much demand on adequate or inadequate resources produces stress. Too little demand on adequate resources likewise produces stress – which is why boredom and unemployment are stressful.

Stressful life events

Much contemporary research on stress has been associated with its role in coronary heart disease. Yet it has long been suspected that there is a relationship between stress and depression.

To die of heartbreak is no mere metaphor. 25 years ago researchers found a significantly increased death rate in the first-degree relatives of 371 men and women who had died in a small Welsh semi-rural community. It is a commonplace observation that depression commonly follows some setback, disappointment, catastrophe. Of course, the association may be coincidental. Or it might be non-specific – that is to say, stress does indeed lead to depression but it leads to all manner of other illnesses and disabilities as well. Or the association might well be erroneous, the depressed person attributing the cause of his depression to the most recent event that he can recall.

Over the past 30 years such issues have been somewhat clarified by research. The result is that an excess of stressful life events has been shown to occur in the months before the onset of depression. A leading researcher in this area, psychiatrist Eugene Paykel has found, for example, has found that the risk of developing depression rises six-fold in people experiencing markedly threatening life events such as bereavement, financial disaster or loss of a job.

Are any particular life events more likely to provoke a depression? Given that depressive symptoms are a normal part of bereavement, it has been suggested that events involving loss – loss of a spouse, of a job, of health, of financial independence - might be particularly potent. In fact, it has not been possible to demonstrate a particular effect for events involving loss. Some life events which do not involve loss (marriage, going on vacation, winning the pools) can provoke depression. What is more, Paykel estimates that of those people in the community who do experience loss events, only about 10 per cent develop depressive disorder.

But there is a link, and it is robust. Furthermore, it also occurs in mania. In a cross-national study of manic patients carried out by Julian Leff and his colleagues (1976), seven out of 25 Danish patients (28 per cent) who were admitted for treatment between 1969 and 1973, and 11 out of 38 London patients (29 per cent) who were admitted between 1965 and 1974, had experienced 'an independent event in the winter before the onset of mania' – twice the incidence in a comparison population. In an American follow-up study, loss-related events, financial problems and employment difficulties were found to occur more frequently before manic episodes (Hall, 1984).

A retrospective follow-up of 67 patients admitted to one English psychiatric hospital during a two-year period with a manic-depressive illness revealed that admission had followed a stressful life event in the previous four weeks in 15 (28 per cent), compared with four (6 per cent) of 60 surgical admissions (Ambelas, 1979). Of 50 first admissions admitted during 1974-81, two thirds had experienced a significant life event in the four weeks prior to admission, compared with 20 per cent of readmissions for mania and 8 per cent of surgical admissions (Ambelas, 1987). The commonest event was the death of a relative, while role loss and work overload have also been implicated as pathogenic life events.

Vulnerability factors

What about stressful events acting as the 'last straw' in individuals who have struggled for some time to keep their heads above water? Two

London sociologists, George Brown and Tirril Harris, have worked hard to establish the scientific standing of 'last-straw' events. In their work they identify long-term difficulties – that is to say, prolonged stressful circumstances - which can themselves cause depression as well as adding to the effects of short-term life events. Brown and Harris also consider vulnerability factors, which they define as predisposing circumstances that do not themselves cause depression but act by increasing the effects of short-term events.

In their classic study of working class women living in Camberwell, South London, Brown and Harris found three circumstances which appeared to act as vulnerability factors: having the care of young children; not having employment outside the home; and not having someone in whom to confide. They also found that events in the individual's past increased vulnerability to depression, most notably the loss of the individual's mother by death or separation before the individual had herself reached the age of 11 years.

These four factors, however, have not been consistently found to act as vulnerability factors. In a study in a rural community in the Outer Hebrides, George Brown was only able to confirm that having three children under the age of 14 years appeared to render the mother vulnerable to depression. Several other studies failed to confirm even that finding.

But another vulnerability factor, the lack of someone in whom to confide, has received more support. A lack of an intimate relationship – or certainly the belief that one does lack such a relationship, whatever the evidence to the contrary – does seem to render individuals susceptible to depression. This may be because the lack of opportunity to develop such a relationship makes a person vulnerable. Then again, it may be that a depressed person has a distorted view of the degree of intimacy that he or she has achieved before becoming depressed. Or it might simply mean that the same underlying problem leads to both a difficulty in being open with people and a vulnerability to depression. The issue remains unresolved.

There has been growing alarm concerning the prevalence of a history of childhood sexual abuse in adult patients presenting with depression. One of the most extensive studies is that undertaken by George Brown and his social research colleagues in London. A community sample of women between the ages of 18 and 50 were studied, all of whom had a child under the age of 16 living at home. Two thirds of the women who reported childhood sexual abuse were depressed at some point during the three-year study compared with 20 per cent of the women who did not report abuse. More of the sexually abused women had chronic episodes of depression lasting 12 months or more. In half of the abused women the perpetrator was a relative. The presence of childhood sexual abuse was associated with other markers of poor parenting experiences such as institution stay, parental indifference and parental violence. The authors suggest that inadequate parental care in childhood produces a higher risk of depression and this parental neglect facilitates relationships with unsuitable others. In addition, the experience of childhood sexual abuse nourishes poor self-esteem, marked lack of confidence particularly in relation to personal and sexual relationships, and intense guilt and feelings of hopelessness. (Bifulco et al., 1991)

Other social stresses

The relationship between other specific social stresses (such as unemployment, poverty, social isolation and immigrant status) and disturbances of mood likewise remains unclear. That such factors play an important role in individual cases is undeniable, but establishing a significant causal link for depressed patients in general is more problematic. In part this may reflect the fact that, while adverse social factors undoubtedly trigger and aggravate disturbances of mood, they are not necessary causes. Many people suffer depressive or manic mood swings without any clear precipitant or adverse social provocation.

But how might stress provoke depression? As already discussed, the psychoanalysts suggest that it is the reopening of scars suffered in infancy and early childhood. The cognitive theorists point to the habitual tendency of the depressed to perceive, respond to and manage stressful situations from a negative and self-denigratory position.

The role of the immune system

The biologists are increasingly intrigued by the possibility that a role is being played by the immune system, the bodily system by which the organism protects itself from, and overcomes invasion by, materials and organisms that are identified as foreign.

The immune system is composed of many elements, including the protective barrier provided by the skin and mucous membrances; the tissue cells involved in self-protection, most notably the white blood cells and cells such as macrophages which ingest foreign material; and the lymph and allied glands of the body, including the spleen, thymus and the bone marrow. The immune system is divided into the so-called humoral system, which responds to threat by producing antibodies, and a cell-mediated system, which responds by direct cell killing – cytoxicity – as well as by the production of substances including interferon which modify the attacking agents. These cells include natural killer cells, which are crucially important in the initial defence against virus-infected and cancerous cells.

A number of studies of depressed patients do suggest, though they do not conclusively prove, that the immune system may be compromised. The ability of certain white blood cells, the lymphocytes, to undergo transformation in response to foreign matter is a measure of their ability to respond to and cope with a threat. In depression, this ability for some reason is reduced.

In one study (Linn et al., 1984), for example, men who had reported most depressed mood following bereavement or serious family illness had a reduced lymphocyte response to injected foreign matter. In another study of psychiatric trainees, in 1982, Dorian and his colleagues reported that the most distressed had a markedly reduced ability to respond to the introduction of foreign material, as evidenced by a reduced lymphocyte response. Cappel and his colleagues in 1978 followed up patients with severe depression and showed that recovery of the lymphocyte response to foreign material correlated with clinical recovery from the depression. This finding does suggest that such immune changes as are found in depression are reversible with recovery. Some studies of depressed individuals have reported actual decreases in the number of lymphocytes circulating in the blood.

Natural killer cell activity is another indicator of the ability of the body's defences to deal with threat, and it too has been studied in depressed populations. In one study of depressed women, in 1987, Irwin and his colleagues found that natural killer cell activity (NKCA) was reduced, compared with age-matched, non-depressed male controls. These immune changes seem most clear-cut in the most seriously depressed patients. They do not appear to occur in other psychiatric disorders, although this has not been unequivocally established.

Such changes may be linked to changes in hormonal functions mentioned earlier. The endocrine system is highly responsive, both to life experiences and to psychological state, and has a significant effect on immune processes. A Canadian research group, with a considerable track record in this area, has suggested a link-up between the corticosteroids, such as cortisol, the immune system and stress (Schleiffer et al., 1985). If true, it may well shed light on what a *Lancet* editorial in 1987 termed 'the importance of the protection provided by a positive approach to life'. The Canadian group points out that a wide range of stressful experiences can induce the release of corticosteroids such as cortisol, and these substances have extensive and complex effects on the immune system, including suppression of the number of circulating lymphocytes. Corticosteroid secretion has long been considered the mechanism of stress-induced regulation of immunity and related disease processes. Clarifying these interactions is a major task for researchers in the coming years. It is yet another research area of promise in the struggle to explain the biological basis of mood disorder.

In summary, we can say that depression does seem to be associated with changes in the immune system. Certain illnesses which involve interference with the system, such as influenza and infectious mononucleosis (glandular fever), are strongly associated with depression. Drugs and treatments such as radiation therapy, which reduce the immune system's ability to ward off infection, often produce depression. In addition, it is now clear that human immune responses can be altered and suppressed by psychological techniques including hypnosis, suggestion and meditation. Controlling for all the factors involved is of course fiendishly difficult, so it is hardly surprising that at this early stage many of the findings are inconclusive. But there does appear to be something there, some strong suggestion that within the immune system itself lies the answer to the question: Does stress cause depression? It looks very much like it does, by way of its effects on the immune and endocrine systems of the body.

OTHER CAUSES

Whenever there is uncertainty about the cause of a condition, theories multiply and flourish. In the case of depression there is no shortage of causal theories, just of established facts. One of the oldest theories is that which suggests that a particular type of personality may be associated with manic-depressive illness. The German psychiatrist Emil Kraepelin argued that people with a cyclothymic personality, by which he meant those of us who have a tendency to oscillate between spells of moody ill-humour and *joie de vivre*, are more prone to develop classic manic depression. Several studies appeared to confirm the suggestion, which anyway had the merit of seeming sensible. In fact, however, when studies have been undertaken involving an assessment of the personality without knowledge of the type of illness under scrutiny, manic-depressive patients have not been found to have mainly cyclothymic personality traits.

Another area that has attracted much interest and controversy is diet. Gross dietary deficiencies, including vitamin deficiencies and iron deficiency, are known to produce depression, which in turn is relieved when the deficiency is corrected. Claims that a particular type of diet can cause depression – for example, a diet rich in sucrose and caffeine – are less easy to substantiate, but individual patients claim benefit from applying various forms of dietary restriction.

Some theories of causation interconnect. The seasonality of depression may relate to monoamine changes and alterations in the biological clock governing sleep, appetite, hormonal output, temperature and mood. A Spanish research group has shown that very marked changes in plasma serotonin occur throughout the year. Plasma serotonin is increased during the summer and decreased during the autumn-winter, whereas its breakdown products show a reverse pattern, suggesting that a faster rate of breakdown of serotonin occurs in cold periods of the year. This might be related to what seems to be a functional deficit of this amine during the winter and early spring. The research strongly suggests that neurotransmitter function, a firm biological factor, may be crucially affected by the environment. In turn this only serves to emphasize that distinctions between physical, psychological and social causal factors have their limitations and that interactions between such factors are likely to be the rule rather than the exception.

CONCLUSION

This chapter opens with the admission that we do not know what causes depression. It closes with the same statement. The absence of a clear and unequivocal cause means that heady claims are often advanced to fill the vacuum. It does seem doubtful, however, that, except in a small number of cases, a single cause will be identified. A number of factors working together – a gene or genes, a provoking stress, a predisposing upbringing, some environmental difficulties or setbacks – seems a more likely bet.

But there may well be a common final pathway, a crucial nexus in the brain where all these factors come together to work their effect on mood. At the present time, the odds are on a biological clock which sets and times our circadian rhythms – a kind of over-riding, control mechanism regulating our waking and our sleeping, our activity and our relaxing, our drive and our rest. The notion of a clock appeals, bringing into the otherwise mind-boggling chaos of the multiple systems of our brain a reassuring stability and order. The molecular biologist and Nobel Laureate, Francis Crick, contemplating the enormity of the problem posed to researchers by the brain, has come to just such a conclusion. Writing of the brain, he observes:

> If the system were as chaotic as it sometimes appears to be, it would not enable us to perform even the simplest tasks satisfactorily. To invent a possible though unlikely example, the discovery that brain processing was run physically, by some kind of periodic clock, as a computer is, would probably constitute a major breakthrough.

In the meantime, researchers, clinicians and sufferers struggle to manage the different causal strands blowing in the wind, chasing one then another in the equally elusive search for the definitive treatment.

5

WHAT CAUSED SPIKE MILLIGAN'S DEPRESSION?

*I*N the light of what is known and not known about the causes of depression, how is one to make sense of an individual case? All these possible causes, all these intriguing theories, all these robust claims are all very well in their own way. But they make it difficult for the individual sufferer to make much sense of his or her individual experience and for relatives and friends to begin to comprehend it.

What happens when we apply what is thought and known about the causes of depression to Spike Milligan's story? What can be said about the origins of his particular manic-depressive illness? Is Spike's illness due to physical disorder, psychological disturbance, social pressure, personality or a combination of such factors?

POSSIBLE GENETIC FACTORS

The Milligan family tree has its fair share of depressed branches. Both his parents appear to have suffered disturbances of mood, although in the case of Spike's father, Leo Milligan, these were not severe enough to warrant treatment. Spike's mother does seem to have suffered depression shortly after his birth and there is a possibility that her own mother may have made a suicide attempt while depressed.

None of it is conclusive but it is enough to make Spike, like many a depressive, worry about the possibility of transmitting the disorder to one or more of his children. His son, Sean, causes him most worry; Spike describes him quite bluntly and clinically as an 'anxiety state – chronic', a worrier who has found it difficult to cope and make something of his life and who clearly makes Spike wonder whether he has some of his own make-up.

FAMILY STRESS

But Spike Milligan's story illustrates the difficulty of disentangling the role of genetic loading from the role of family stress. For example, Spike's mother encountered serious problems delivering and feeding her infant son. His first year was spent not in the family home in India but in an alien Britain, with a mother who was far from well. Such a start would be grist to the mill of any psychotherapist – consider the unsettled nature of that year, the anxiety, the insecurity, the unpredictability. Was this, rather than any genetic factor, the origin of the anxiety he repeatedly refers to? It appears to have manifested itself early on (note his persistent bedwetting and temper tantrums) – and is still a feature of his personality.

He describes both parents as temperamental and dramatic, and so, of course, is he. His father was a gifted musician, singer, actor and comic. He was also inclined to be moody and could break into fearful rages like his father before him, William Patrick Milligan. Spike's mother, Florence Kettleband, had a beautiful contralto voice and was an accomplished pianist. Her sister, Spike's Aunt Eileen, had similar striking looks and talent (even if her temperament was somewhat more subdued – Spike describes her as 'bovine'). Florence's brother, Uncle Hughie, played the ukelele and banjo and was, in Spike's view, 'a marvellous musician'.

The Kettlebands were indeed talented performers and, after they were married, Leo and Flo Milligan undertook several professional appearances, courtesy of generous army leave for Leo. But dramatic and temperamental people are not easy to live with. Their very unpredictability, mercurial changes of mood and tendency to self-absorption engender stress and tension in their children. There were terrible rows between Spike's parents, which to this day have left him with a horror of rows. Spike described their relationship to me thus:

> My father and mother loved theatricals. They were given time in the army in those days. But they rowed – the sound of rows always upset me. I can remember my mother and father having a row in Rangoon which upset me. I can still hear it ringing in my ears, this terrible screaming and shouting. I have always been hypersensitive to noise. We had just come from Poona to Rangoon, where my father had already been posted in advance of us, and I think he had been having an affair with an Anglo-Indian girl, a slant-eyed temple maiden of Kipling, and he was saying 'I only took her out dancing' and this screaming match went on which frightened me very much.

A domineering and possessive mother

His mother's change of mood were indeed mercurial. While Spike does not remember her depressed, he does remember her as a very domineering woman, always shouting, always very changeable. Here is how Spike described the impact of his mother's capriciousness to Pauline Scudamore:

> She was always either hugging me close and loving me to death or hating me and screaming at me. I couldn't understand it. I didn't understand the extremes of temperament. I couldn't cope with it at all.

Children rarely can, unless there is an alternative source of stability and comfort at hand. But Spike does not describe his childhood home as comfortable, reassuring, stable. His mother was possessive of her son and, with his father away on duty so frequently and no younger brother for seven years, Spike was very much the centre of her attention. Right into his teens she exercised a powerful influence.

> When I stopped going to Church – I was 18 at the time – she started an unending attack on me every Sunday as to why I wouldn't go to Church such that eventually I left home and went to stay with Harold Fagg [a friend]. She could be very demanding.

He recalls too an incident in childhood suggesting turbulent and confused feelings antedating the possessiveness and jealousy he recognizes are part of his adult personality.

> I was about six and a picnic was going on. She was very beautiful and I remember one of the chaps who was with her pulled her head right back and it upset me so much that I ran inside the house and cried, I don't know why. Did I love her? Was she my girlfriend deep down? I was jealous.

His mother sent the young Spike to a girls' convent school instead of a boys' school, which Spike attributes to her possessiveness and desire to keep him infantilized and hers alone.

> She seemed to fuss over me all the time. In fact I wasn't able to take responsibility. She did it all, everything. She used to make my bed in the morning, clean my shoes, make my breakfast and I used to take it as normal.

Absence of his father

There were obvious marital tensions which Spike in retrospect wonders might have been sexual in origin. Was Spike a surrogate, a sexual substitute for the father that was never there? 'My father was away a lot,' Spike observed when reflecting on his childhood in the *In the Psychiatrist's*

Chair interview.

> He was a soldier and he was away a lot from home. My mother was very highly strung and not cruel but used to beat me sometimes quite violently, and I think there was this resentment that I didn't have anybody to go to. I thought when you got beaten by your mother you went to your father and vice-versa. I don't know – it's a mystery. I'd like to be put to sleep one day and asked about it.

Later, commenting on his childhood bedwetting, he told Pauline Scudamore:

> I don't know what it was all about. I believe I wished my father was with me more. I think I wanted some extra attention. I remember it was very awful lying there all wet. And then I remember being picked up and dried and powder being put on and clean pyjamas, and then being tucked up again in fresh sheets, and it was a very wonderful thing indeed to be put back to sleep again, clean and dry and warm.

And how did Spike get on with his father when he would return from army duties?

> He would come back and we would all have a jolly time shooting deer. Actually I didn't like that. I remember one was pregnant and it was like an arrow in my head. I think that is why I am a vegetarian.

Virtually every time Spike recalls his father there is a shadow. It is his mother who, for all her temperamental change of mood, made the strongest impact. In many ways it had the makings of the classical Oedipal triangle – the military father and the jealous son competing for the favours of the beautiful if unapproachable mother.

Relationship with his brother

Spike insists he wasn't jealous when his brother Desmond arrived. Yet it was clear that he was put out. The birth was unexpected. He was more than a little baffled by the coming and going. He has a touchy relationship with his younger brother to this day, nearly 70 years later. During his mother's last months and days he and Desmond fell out, significantly over how much each had or had not done for her. The family constellation, with its absent father, dominant and possessive mother and the unexpected arrival of a younger male rival seemed tailor-made to foster jealousy, insecurity and resentment. It did.

A sense of loss

Then add loss to the mix. As we have seen, loss plays an important role in theories concerning depression and it is certainly a feature of Spike Milligan's life story. His early years were marked by the periodic absence or loss of his father. Before that there had been an earlier, somewhat mysterious separation. Shortly after his birth his mother became ill 'with some kind of bronchial complaint' and, according to Spike, 'She went blind and had to stay in hospital.' By this time they were both in England and the infant Spike was looked after by his Auntie Madge, 'my bovine grandmother's sister'. Apparently, however, Spike became so distressed he wouldn't eat and drink, lost weight and was inconsolable. His mother was in hospital for two or three months.

> My father thought my mother was dead. In fact, she recovered. I don't know how deep the wound in me was but I do often wonder whether it all started there and then.

One of his aunts told him of this episode many, years later.

> I was about two or three. My mother was in hospital. Apparently I cried all day, all day. I could not be consoled. It was dreadful. They tried to calm me, distract me but without effect. I often wonder whether that or similar experiences did something to me. I think it could have made me very sensitive about losing things, about loss, about the passage of time, about losing people, friends.

What may have started there and then was Spike's temperamental tendency to expect to be let down, particularly by people close to him. But he was to be exposed to more irritating, niggling losses throughout his childhood. His first 'gleamings of remembrance', as described to Pauline Scudamore, are memories of loved possessions thoughtlessly discarded:

> I suppose I was four or five. I remember being given a *chota bazri* – the Indian for small breakfast – on a tennis court where our beds had been taken out at night because of the great heat. And I remember the toys my father gave me, he had them carved out of wood for me by his Indian carpenter – but I had one toy I really loved, he was called Mickey, a huge donkey – a caricature of a donkey – who used to sit up at the front whenever we all went for a ride in a gharry or a Victoria or a tonga. I don't know what happened to him. My parents always threw everything out, gave everything away. I'm surprised they never threw me away. That's why I've always kept my children's things. My parents had no feelings for belongings.

'I'm surprised they never threw me away' – Spike's lament makes his tendency, particularly evident when he is depressed, to suspect that in the end everyone will throw him away, even those closest to him, even his best friends, even old Harry Edgerton, just that little bit more understandable.

And he does indeed keep his children's things. In his room in his lovely Sussex home, there are toys and shoes, teddies and birthday cards, school reports and prize certificates belonging to his children and exhibited as a permanent reminder to him of their childhood – a poignant, painful reminder when he is low, a reassuring and proud memory when he is well. In those possessions he retains a little of his children as they were. In the rejection of his childhood possessions he still feels his parents rejected him. He knows it is probably unrealistic but he feels it still.

Another seemingly traumatic loss was India. Whatever his memories of his family, those of India and Burma remain uniformly warm and golden, bathed in a potent glow of nostalgia. The abrupt transfer to grimy, cold and comfortless pre-war Lewisham still moves Spike to tears. His childhood India was the Raj with all its glamour, style, power, privilege and hierarchy. His family were accustomed to servants and service. Coming back to an England of the '30s was quite a change. Leo Milligan was one of the victims of the Ramsay MacDonald government cuts, which reduced the armed forces and put him out of a job. Spike recalls playing soldiers with his brother Desmond in their Lewisham attic, keeping the Empire going, while the real army was stripped down. Yet for all his fond and intense memories of India he has never returned and does not plan to do so. Like childhood, it can be recalled but not regained. The memory remains unsullied and intact – and painful.

> I remember leaving Rangoon, I was 14, and I stood on the deck of the ship and I burst into tears but my mother never knew nor my father, nobody ever knew. I didn't let on. I kept that sort of thing to myself. Odd thing but the only other time I remember crying like that was when I was on the boat that was going to take us on the invasion of North Africa. It was late night in Liverpool and all the soldiers had gone down below deck to their hammocks and I stayed on deck looking at the water and I burst into uncontrollable fits of crying. Perhaps I recalled the previous trip. I am not very good at leaving things.

PERSONALITY OF THE YOUNG MAN

A family loading for moodiness, depression, irritability, dramatic ability and a fair share of separations, losses, perhaps rejections. What of Spike's personality? It is difficult to obtain a clear view of his personality before the war and his war injury. Spike himself says:

> I think sometimes when I was young, in my 20s and 30s, I was manic and rattled away and talked very fast and joked and all that but I wasn't in a state of illness at that time. But the personality was there.

He also could recall periods of feeling low and lacking in drive, but the episodes never lasted long and were never severe. In other ways, he was gregarious and agreeable, made some good and lasting friendships, including girlfriends, and sustained a series of jobs before joining the army just before the fall of Dunkirk in 1940.

But there is more than a suggestion of a cyclothymic personality – a personality marked by traits of moodiness, with rapid alternation between cheerfulness, activity, optimism and productivity on the one hand and gloominess, inactivity, pessimism and indecision on the other. Such a personality, as we saw in Chapter 4, was once thought prone to develop manic depression under stress. This certainly is a currently popular model of causation, not merely in the case of manic depression but in the case of many different psychiatric disorders. A genetic factor, an early family environment conducive to creating anxiety and 'nervousness', a personality predisposed to a certain kind of illness under stress – and then the stress. In Spike Milligan's case, the stress came with the war. To be more precise it occurred on 22nd January, 1944.

THE WAR TRAUMA

Gunner Terence Milligan was with D Battery of the 50th Heavy Regiment of the Royal Artillery, fighting its way up Italy and towards Monte Cassino. He had joined the army on 2nd June, 1940, and had seen action in North Africa. While he had missed his family and friends on joining up, he had escaped from drab suburbia, initially to the space and beauty of the English countryside around his barracks in Bexhill and then abroad. In the preface to Volume I of his autobiography, *Adolf Hitler: My Part in His Downfall*, Spike Milligan wrote, 'The experience of being in the army changed my whole life.'

On 22nd January, Milligan was on his way to an operation point, in some considerable pain from bleeding piles. There was heavy mortar shelling and he was wounded in the left leg. The soldier with him carried him to the nearest first-aid post. Gunner Milligan was by now shaking, weeping and incoherent. A sarcastic major lectured him for failing to reach the operation point. Of that moment Pauline Scudamore has written:

> The words, and the implication, were to live in Spike's memory. At the back of his mind the fear that he might, at some level, have acted in a cowardly way tormented him. Milligan is fundamentally a courageous man – the lifelong battle he has fought with his manic-depressive illness would seem to confirm this – but he has never quite assuaged the self-doubt that began that day.

After a few hours in a dressing station, he was sent to a reception centre for the wounded at Naples. He was weepy, frightened, lethargic and ill. Nearly 40 years later I asked him to recall the experience:

CLARE: When you had your first breakdown were you invalided out of the army?

MILLIGAN: No, they gave me some tablets. It was the early days of deep narcosis; they gave me some early tranquillizers, I think, which sent me to sleep, sent me out of the lines for seven days. Then they sent me up to the guns and as soon as I heard them go I started to stammer. I don't know to this day whether I induced the stammer myself because having failed to get out of the army one way I thought the stammer might do it. I don't know if I am making this up or not, but I've always been guilty about the fact that I might have run away – and I should hate to think I did, because I didn't want to. I thought it was a just war for a just cause.

CLARE: And what happened then?

MILLIGAN: Then, in the sort of state I was in, they took me out of the line and I went to a psychiatrist. And he said, 'I'm sorry, it would be dangerous for you to go up the line in this condition. It wouldn't be fair to your comrades.' And I said, 'I see that. Will it get better?' He said, 'I don't know. On the whole it doesn't seem that people like you do. We'll put you at a base camp.' So I went to a base camp and had a couple more breakdowns while I was there and that put paid to me. I did try to get back to the regiment, though. I wrote to the major but they wouldn't have it, which I understand now. Can't have duff people in the firing line.

CLARE: Did you feel a sense of failure?

MILLIGAN: Yes, and the major stood me up and said, 'You're a coward.' That was an appalling thing to say to a man. No crime in being a coward, mind you, but I didn't think I was a coward inasmuch as I'd been in action all through the North African campaign and all the way up to Cassino. If I'd been a coward I would have run away the first day, wouldn't I? I think I just ran out of steam, that's all.

That was in 1982. Nearly ten years later we again discussed the events of 22nd January, 1944, and the whole dreadful business seemed as vivid as ever. He remained troubled by the accusation of cowardice, shaken by what it suggested about his character.

A thing that worried me very much, Anthony, was coming from a soldier family, even though I got mentioned in dispatches at the beginning of the war and I was promoted in the field, when I finally folded up in action I formed this terrible mental image of being a coward. The major demoted me at the time as unsuitable – of course I was unsuitable. I was ill! But he came and court-martialled me, this bastard, in a tent in the front line. And me – I didn't know what day it was – it was the 22nd January, 1944. I don't think I was a coward.

Post-traumatic stress syndrome

For some months Spike Milligan suffered the psychological consequences of the mortar blast. There were recurrent intrusive recollections of the event, nightmares, a marked lack of interest in life, a persistent and nagging guilt at having let himself and others down, considerable difficulties concentrating and avoidance of anything that served to remind him of what had happened. This cluster of symptoms is now recognized as post-traumatic stress syndrome. Then it was lumped under the general term 'psychoneurosis' and deemed to be largely untreatable. To this day Spike wonders whether he might have suffered a personality change as a result of this experience. He lost his temper easily, behaved self-destructively, cutting himself on one occasion with razor blades. But eventually he recovered.

Did this experience cause his manic-depressive illness? I doubt it very much. He was not to experience the first serious episode of that illness for a further nine years. In the meantime he was demobbed and slowly but surely developed his career as a writer, comedian, musician and performer. Throughout those years he survived various vicissitudes, but he cannot recall, and I am unable to find, any evidence that he suffered mood swings of any noticeable severity.

Of course the war injury didn't help. It certainly affected his ability to cope. It massively assaulted his confidence. He was a military man from a military family; and he had been accused of being a coward. To this day, when Spike encounters a particularly stressful, psychologically painful situation, he is certainly tempted – out of a lack of confidence in himself – to opt out, swallow a large dose of sedatives and take to his bed until the problem passes.

So, thus far, how does it look? A genetic loading, a series of separations and losses, a traumatic war injury – all contributing to a personal fragility, a predisposition to crack under strain. And there came, indeed, a mighty strain. It might not seem in the same league as a bomb explosion but its effect on the life and family of Spike Milligan was to prove even more traumatic.

SCRIPTWRITING AT FEVER PITCH

On 28th May, 1951, the first *Goon Show* was broadcast by the BBC. Before Spike Milligan's brilliant inventive skills as comic and scriptwriter were joined with Harry Secombe, Peter Sellers and Michael Bentine (who was to drop out after the second series), he had already established himself as a burgeoning talent, not least with the successful radio series *Crazy People*. The Goons were to ensure him radio immortality.

Yet Spike Milligan has much reason to regard his period as scriptwriter with the Goons with considerably mixed feelings. His was the responsibility to devise and write the scripts, to indicate the sound effects, and then bully, cajole and plead with an often unhelpful BBC Sound Effects department to produce the goods. He would write the script for the next week's show in a fever of creative inventiveness, working right up to the deadline and right into the night. During this time, he manifested in full measure one of the characteristic traits of the manic-depressive, certainly during a hypomanic phase – the ability to function on a few hours of sleep and to operate at a high energy level for hours on end.

Reflecting on those weeks 40 years later, Spike Milligan still winces at the toll the process took of his physical and mental health. He recalls the irritability, the haunting deadline and the enormous sense of pressure he felt. The whole show, the performance of the other three, the quality of the material, the very humour itself depended on his ability to dredge up out of his often weary mind novel, idiosyncratic, incongruous and hilarious comic material.

At times his frustration was vented in outbursts of rage and weeping. He felt continuously on edge. What kept him going? Quite simply, it was the fear of financial disaster, he insists. It compelled him to churn out *Goon Show* scripts at a rate of 26 a year from 1953 to 1959.

While at times Spike Milligan is tempted to identify the war trauma as the beginning of his illness, more frequently and more convincingly he points the finger at this extraordinarily stressful period in his life. Nearly 40 years after the beginning of that remarkable series, he replied to my query about the valuation he put on the whole experience with unexpected bitterness:

> I was so ill when I wrote those scripts, particularly at the beginning, that now, when I think back, that is what I remember. Of course I take pleasure in the fact that I made people laugh and the scripts still do. But it was at a terrible price for me. If I could choose now, which of course I cannot, I think I would choose to be free of the illness and not to have written the Goons. It took that much out of me. It caused me that much pain – and pain to my wife and children too.

As we have seen in Chapter 4, stressful life events frequently precede the onset of a severe psychiatric illness, and Spike Milligan's illness was no exception. Consider the events around the time of his breakdown. He had not been long married. He was just about coping with his first wife, June, his newborn first child, Laura, and the need to keep writing. And there was to be a 'last straw' stress too. It was that stream of letters from the BBC, concerning the late arrival of his scripts, which he himself is convinced broke him. Pauline Scudamore describes how one particularly distressing letter arrived after a dreadful night during which his wife had been in great discomfort from a breast abscess and the baby had cried without pause. Spike, exhausted and sleepless, was working on the latest script. The letter read:

> Dear Mr Milligan,
> It has been reported to me by Mr Peter Eton that despite his constant requests for early delivery, your scripts for the above production continue to arrive late – in some cases not until the morning of the pre-recording.

'Perhaps the letters were the last straw,' writes Pauline Scudamore.

Poor Spike clutched his head, felt he was going mad, couldn't go on. The episode with Peter Sellers and the knife followed, and Spike ended up hospitalized.

OTHER POSSIBLE FACTORS

What about the other causes which have been suggested in manic depression? There is no seasonal pattern to Spike Milligan's illnesses, no apparent relationship with physical ill-health. He was not taking stimulants at the time of the onset of his first illness (although one might not have been surprised to learn that he had been taking them, given the need to avoid sleep and keep working). Sleep deprivation itself can provoke manic and depressed swings in some individuals, and lack of sleep may well have been an important provocation in his case. More often, however, disturbances in sleep are symptoms rather than causes of the mood swings.

The secret son

While I was writing this book, it emerged that for 17 years Spike Milligan had had a child by another woman. During the early 1970s, while he was married to his second wife, Paddy (Patricia Ridgeway), Spike, then in his mid-50s, had met a 26-year-old artist, Margaret Maughan, and began an affair that was to last eight years. In an article in *The News of the World* (19th January, 1992), a claim was made to the effect that the strain of his secret son and the stress of public life led him to a nervous breakdown. 'I've been a manic-depressive for two years now,' Spike was quoted as saying, 'and go to a group for help. I'm 73 but going on 90.'

While having to conceal the existence of his son hardly helped him cope with his manic-depressive illness, there is little to suggest that it caused it. Spike's first illness occurred some 20 years before the affair, and he had already had a number of breakdowns and hospitalizations in a variety of mental hospitals before he met Margaret Maughan. Indeed, in 1970, not long before he met her, he appeared in a documentary for Granada Television entitled *The Other Spike*, produced by John Goldschmidt. In it he appeared as himself and as his own psychiatrist and relived his experiences, agonizing and therapeutic, of isolation wards and mental hospitals. It was one of the first attempts by a sufferer to explain the mysteries of manic depression to the general public.

When I talked to Spike about his son James, the story had broken some weeks before, and father and son had just met each other for the first time.

MILLIGAN: Yes, I had a child by Margaret Maughan. Silly moment in time, you know. I had him up here for his holidays. He is 15, 16 now. I supported him.

CLARE: Who would have known?

MILLIGAN: Only me and his mother; Shelagh knew.

CLARE: Were you upset when it was revealed?

MILLIGAN: I wasn't upset. The journalists tried to make me deny it. I told them, 'I'm his father.' I told them I maintained his schooling and education, etc, gave an allowance. It was just one of those things. But they wanted me to deny it – 'It's not my child' – it wouldn't make a good story otherwise. One chap came all the way out here [to Sussex] and said, 'Don't you deny it?' I said, 'No.' He went away flabbergasted.

CLARE: But why had you denied it for so long?

MILLIGAN: I don't really know. I worried about people who didn't know. I am glad that my mother and father weren't alive when it came out. They thought I was the acme of purity. I had my own wife and children at the time – I wanted to spare them and me the publicity. I didn't meet him because I just didn't believe I could cope with it.

CLARE: His mother honoured the secret for 16 years. Why do you think she broke it now?

MILLIGAN: She went to the newspapers. For some money, I suppose. Good luck to her.

CLARE: Did you have any inkling that she was going to do this?

MILLIGAN: None at all. Although it's silly. You can't be father to two separate families. You can't have two wives. One has to go by the board. I helped her as much as I could. I stayed in touch. Now here I am talking about overpopulation! I haven't a ghost of a chance in the witness box!

CLARE: What does James make of you?

MILLIGAN: When we met for the first time, he called me Spike. We went out for dinner together. He likes football. He knew I was his father from the beginning, I think.

In fact, Margaret Maughan insists that she broke the secret because her son desperately wanted to meet his father, of whom he is very proud. At the time of the newspaper articles she expressed the fervent wish that they would meet. 'It would,' she said, 'be the perfect ending to a very sad episode.'

When the news broke of his secret son, Spike was beginning to recover from the depressive swing that had commenced after the death of his mother 18 months earlier. Interviews published in the papers at the time, and before he had met James, suggested that Spike was a broken man. He was reported as declaring that other people appeared to have sorted out their lives, but his appeared a mess. He was quoted as saying that he worried about everything, 'from money to the state of the environment'.

He fretted over a book he wanted to write but just could not get the inspiration 'because of the way I feel'.

Four months later, when I returned to the subject of James, he was better. His book *Peace Work* had been published, he had met his son and he had told his other four children of James's existence. He still regretted that it had happened, yet could joke, 'It was Chateauneuf du Pape that did it. I'm going to sue the company!' Yes, he accepted that it had been difficult, painful, even emotionally damaging for James to have known that Spike was his father, to have seen him on television, yet not to have been able to see him, talk to him, be acknowledged by him as his son. But he had not known what else he could do. 'I think he can cope now, he is a young man. I can cope now although I am an old man. I hope his mother can cope.'

Just what Spike felt like at the time can be gained from reading a letter he wrote to Margaret Maughan two weeks after James was born. He writes:

> You have a baby – I am the father. I should come and see you but I'm not like any other person in the street, everybody recognizes me. I'm well-known so if anything scandalous occurred in my life . . . It would make great newspaper copy if it got out that I was father of your child.
>
> It would be on the front page of every daily paper . . . it would destroy me, my wife would sue for a divorce. I would be separated from my children, you and the baby would be front-page news . . . it would destroy all the relationships . . . no one would get anything.

Margaret Maughan kept the secret and Spike Milligan stayed away. The affair ended with Spike asking that his son's second name be Turlough (what he called 'the Anglo-Irish for Terence', his own name). Paddy, his wife at the time, was dying of cancer. Jane, his daughter by her, was only ten. Laura, Sean and Sile, his children by his first wife, were 20, 18 and 16 respectively. He was desperate to keep the affair and child from them, and it did take its toll. It is clear from letters he wrote at the time that he was depressed. 'I have no desire to live or go on . . . I did the Newcastle Jazz – it was agony to try and appear carefree and happy. I don't see any future for myself,' he wrote in one. 'It's like running the hundred yards with broken legs,' he wrote in another. Yet he survived and recovered until the next stress, the next episode triggered him off into another low.

I do not believe that his affair and secret son made Spike Milligan a manic-depressive. Not everything that happens to someone with manic depression is linked with the illness. It is true that some sufferers, particularly when manic, engage in transient extramarital affairs, but Spike's affair does not appear to have been that kind of relationship. It lasted not weeks nor months but eight years. Both parties testify to its seriousness. Spike sustained it through highs and lows, and no matter how high or low he was, he never revealed it – not even to doctors, relatives or friends.

PSYCHO-ANALYTIC THEORIES

How do psychoanalytic theories relate to Spike Milligan's illness? As we saw in Chapter 4, Freud suggested that the self-reproach which is such a feature of depression is in fact misdirected. It is actually intended for some person the patient loves. The self-reproach is shifted from this loved one and redirected on to the self. In Spike's case, his mother appears the likeliest candidate. Time and again, as he spoke of her a profound ambivalence showed. He clearly loved her yet resented the extent to which she dominated people around her, including him.

> I found her difficult to handle. She was very house-proud. I don't remember bringing home any friends to the house. She was enormously sensitive to what people thought – especially people in authority, doctors, lawyers, priests. Her feelings wildly oscillated. It was not easy to be absolutely relaxed when she was around.

Or again:

> She was quite a character out in Woy Woy [Australia]. Everyone knew her. She was quite proud of me and I suppose I was of her. She was a survivor, you know, a survivor.

Yet it was clear from what he said that her death had been a blow and a loss that provoked another severe depressive swing. She had been ill for some time, and in June 1990 she died. Spike had flown out to visit her in Australia earlier that year. Had he tried to prepare himself for her death?

> Isn't it funny, I couldn't imagine her dying. There seemed a permanency, and the shock now of realizing that she's dead is having a depressing effect. I didn't say goodbye to her before she died. I couldn't bear saying, 'Goodbye forever, Mum' – she was in hospital in a bed and I said, 'I'm going now, Mum, bye bye,' and she said, 'Bye bye, son' and that was it. I feel like that Dylan Thomas poem – 'Do not go gentle into this good night. Rage, rage against the dying of the light.' She died about ten days after I got back to Britain.

Psychoanalytical psychotherapy would unquestionably focus on Spike's relationship with his mother, his feelings of loss and resentment, his ambivalence and possessiveness concerning her and feelings of jealousy and loss following his brother Desmond's birth. Spike admired his mother's stamina and vitality. He resented the difficulties she had in expressing her feelings for him, particularly as these difficulties had affected him in earlier life. He was prepared to consider the possibility that some of his anger and hostility had been turned inwards and fuelled his depression.

As we noted in Chapter 4, Karl Abraham emphasized the withdrawal of love during infancy as a factor in melancholia – Spike's mother had been ill and temperamental. Melanie Klein made much of disturbance during the infant's first year and the tendency for the growing child to split mother into a good and a bad object – there is not much disagreement over the fact that Spike's first year was a particularly unpredictable one. So the possibility that his adult melancholic swings reflect a personality, an attitude, a predisposition laid down in early childhood, is plausible. The problem is that, while such psychoanalytic theories are often plausible, applying them rarely results in significant improvement of a severe mood swing. As for Spike, 70 years on, he finds it difficult to confirm or deny my suggestions, speculations and interpretations concerning his early experiences and memories.

MILLIGAN'S ATTITUDE TO LIFE

What of Aaron Beck's suggestion, also discussed in Chapter 4, that it is the way we look at the world that makes us depressed rather than the other way around? It is certainly true that Spike Milligan's thoughts when he is depressed are appallingly gloomy and incorrigibly pessimistic. When he is feeling well he retains some of the pessimism and a fair dollop of gloom, particularly about the human race. But he has strongly positive views of his talent, his abilities, his professionalism right through health and illness. It would be a mistake to believe that even when profoundly depressed Spike Milligan is uniformly self-denigratory and destructive. It is easier to see how his general attitude to life – one of scepticism, suspicion and pessimism – can aggravate a depression when it occurs than to see it actually causing the depression to occur.

Take, for example, his pugnacious views on overpopulation. When I first came to interview him in November 1990, he was seriously depressed, irritable and incorrigibly gloomy. Nonetheless, having asked me how many children I had and on learning I had seven, he launched into a passionate and animated attack on my irresponsibility:

MILLIGAN: How can you bring so many children into a world that is grossly overcrowded, polluted, packed like sardines? How can you be so irresponsible? The world has too many people as it is! Cecil Parkinson said that on Easter Monday there were so many people on the Underground platforms they had to shut them. I suggested that they should join the platforms together so that the passengers could just walk from one Underground station to the next! Peter Bottomley, this is the Minister for Roads, he says, 'There is nothing I can do about the traffic jams in London. It is a sign of prosperity.' So when everything comes to a grinding halt, we are going to be amazingly rich! People are ruining the planet with their plastic rubbish, their pollution, noise, garbage. And you go and bring another seven into what is already an overcrowded mess.

CLARE: You make people sound like vermin. I have just come back from Hungary. There is a country which is hardly reproducing itself.

MILLIGAN: You mean we haven't enough people! What about China? What about India?

CLARE: The number of children I have is unlikely to affect the economy of India. Ireland is not India.

MILLIGAN: So you are waiting until Ireland gets like India.

CLARE: Unlikely – the Irish birth rate is falling, you will be pleased to know. Europe is not particularly overpopulated. West Germany is actually in negative growth. Some societies are clearly overpopulated, some underpopulated. But I need to talk about you, not about overpopulation.

MILLIGAN: I want to talk about overpopulation, being an environmentalist.

CLARE: So am I.

MILLIGAN: You can't be, you can't be, Anthony. Everything you are saying is death to the planet.

CLARE: But people aren't death to the planet. What is the value of human life?

MILLIGAN: None at all.

CLARE: That's where we disagree.

MILLIGAN: What's so valuable about human life when a quarter of the living children are chucked on to the streets? What's so valuable about it? What's so valuable about giving birth to starving children?

CLARE: Clearly they shouldn't starve. But the notion that Europe, by curbing its birth rate and reducing its population, would change that is arguable.

MILLIGAN: People are getting used to overcrowding. In Mexico I saw children swimming in sewage. What I am saying is that what population does is it reduces the quality of life very gradually, so much so that you see somebody pay £40,000 for a broom cupboard in London to live in. People are getting used to swimming in shit. The quality of life is going down. Sensitivities are going down. Music is noisier and more obscene than ever. Our best painter, Francis Bacon – my God, all his paintings are tortured; sensitivities are going down. Think about it, Anthony.

We argued in a similar gloomy vein for some time before returning to the topic of his own depression. Throughout the discussion, however, he remained courteous and made his points with no great animosity. But there were few flashes of wit, and such humour as he showed was bleak and pitiless.

Some 18 months later, when the story of his secret son broke, we returned, perhaps predictably, to the subject of overpopulation. By now he had recovered from his depression, and much of his old lightness and jocularity had returned. He was still passionately concerned about overpopulation and still robustly disapproving of my reproductive irresponsibility. But he was able to laugh. His approach did not quite possess the bite, the vehemence, the rancour. It seems that Spike's moods do not change his ideas and convictions; it is the way in which they are expressed that alters. I asked him if he agreed, and he replied:

Yes. Even when depressed I do have the satisfaction of feeling that I am right, that all the philosophies I have put together are right. Being depressed does not affect me. My views of the world don't greatly change. Perhaps I find the world less easy to accept. But the ideas remain constant. I retain my beliefs. I keep them. They are sacrosanct to me insofar as they concern the whole world.

CONCLUSION

In Spike Miligan's case we are back to a cluster of possible causes interacting to produce the disorder manic depression. There is a family history. There is a history of a somewhat unsettled infancy, family dysharmony and childhood anxiety. The young adolescent Milligan may have had a somewhat moody personality; he certainly had a traumatic war. Perhaps these factors together constitute an Achilles' heel, a hairline fracture waiting for the fundamental stress, which when it comes ruptures everything. For Milligan, it appears to have been the constellation of stresses occurring shortly after the birth of his first child – a traumatic period not merely for women. Once uncovered, Spike Milligan's manic depression has waxed and waned in response to the normal and not so normal strains of his turbulent life. It has been relieved and has then recurred, as manic depression classically does.

6

MANIC DEPRESSION AND CREATIVITY

SPIKE Milligan is an exceptionally creative man, a comic genius in the view of many. It is certainly arguable that the three Goons – Peter Sellers, Harry Secombe and Spike – were the parents to a whole new family of British humour, of which *Beyond the Fringe, Monty Python, Fawlty Towers* and *Blackadder* are just some of the progeny. Spike's role in this was pivotal – he was, as the major scriptwriter, the driving force behind the *Goons*. It was his extraordinary blend of inspired inventiveness, anarchic humour, savage satire and manic energy that provided the fuel propelling the radio series to the very top and making it a landmark of British comedy since the war. On the occasion of his 70th birthday, in 1988, Richard Ingrams in *The Independent* hailed him as 'the great father figure of modern British humour'. As one collaborator put it, 'Spike changed humour in the same way that the Dadaists changed modern art.'

But Spike Milligan's claim to fame does not rest there. There is his television work, which demands but has yet to receive appropriate study. He has used the medium quite brilliantly, pioneering television comedy with *A Show Called Fred*, which won him a British Academy Award in 1956. He helped launch the satire boom and the flowering of *Beyond the Fringe, That Was the Week That Was* and *Private Eye*. Several of his shows wonderfully and uniquely exploited television's ability to project zany visual and verbal humour.

Yet, as his biographer Pauline Scudamore astutely notes, there is a remarkable unevenness about the work, oscillating as it does from fertile inspiration to bland ordinariness. Her explanation – that 'Milligan is a master of spontaneity and a victim of the rehearsal room' – fits his psychology. Spike produces his material on the run and responds poorly to attempts to control and regulate this creativity.

His writing too has been rich and prolific. In 1987 he published four wonderfully comic books – *Puckoon* is a classic of its kind – permeated by a self-deprecating style and mercurial mood, which may account for the relative neglect by the critics of their value and complexity. He has written a number of delightful books for children. My own children, in common with thousands of others, turned to *Badjelly the Witch* and *Silly Verse for Kids* in preference to many of the supposed children's classics. Indeed, hardly a year goes by without a major book. In addition, he has starred in nearly 30 films, and he has acted on stage as well.

An Occupational Hazard?

Spike Milligan's richly creative life and his crippling psychiatric illness resuscitate an ancient question: are creativity and mental illness related? The lay person certainly seems to think so. The average man in the street appears to believe that having an artistic sensibility predisposes one to mental instability. How else is one to explain the fact that insofar as anyone can admit these days to having, or having had, a psychiatric illness, artists can. Indeed, psychiatric illness seems to be envisaged as a sort of occupational hazard of the artist. Nobody holds mental illness against the painter, poet, musician, sculptor, actor, playwright, novelist quite as they would against a banker, priest, doctor or prime minister. In our time, those public figures who have testified to suffering from psychiatric ill-health have been predominantly artists.

Over the years psychiatrists and psychologists have constructed lists of artists and other achievers who have made substantial contributions to Western culture but whose psychological constitution and mental health have been seen as suspect in some way or other. As early as 1944, R R Madden wrote *Infirmities of Genius*, in which he subjected to psychological examination a number of writers, including Burns, Byron, Cowper, Dr Johnson, Pope and Scott. Finding evidence of psychopathology was merely a prelude to explaining the creativity. In Byron's case, for example, Madden simply attributed the creativity to epilepsy!

The 19th century, as Ekbert Faas pointed out in a 1988 study, was a period of intense interest in the relationship between psychiatry and creativity. The Romantic poets themselves were intrigued by the insights being provided by the fledgling science of psychological medicine, while psychiatrists increasingly speculated about the precise mental status of many of the more eccentric, unusual and idiosyncratic artists of the day. Since that time, it has become fashionable to construct lists of artists strongly suspected of psychiatric disorder.

Such lists almost invariably include Goethe, Mill, Nietszche, Luther, Comte, Rousseau, Isaac Newton, Pascal, Van Gogh, Blake, Coleridge, Strindberg, De Quincey, Dostoevsky, Gogol, Maupassant, Balzac, Lamb, Swift, Ruskin, Strindberg, Kafka, John Clare, Donizetti, Tchaikovsky, Schumann and, in our time, Virginia Woolf, Ezra Pound, Robert Lowell, Sylvia Plath, Scott Fitzgerald, John Berryman, Ernest Hemingway, Anne Sexton, John Cheever, Dylan Thomas and Samuel Beckett.

Before concluding from such an impressive list that the association is confirmed, there is a need to consider the problems involved. First, psychiatric illness is a common affliction. To show a significant connection between it and creativity requires that it should occur in the creatively gifted to a significantly increased extent. After all, a pretty impressive list of artists whose psychiatric stability seems reasonably well established could with equal facility be drawn up. Second, it is worth noting that in many of the artists listed, their mental disorder became manifest long after they had done their best work. Third, some of those judged retrospectively to have suffered from mental ill-health now appear to have been afflicted by particular forms of physical disease.

Jonathan Swift's illness

Jonathan Swift is a case in point. During the last years of his life Swift's mental faculties declined. He became increasingly deaf, giddy, driven to distraction by noises in his ears. His memory and understanding began to fail, he suffered a series of strokes and eventually a committee was set up to administer his affairs. Following his death in 1745 at the age of 78, a fertile industry grew up, fostered to some extent by Samuel Johnson, which argued that Swift had been mad and had expired a 'driv'ler and a show'. It did not help that Swift left all his money to found a psychiatric hospital, St Patrick's, nor that some years before, in his own epitaph, 'Verses written on the death of Dr Swift', he had penned the lines:

> He gave the little wealth he had,
> To build a house for fools and mad.
> And shew'd by one satiric touch,
> No nation wanted it so much.

The myth merely grew. Swift, it was claimed, had been exhibited to a curious public by his servants for a shilling a time. He was said to have been the first patient admitted to his own hospital (a somewhat difficult achievement seeing that the hospital did not open for a decade after his death). His masterpiece, *Gulliver's Travels*, was cited as evidence of his madness. The Johnsonian diagnosis of insanity, as Michael Foot recently pointed out,

was subsequently adopted and approved by a long list of distinguished writers, including Scott, Macaulay, Thackeray, Yeats, D H Lawrence, George Orwell, Malcolm Muggeridge, and A L Rowse until it became accepted as an incontestable piece of common knowledge.

Common knowledge it may have been, but it was wrong. It had taken a careful investigation and refutation of Dr Johnson's theory by Sir William Wilde, a distinguished ear, nose and throat specialist and father of Oscar, to show that Swift had not been mad but had suffered in the final years of his life from the distressing complaint of Menière's disease. This is a condition in which the inner ear is diseased and the sufferer afflicted by disabling paroxysms of vertigo, deafness and tinnitus.

There is, then, a need to be certain as to the status of the diagnosis of psychiatric ill-health in connection with any particular artist and a need to show that the creative artist is more likely than chance to suffer from such ill-health. It is not an easy task, but a number of intriguing studies have been undertaken.

THE EVIDENCE

The classic approach to studying the relationship between creativity and psychiatric illness is biographical – that is to say, the retrospective analysis of the psychology of famous historical figures who, on account of their achievements, can be deemed to be outstandingly creative.

Retrospective studies of eminent people

In the 19th century, the Italian psychiatrist Lombroso and the French psychiatrist Moreau de Tours took up the cudgels on behalf of an association. Lombroso had based his claim of a pathological basis for genius on a study of such achievers as Newton, Rousseau, Schopenhauer and Julius Caesar. Again, his work was compromised by the fact that many of his subjects would now be considered to have suffered, like Swift, from gross physical disorders. Caesar, for example, suffered from epilepsy, a condition which until this century was classified as a psychiatric and not a physical disorder. Lombroso took a pretty gloomy and negative view of genius, equating it with antisocial behaviour (he is better remembered for his studies of criminality) but his work sowed a fruitful seed.

Ernst Kretschmer, an influential psychiatrist of this century, concluded after an extensive review of the evidence that men of genius:

> show in their psychological structure an unusual instability and hypersensitiveness, together with a very considerable liability to psychoses, neuroses and psychopathic complaints . . . The loosening of mental structure, the plasticity, the hypersensitiveness to find distinctions and remote relations, the frequently bizarre play of contrasts in the innermost parts of the personality – all these things, conditioned by the passionate quality of genius, its restless internal production, and its immense intellectual range, are part of the daemonic element which is identical with the psychopathic structures in the personality . . . For some types of genius, this inner dissolution of the mental structure is an indispensable prelude.
>
> (Kretschmer, 1958)

Kretschmer concluded that if the 'daemonic unrest' and the 'mental tension' were to be removed, nothing but an ordinary, talented individual would remain. If Kretschmer is right then Spike Milligan's manic depression becomes essential to his art. Without it he would be just another 'ordinary talented individual'. But is Kretschmer right?

One of the earliest studies, and one that dissented from the proposition that mental ill-health and creativity were related, was that undertaken by Havelock Ellis at the turn of this century. He examined 'British genius' by studying the psychological, physical and social characteristics of over 1000 people listed in the *Dictionary of National Biography*. He found only a modest rate (about 4 per cent) of frank psychiatric disorder among his subjects, and even that included some examples of gross brain disease. The problem, however, as has been pointed out in a recent detailed discussion of the issue, is that Ellis's survey did not actually include people of outstanding creativity but covered people whose achievements were rarely so enduring 'as to place them in the class apart to which we would assign the truly original thinkers in history' (Claridge et al., 1990).

A somewhat similar analysis was undertaken by Catherine Cox. She collected full biographical data concerning 301 of the most eminent people who have lived between 1450 and 1850, eminence being judged by the space accorded them in encyclopaedias and biographical dictionaries. She estimated their IQs and reported that the philosophers topped the list with IQs in the 170 range, followed by poets, dramatists, novelists and revolutionary statesmen (IQs of 160), then the scientists (IQs of 155) and the musicians (IQs of 145). The majority were above average in force of character and social attributes and, in Cox's view, did not differ significantly from the average in terms of their emotional balance and mental health.

Again there are problems. Cox does not appear to have approached the issue with an open mind – otherwise how would she have concluded from a somewhat cursory examination of the life of Isaac Newton that he was psychiatrically sound? Newton was in fact decidedly odd; Anthony Storr, in a cautious review, concluded that Newton was a remarkably eccentric man who at one stage became frankly paranoid. Claridge and his colleagues suggest that Cox, who was a participant with Terman in one of the most extensive studies of gifted children ever undertaken in the United States, was emotionally committed to the idea that mental health rather than ill-health predisposed to creativity. Certainly the 1500 highly gifted children which Terman and Cox followed into adult life showed very little evidence of mental ill-health. But they showed very little evidence of startling creativity either. A high IQ may be necessary for creativity but it is certainly not sufficient.

A somewhat more restricted group of eminent men was reported on by Adele Juda in 1953. Her collection of eminence included the most outstanding scientists and artists of the German-speaking countries since 1650. The sample consisted of 113 artists (painters, sculptors, architects, musicians and poets) and 181 scientists (a group which included theologians, philosophers, jurists, historians and 18 Field Marshals, statesmen and inventors!). She failed to find an association between mental ill-health and creativity. Her data indicated that the artists and their families were relatively free from psychiatric disorder. The scientists were even healthier as a group, leading Juda to conclude that:

> there is no definite relationship between highest mental capacity and mental health or illness, and no evidence to support the assumption that the genesis of highest intellectual ability depends on psychological abnormalities ... Psychoses, especially schizophrenic, proved to be detrimental to creative ability.

Growing doubt

Influenced by work such as that by Ellis and Juda, many psychiatrists have doubted the existence of a significant link. Aubrey Lewis, one of Britain's most eminent psychiatrists, remained unsure of the connection. All men and women of outstanding gifts and achievements, he argued reasonably enough, are statistically abnormal. What is distinctive and lasting in a work produced by a psychiatrically disturbed individual, he claimed in 1960,

> is not the conflict but the manner and form of its expression ... the artist's or scientist's abundant power to conceive and develop and conclude his work is healthy no matter what mental disabilities he may also have.

Anthony Storr, who has written extensively on the dynamics of creativity, likewise remains ambivalent. He argues on the one hand that for many artists creativity can be a particularly effective way of protecting them from depression, and on the other that creativity may be more closely bound up with what he terms a 'dymanic of the normal' than with psychopathology (Storr, 1972).

Silvano Arieti, a leading expert on schizophrenia and creativity, has been intrigued by the similarity between certain types of schizophrenic thinking and the creative process, but he too has refrained from drawing clear-cut conclusions. In general, his attitude seems to be that of Carl Jung. Confronted by the tortuous complexity of James Joyce's *Finnegan's Wake*, and the fact that Joyce's daughter, Lucia, was undeniably a schizophrenic, Jung concluded that the difference between the sane artist and the sick daughter was the difference between someone diving and someone drowning – ie the extent to which the artist, unlike the psychotic, is in control of potentially pathological processes.

Looking beyond the individual

More recently, however, there have been signs of a change. Renewal of interest in the issue came from the growing use of techniques to study familial transmission of various illnesses. These include evaluation of first-degree relatives of creative individuals and the examination of biological and non-biological adoptive relatives of creative individuals adopted at birth. The striking number of suicides by a series of contemporary writers – including Ernest Hemingway, Sylvia Plath, Virginia Woolf, Anne Sexton and John Berryman – also stimulated interest.

One intriguing study is that by Nancy Andreasen, professor of psychiatry at the University of Iowa College of Medicine. Andreasen is especially interested in the psychology of creativity; before she turned to medicine and psychiatry she was a distinguished academic in literature studies. Her contribution to the creativity-mental illness argument involved a systematic evaluation of a sample of creative writers at the University of Iowa Writers' Workshop. The workshop is the oldest and most respected creative-writing programme in the United States. Its students and faculty have included over the years such writers as Philip Roth, Kurt Vonnegut, John Irving, Robert Lowell, Flannery O'Connor and John Cheever.

Andreasen assessed 30 faculty members (27 men and three women) with a structured interview to determine their patterns of creativity, their history of mental illness and the prevalence of these traits in first-degree relatives. She matched the writers for age, sex and educational status with an occupationally varied group made up of hospital administrators, lawyers, social workers, etc.

Andreasen's findings suggest a strong and significant association between creativity and mood disorder. A remarkable 80 per cent of the writers had had an episode of some form of mood disorder at some time in their lives, compared with 30 per cent of the control subjects. 43 per cent of the writers had had bipolar manic-depressive disorder, in comparison with 10 per cent of the control subjects. In addition, the writers had significantly higher rates of alcoholism (30 per cent) compared with 7 per cent in the control subjects. The rates of illness for the writers were substantially higher than Andreasen expected. So, indeed, were the rates for the control subjects. Andreasen points out, however, that the controls, having been matched for social status, represented an educationally and occupationally advantaged group. Woodruff and his colleagues at St Louis University about 20 years ago had reported an association between bipolar manic depression and occupational achievement, an association which might explain the somewhat higher levels of mood disorder in Andreasen's control group.

Nancy Andreasen also found higher than expected rates of manic depressive illness in the first-degree relatives of the writers. In order to clarify the relationship between creativity and illness further, she examined the patterns of creativity in the writers' relatives and found that 41 per cent of the siblings of the writers displayed some creativity, compared with 18 per cent of the control siblings. Relatives were classed as somewhat creative by Andreasen if they pursued occupations 'such as journalism or teaching music or dance', and definitely creative if they had an acknowledged level of creative achievement, such as writing novels, dancing in a recognized company, performing as a concert artist or making a major scientific contribution such as an invention. The families of the writers in this study were, in Andreasen's words, 'riddled with both creativity and mental illness', whereas in the families of the control subjects creativity and mental illness were randomly distributed.

No study in this area is perfect, and Andreasen's is no exception. She was not blind to the status of her sample, which means that she may have been biased in her asssessments of the writers and their relatives. It is interesting to note in this regard, however, that Andreasen set out to test a somewhat different hypothesis, namely whether there might be an association between schizophrenia and creativity, so the discovery of a strong link between manic depression and creativity came as a considerable surprise to her.

Another researcher interested in the association was the Icelandic geneticist, J K Karlsson. To the usual list of allegedly afflicted artists assessed retrospectively he added the names of Scott, Tolstoy, Pope and Poe. Karlsson claimed that 25 per cent of his international sample of creative geniuses had suffered from severe psychiatric ill-health (Karlsson, 1978). In another retrospective study, he analysed the professional standing of the first-degree relatives of psychiatric patients admitted to hospital in Iceland between 1851 and 1940. Comparing this group with the general population over the same time frame and examining available records, which included the Icelandic version of *Who's Who*, Karlsson showed that the relatives of the psychiatrically ill patients entered creative occupations to a statistically increased extent (Karlsson, 1984).

Creativity and mild mood swings

A somewhat similar approach was adopted in a more recent study (Richards et al., 1988). Once again the sample studied was made up of psychiatric patients and their first-degree relatives. The patients were deemed to be suffering either from full-blown manic depression or from mild, subclinical mood swings, sometimes referred to as 'cyclothymia' as mentioned in Chapter 4. Using an inventory designed to assess creative ability and application, these researchers claimed to find a raised prevalence of creativity among those judged cyclothymic (though not raised among those suffering from frank manic depression). This echoed some earlier work by the distinguished British psychiatrist and geneticist, Eliot Slater, who with Adolf Meyer carried out a study of 27 famous German composers, and found that only three had ever been psychotic (all due to gross brain disease), whereas eight of the 27 had been cyclothymic. Slater went on to argue that the regular oscillations from mild depression to mild overactivity characterizing cyclothymia did not account for the creativity of his subjects but only for the observed considerable fluctuation in productivity.

Creativity and personality disorder

Another British psychiatrist perplexed by the issue is Felix Post. In 1989, he selected world-famous people with outstanding and original achievement who had been alive during the previous 150 years and 'for whom expertly researched biographies, written after their death, had become available to me'.

Post extracted the 'factual' information from the biographies, firmly eschewing the biographers' speculations and interpretations concerning their subjects' psychological make-ups. He compared innovative and world-famous novelists and dramatists with famous scientists. Of note was Post's comment to the effect that it was relatively easy to select his 55 writers but much more difficult to find scientists who had 'attracted' biographies of high quality. Indeed, to bring his numbers of scientists up to a reasonably acceptable level, he had to bring in applied scientists and doctors. Even then, out of some 60 such 'scientists', only 35 had had biographies written of sufficient depth as to enable Post to include them in his study.

Post analysed his data in terms of (1) life-long characteristics (personality disorder), and (2) episodic impairment of mental health (illness). 12 per cent of the scientists and 30 per cent of the writers had a history of having suffered episodes of mild psychiatric symptoms, while 33 per cent of the scientists and 54 per cent of the writers were classified as having a history of definite psychiatric illness. One scientist and one writer had received a diagnosis of manic-depressive psychosis. When Post examined his data and added psychotic depression and severe non-psychotic mood disorders together, he found that 30 per cent of the writers had severe disorders and nearly one in six had a history of suicidal behaviour. Only 15 per cent of the scientists had at times been seriously ill and only two of them had ever attempted suicide.

In addition to severe mood disorder, artistic creativity in this study has strong links with personality disturbance! Nearly one in three of the writers were classed by Post as having a disordered personality, compared with one in eight of the scientists. In addition, 36 per cent of the writers had been heavy or problem drinkers, and 16 per cent had regularly abused other substances, whereas only two scientists abused drugs and none seemingly abused alcohol. Marital difficulties too figured more prominently among the writers – 52 per cent had had broken marriages against only 12 per cent of the scientists.

Prize-winning artists and writers

One of the most energetic attempts to establish a link between creativity and mental illness was undertaken by the American psychiatrist and researcher Kay Redfield Jamison. She not only studied mood disorder in a group of outstanding British writers and artists but looked too at seasonal variations in mood and creative output. She chose her subjects for study on the basis of their having won awards or prizes in their field. These included the Queen's Gold Medal and the Cholmondeley Award for poets, the New York Drama Award and the Evening Standard Drama Award for playwrights, and the James Tait Black Memorial Award for biographers. The artists and writers were asked whether they had ever received treatment, and, if so, what kind of treatment, for a mood disorder.

In all, 47 writers and artists were studied – made up of 18 poets, eight playwrights, eight novelists, five biographers and eight painters and sculptors. 38 per cent had received treatment for an affective disorder. 75 per cent of those treated had received antidepressants or lithium or had been hospitalized. Poets were the most likely to have received medication and were the only ones to have been hospitalized, received ECT or been treated with lithium for mania. A very high percentage of the playwrights had received treatment for mood disorders but the majority had received psychotherapy alone. The high rate of mood disorder in this sample (38 per cent) compares with the American lifetime prevalence of 1.2 per cent for manic depression and 4.4 per cent for unipolar depression.

In summary

Summarizing the evidence, the bulk of it favours a statistically significant association between mental illness and creativity, although there is a substantial minority report critical of the samples studied and casting cold water on the results. Little convincing evidence exists to link schizophrenia and creativity – it is manic depression that is the psychiatric illness most notably associated in those studies supportive of a link.

CREATIVITY AS ILLNESS

But if there is indeed a link, what is its nature? There are a number of explanations. One possible explanation which merits particular scrutiny is that creativity is itself a form of psychopathology, a distorted and socially acceptable way in which the affected individual can express psychotic and neurotic fantasies and preoccupations. According to this theory, it is not surprising that psychiatric illness is associated with creativity because creativity itself *is* illness.

If art to the Greeks resulted from an external, mystical, heavenly spirit or fury, it has been portrayed by psychiatrists of a Freudian persuasion as emanating from within the individual, deep in the unconscious. The psychoanalytical theory holds that neurosis for most people results from an unsatisfactory negotiation of, and adaptation to, the traumas of infancy and childhood. But for some individuals the result is not so much a frank neurosis as a sublimated one – artistic creativity.

Freudian wish-fulfilment

The most powerful advocate of the art-as-illness theory was without doubt Sigmund Freud himself. Art, he told his disciples, is a 'substitute gratification', an illusion in contrast to reality. While Freud regarded the illusions of art as harmless, indeed beneficial, he regarded the artist as virtually indistinguishable from the neurotic. Consider this passage from his introductory lectures:

> There is, in fact, a path from phantasy back again to reality and that is – art. The artist has also an introverted disposition and has not far to go to become neurotic. He is one who is urged on by instinctive needs which are too clamorous; he longs to attain to honour, power, riches, fame and the love of women; but he lacks the means of achieving these gratifications. So, like any other with an unsatisfied longing, he turns away from reality and transfers all his interest and all his libido too, on to the creation of his wishes in life. There must be many factors in combination to prevent this becoming the whole outcome of his development; it is well-known how often artists in particular suffer from partial inhibition of their capacities through neurosis. Probably their constitution is endowed with a powerful capacity for sublimation and with a certain flexibility in the repressions determining the conflict. He is not the only one who has a life of phantasy; the intermediate world of phantasy is sanctioned by a general human consent and every hungry soul looks to it for comfort and consolation. But to those who are not artists, the gratification that can be drawn from the springs of phantasy is very limited . . . a true artist has more at his disposal.
>
> (Freud, 1917)

Frued's theories, seized on with even more avidity by artists, particularly writers, than by psychiatrists and psychologists, portrayed creativity as wish-fulfilment, sublimation, a substitute for living. However, many Freudian psychonalysts were aware of the somewhat negative implications of this portrayal of creativity as neurosis and struggled to solve the many dilemmas this posed. One is the fact that, if indeed much art is neurosis, then presumably the artist on being successfully analysed loses his motivation for his creativity, ceases to create, turns from the 'phantasy' of art to the 'reality' of living. Ernest Jones, Freud's biographer and a fervent follower, suggested his own solution to the problem when he wrote:

> Many artists, both first-rate and second-rate, have now been analysed and the results have been unequivocal. When the artistic impulse is genuine the greater freedom achieved through analysis has heightened the artistic capacity, but when the wish to become an artist is impelled by purely neurotic and irrelevant motives the analyst clarifies the situation.

The problem remains, however, that it is not always so easy to distinguish between neurotic and genuine artistic impulses. Nor has analysis been able to distinguish between good and bad art or, more importantly, between a work of art and a neurotic symptom. As Anthony Storr has neatly put it, 'The achievements of a Beethoven or a Tolstoy are not to be put upon the same level as a masturbatory phantasy, however much it may be true that the sexual drive enters into these achievements.'

This is not to deny that some artists might indeed be expressing infantile, sexual and neurotic fantasies through their art – Storr chose Frederick Rolfe and Ian Fleming as examples of writers whose creativity betokened a wish-fulfilment; Franz Kafka as one whose creative activity was a particularly apt way for him to express his profoundly schizoid personality; Balzac and Schumann as artists whose manic-depressive temperament profoundly coloured their art.

Such observations have led to attempts to seek a particular constellation of early-childhood experiences within the lives of creative artists. One of those who strove most energetically to establish a foundation for the Freudian view of art was the poet W H Auden. In an essay entitled 'Psychology and Art Today', Auden argued that the artist is like 'a man struggling for life in the water, a schoolboy evading an imposition or a cook getting her mistress out of the house'. We only truly think when we are prevented from feeling or acting as we would like, and perfect satisfaction is complete unconsciousness. Most of us, however, fit too neatly into society, and so the stimulus to struggle arises only in a crisis, such as falling in love or losing all our money. It is struggle which produces the artist, and, while the possible early childhood and family situations that may produce the artist or intellectual are innumerable, there are, in Auden's view, some that are more commonly found. He enumerated them somewhat naïvely as follows:

(1) When parents are not physically in love with each other. There are several varieties of this: the complete fiasco; the brother-sister relationship on a basis of common mental interests; the invalid-nurse relationship when one parent is a child to be maternally cared for; and the unpassionate relationship of old parents.

(2) The only child. This alone is most likely to produce early-life confidence which on meeting disappointment turns like the unwanted child to illness and antisocial behaviour to secure attention.

(3) The youngest child. Not only are parents old but the whole family field is one of mental stimulation.

The problem, even if one were to accept Auden's assertion of specific kinds of early childhood experience being associated with creativity (and the examples he provided are not exactly specific), is that it fails to explain why the individual ends up creative rather than criminal, artistic rather than numerate. In truth we are no further forward from Freud's simple assertion that creativity is a variety of psychological instability.

One critic who subjected Freud's theories of art as neurosis to particular scrutiny is Lionel Trilling. Confronting Freud's equation of the artistic creation with dreaming and neurosis, Trilling acknowledges that they do indeed have certain elements in common. Unconscious processes are at work in both. They share in various degrees the element of fantasy. But Trilling notes a vital difference and quotes Charles Lamb in support: 'The . . . poet dreams being awake. He is not possessed by his subject but he has dominion over it.' (Trilling, 1950).

It was this notion of the artist in command of his fantasy, in contrast to the psychiatrically ill, that Jung echoed in his famous diving/drowning metaphor. Trilling goes on to argue that the artist, as opposed to one who is psychiatrically disturbed, utilizes the illusions of art to serve the purpose of a closer and truer relation with reality rather than as a means of evading it.

Spike Milligan's creativity

What of Spike Milligan's creativity? He certainly had an early childhood environment that Auden would have classed as a likely crucible for adult creative achievement. In some of his work (most notably his children's books) and in some of his statements (for example, his rejection of adulthood and his glorification of the world of the child) Milligan might be seen to seek in his art a return to a simpler world of instinctual gratification. In his comic material the analyst would see evidence of a partial satisfaction of sexual and aggressive impulses. Within such a model, Milligan when depressed self-destructively turns his aggression and sexual tension inwards in the form of self-loathing and despair. When manic he turns them outward in the socially acceptable form of Goon humour and verbal pyrotechnics. Within such a model, Milligan's illness and his artistry are one and the same.

But are they? Trilling's observation has relevance here. Spike Milligan himself insists that his manic-depressive swings are not consciously under his control. They occur often at highly inconvenient moments and cannot be banished by an act of will. The last time I saw him profoundly depressed was when he had had to cancel his appearance as Baron Hardup in the local pantomime, the first such cancellation in his long career. He was bitterly disappointed and savagely self-destructive. There was no reason to suggest he would, under the guise of illness, 'want' to get out of such a role. He has played in pantomime for many years; he loves it as a theatrical form and as a vehicle for his particular brand of humour.

His comic inventiveness, on the other hand, is under his own control, at least to a partial extent. But – and it is an important but – what makes Milligan of particular interest is the fact that there have been well-documented occasions when, while clearly manic and seriously out of control, he has been magnificently creative. Take the early years of the Goons. Remember his own words: 'The best scripts I wrote were when I was ill.'

However ill he was, Spike Milligan was still able to subject his surging, teeming brain to the discipline of getting ideas, thoughts and imaginings down on paper and delivering them in a more or less coherent form to the BBC production team each week. Eventually his state worsened and required hospitalization – he presumably moved from a milder form of mania, so-called hypomania, to the full-blooded form.

The case of Robert Schumann

In this respect Milligan's experience recalls that of the composer Robert Schumann. During the greater part of his life Schumann suffered from what in retrospect appears to have been classic manic-depressive illness. Periods of intense activity, exaltation and enthusiasm were followed by periods of dreadful gloom, despondency and listlessness. Schumann had his first breakdown at the age of 23. It was preceded by a malarial infection, and by the deaths of his brother Julius and his sister-in-law, Rosalie. He became intensely melancholic and revealingly described his feelings in a letter written to his mother in November 1833:

I was hardly more than a statue, without coldness, without warmth. Only by forcing myself to work did life return, bit by bit . . . Can you believe that I don't have the courage to travel to Zwickau by myself, for fear that something could happen to me? Violent flushing, unspeakable dread, shortness of breath, and momentary lapses of consciousness fluctuate rapidly, although less now than in days gone by. If you had an inkling how depression has totally shattered my peace of mind, you would surely forgive me for not writing.

That particular episode of depression lifted but he was to be plagued by mood swings for the rest of his life. When euphoric or 'high', Schumann, in Ostwald's phrase, 'seems to have felt like the passive recipient of his own creative energies'. The composer himself described music pouring into him 'which often made [him] feel like bursting'. He began to hear voices and musical tones. Many times during his life he was able to transform these into compositions. For example, in 1840 and again in 1849, when his manic swings were at their most extreme, he was at his most productive, adding a record number of opus numbers to his body of musical composition. During 1844, in contrast, when he was seriously depressed, he produced nothing.

Early on in his illness Schumann was able to respond to the inner voices and utilize the hallucinated musical phrases. Some of his best works, including the Manfred Overture (Op. 115) and the Spring Symphony (Op. 38), were written in such circumstances. By 1854, however, he had become unable to control his symptoms. On 12th February he was constantly tormented by hallucinations. His wife, Clara, described his hearing 'one and the same tone and from time to time another interval as well'. He claimed to be hearing 'music that is so glorious and with instruments sounding more wonderful than one ever hears on earth'.

In his own diary, he specifically mentioned a Bach cantata, 'Ein Feste Burg'. Glorious it might have been, but it made it impossible for him to organize his mind and concentrate on his own work, and became, in his own words, 'exquisite suffering'. Clara Schumann wrote:

> His auditory disturbance had escalated to such a degree that he heard entire pieces from beginning to end, as if played by a full orchestra, and the sound would remain on the final chord until Robert directed his thoughts to another composition.

She said that he threatened to destroy himself if it didn't stop. Just over two weeks later, Schumann threw himself from a bridge into the Rhine and was drowned.

Schumann's creativity and his mental illness at times were certainly inextricably mixed, but at no stage could it be said that one depended on the other. Furthermore, for considerable periods of his life as a composer he was free of mental disturbance. What seems clear from Schumann's experience is that psychiatric illness up to a certain level of disturbance is not incompatible with creative application and achievement. Up to a point it may, as in mild mania, facilitate it. But beyond that point, when manic energy and symptomatology overwhelm the ability of the individual to contain it, or when depression reaches a paralysing pitch, then it can be said that psychiatric illness and creativity are incompatible.

A matter of degree

Spike Milligan's manic depression and creativity seem similarly related. Examining his psychiatric history, there is evidence, particularly in the Goon years, strongly suggesting a relationship between his surges of manic energy and his comic productivity. Up to a certain point of mood elevation, Spike Milligan appears to have been able to harness the energy, the drive, the heightened sensations, the accelerated fluency of word, thought and association and to fashion the idiosyncratic 'manic' humour that is a characteristic, perhaps *the* characteristic, of the Goons. But beyond the level of hypomania, with the onset of mania itself, Milligan lost the ability to mould it into humour and lost his own power to control his day-to-day life and feelings.

'Skinlessness'

In a recent examination of ten authors who suffered from severe psychiatric illness, Gordon Claridge, a psychologist, and two literary academics, Ruth Pryor and Gwen Watkins, note the personality qualities and traits so often manifested by psychiatrically ill and creative individuals (Claridge et al., 1990). The most general common feature identified in their sample of ill writers was a 'skinlessness', ranging from a hypersensitivity to sensory stimulation, to nervous irritability and bodily complaints. John Ruskin was hypersensitive to noise. John Clare, who was also exquisitely sensitive to noise, described his head as being 'stung as though nettled'. Virginia Woolf's father, Leslie Stephen – himself a nervous, irritable, peevish insomniac – actually called himself 'skinless' to describe his sensitivity to emotional stimuli. Some manage to cope with a lack of robust buffer between their fragile self and the outside world. For others, the balance is precarious. E J Anthony, an American child psychiatrist who first applied the term 'skinlessness' to the area of psychiatry and creativity, observes of the vulnerable group:

> From the very beginning, they seem to lack the 'protective shield' and the constitutional buffering between themselves and the world around. The hypersensitiveness that permits such free exchange between outer experience and the psychic interior may conduce to two outcomes: 'breakdown' when the primitive content takes over and allows the milieu of irrationality and unrealism to prevail without constraint, and an upsurge of creative productivity delicately controlled by the ego.

One of the striking characteristics of Spike Milligan's personality is his 'skinlessness'. He complains bitterly and repeatedly of noise. 'Noises,' his daughter Laura declared in an interview, 'really get on his nerves.' He reputedly tore the Tannoy off the dressing room wall while waiting to go on the Jonathan Ross television show. 'It kept squawking on and on,' he complained, 'with messages for people I had never heard of.' In the celebrated interview with Lynn Barber he revealed that his hypersensitivity to noise had virtually rendered him a 'social invalid', who needed to keep himself away from people because 'I can't live in the noise and pollution that goes on outside'.

Norma Farnes, Spike Milligan's agent and long-term supporter, confidante and friend, eloquently described to me the exquisitely sensitive nature of his reponse to noise:

> When I say noise I mean such things as a telephone ringing, a knock at the door or a hoover – any form whatsoever. Anything. He had ear plugs that I used to get from the Noise Abatement Society which he would use to try and drown out the noise.

He seems physically to feel pain when he reads of distressing events affecting children, animals, the planet. At times, as he talks, he sounds like a man who has been stripped of the normal rough, protective layer on which most of us unthinkingly depend, the layer that enables us to cope with the constant, relentless, often disturbing bombardment of sensory images, impressions, illusions. 'You would have to be a total idiot to be happy today,' he once observed.

Gordon Claridge and his colleagues argue strongly that the 'skinlessness' manifested by many creative people actually facilitates their imaginativeness, their capacity to respond to profound, internal, preconscious associations and impulses. But in turn such imaginativeness has serious implications for mental peace. Milligan agrees. He speaks of torment and anguish. 'A breakdown,' he told Yvonne Roberts in *The Observer* in 1991, 'is like being burnt alive. You come out of it with a higher degree of sensitivity.'

Insensitive behaviour

Yet cohabiting with this 'skinlessness' in many creative individuals is a seemingly contradictory insensitivity. Claridge, noting this trait, suggests that the psychiatrically disturbed individual 'may be unable to acquire the "insincere" behaviour demanded by social courtesy'. His response, which may appear insensitive, in fact 'represents the true, raw feeling unadmitted by more "normal" individuals'.

Spike Milligan's behaviour can certainly appear insensitive. His insensitivity cohabits with his hypersensitivity and, in manifesting that curious contradiction, he is in line with Claridge's theory. In this strange, tortured, gifted man, illness and creativity cohabit, though it is impossible to assert with any degree of confidence that creativity depends on illness.

Whether creativity is but mental illness in a distorted, sublimated form affects not one whit the work of art created. As psychologist William James observed in relation to the subject matter of religion, where such diagnoses as 'hysteria', 'epilepsy' and 'mania' are often applied:

> St Teresa might have had the nervous system of the placidest cow and it would not save her theology if the trial of the theology by these other tests should show it to be contemptible. And, conversely, if her theology can stand these other tests, it will make no difference how hysterical or nervously off balance St Teresa may have been when she was with us here below.

MENTAL ILLNESS FACILITATES CREATIVITY

Another possible explanation for the link between manic depression and creativity is that psychiatric illness in a talented and intelligent person can in some way stimulate artistic insight and creativity. It is, in Ernst Kretschmer's words, 'not merely a regrettable, non-essential accident of biological structure but an intrinsic and necessary part, an indispensable catalyst, perhaps, for every form of genius in the strict sense of the term'.

Schumann's illness, at least in its manic phases, stimulated his musical productivity. Spike Milligan's period as a scriptwriter coincided with a serious manic swing. Could the association between manic depression and creativity, noted by Andreasen and others, be explained simply as an interactive effect – the coming together in one individual of an innate talent and a predisposition to manic swings of energy and drive? The insights derived from the psychiatric illness together with the energy (at least in mania) would combine to produce a driving, achieving, restless, creative talent.

Such an idea has enlisted formidable support. T S Eliot, long interested in the relationship between creativity and illness, suggested in his conclusion to *The Use of Poetry and the Use of Criticism* that some forms of 'debility, ill-health and anaemia may produce an efflux of poetry'. Elsewhere he wondered whether certain kinds of ill-health might favour not only 'religious illumination' but also 'artistic and literary composition'. (His biographer, Peter Ackroyd, speculates somewhat convincingly that Eliot appeared to believe that artistic creativity had to do 'with the satisfaction of obscure and uncontrollable personal needs'.)

Eliot was not alone. Thomas Mann, in a speech in Vienna in 1936 honouring Freud's eightieth birthday, quoted with approval Nietzsche's assertion that 'there is no deeper knowledge without the experience of disease'. Victor Hugo's declaration, 'L'humanité s'affirme par l'infirmité,' Mann declared, 'frankly and proudly admits the delicate constitution of all higher humanity and culture and their connoisseurship in the realm of disease'.

In Jamison's study of prominent British writers and artists, an attempt was made to establish whether there is any association, any 'connoisseurship' between certain aspects of manic depression, most notably the heightened mood, word fluency, thought acceleration and increased energy, and creative activity and output. Almost all of the 47 subjects reported having experienced intense, creative episodes, the duration of such episodes varying from 24 hours to over a month. These episodes were characterized by increase of energy, enthusiasm, fluency of thought and a sense of well-being. About half the subjects reported a decreased need for sleep and an increased sensory awareness.

Asked specifically about changes occurring before these intense creative periods, nearly 90 per cent reported less need for sleep, while 50 per cent reported a sharp increase in mood just before the creative surge. When asked whether these mood changes were important to their work, about 90 per cent stated that they were essential or very important.

Milligan's fluency of thinking

This issue – the possible facilitation of creativity by elevated mood swings – is raised again in any consideration of the work of Spike Milligan. Spike Milligan's very personal sense of humour relies to a quite extraordinary extent on verbal dexterity, punning, rhyming, the juxtaposition of strikingly incongruous images and ideas, a remarkable fluency of thinking. A systematic study by J P Guilford of the nature of creativity concluded that one of the several components is fluency of thinking, including:

(1) word fluency: the ability to produce words

(2) associational fluency: the ability to produce as many synonyms for a given word as possible

(3) expressional fluency: the ability to produce and juxtapose with rapidity phrases or sentences

(4) ideational fluency: the ability to produce ideas to fulfil specific requirements in a given time

Guilford also describes spontaneous flexibility (the ability to produce a rich variety of ideas and to switch from one area of interest to another) and adaptive flexibility (the ability to come up with unusual ideas or solutions). In all of this, fluency and flexibility are stressed. There is more than a suggestion that they can be heightened or facilitated by the sort of quickening of cognitive processes and the surges of mental energy that are a feature of hypomania.

Is it in this hypothesized link between hypomanic drive and fluency of thinking that the clue to the assumed association between comedy and melancholia lies? Consider Spike Milligan's humour once more. In one of the classic *Goon Show* sketches, a team is setting out on an expedition and proceeds to enumerate the items that will be needed:

one portable plastic and gravel road
one long, bent thing with a sort of lump on the end
one waterproof cover for same
33 boxes of yellow kosher boots
another bent thing with a sort of lump on the end
one leather trilby with sugar feather
one 60-foot explodable granite statue with built-in plunger
detailed plans of what to do with long bent thing with sort of lump on the end

Spike Milligan's humour relies heavily on speed of thought, verbal fluency, play, incongruity of association, a leaping from one concept to another and from one category to another, metaphor, pun, sheer quantity of thought. There is a delight in playing with the texture and the sound of words, as in this example:

In 1296 there was a plague on the Isle of Yew.
Where?
The Isle of Yew.
I love you too. Shall we dance?

Yesterday, Lurgi [a Goon disease] claimed its first victim in Britain.
You jest.
I jest what?
You jest said the disease claimed its first victim in Britain.

I want you to accompany me on a safari.
No. I have never played one in my life.

Spike Milligan particularly loves painting a scene which is absolutely straight and conventional in its content save for one key component. Take his 'Auction at Christie's' joke:

There's this auction at Christie's and there is this Monet painting with an asking price of £1 million.
The auctioneer gets up and asks, 'What do I hear?'
This voice from the back shouts, 'You can hear the traffic in Bond Street.'
'Any advances on the traffic in Bond Street?' goes the auctioneer.
Someone else shouts, 'I can hear the buses going up Dulwich Hill.'
And someone else shouts, 'I can hear a ferry going from Dover to Calais.'

'It's completely mad,' observes Milligan levelly. Indeed. His is precisely the kind of infectious verbal play that manic patients display. Take another example:

Two men dressed as vicars knock on a door with stocking masks over their faces. 'We are Jehovah's burglars,' they say. 'We are being persecuted by the police for our beliefs.' 'What beliefs are they?' 'The belief that you have a lot of money in your house.'

Psychiatrists identify precisely these patterns of humour in the thought forms of classically manic patients. Here is a typical description of a classic manic patient, from one of Britain's most noted psychopathologists, Kraupl Taylor, in 1979:

He is never silent but pours out a torrent of words in which a fitful flight of ideas is more conspicuous than any steadfast meaning; no train of thought is verbally expressed for long before it is hustled aside by remarks that go off at a tangent; and when ideas fail, the production of words can go on, though they are strung together for the most casual reasons, perhaps because they rhyme, have a similarity of sound, or convey a precarious pun.

Milligan confesses to firing creatively when he is surging with energy, his mind seething with alliteration, assonance, incongruity. In performance he makes up much of the material as he goes along. The adrenaline flows. When depressed, the creative spark missing, he relies on old, established material.

Does the mania merely supply the energy, stimulating the productivity, or does it actually affect the creative process itself? The kind of humour produced by Milligan makes this question peculiarly difficult to answer. Some Goon humour seems to consist of mental imagery speeded up and verbalized uncensored. Milligan's own account of the whirlwind production of Goon scripts in the early 1950s when he hardly ate or slept recalls Schumann's fevered composition of his Three String Quartets in 1842, when he sometimes began one quartet before he had completed the preceding one. Schumann may well have transcribed hallucinated musical notes and phrases on to the page during manic swings. Milligan certainly notices that, when high, his mind teems with images, words, ideas, which he almost unthinkingly produces as comic material.

CONCLUSION

So is manic-depressive illness the price Spike Milligan pays for his comic genius? The nature of his humour strongly suggests a crucial link. Milligan himself doubts it, pointing out that the Manic Depression Fellowship, a patient support group of which he is patron, contains many people who are not particularly talented yet who have the disease. One thing of which he is certain, however, is that his comic genius is not worth the manic-depressive agony. Yet that begs the crucial question: is the evolutionary purpose of the manic depression gene its role in creativity? For if, as the evidence and Milligan's own life history suggest, manic depression and creativity are indeed causally related, then the question, 'Why does manic depression exist?' may have an answer.

What remains unanswered, however, despite psychiatrists' efforts since the middle of the last century to explain it, is the nature of creativity itself. And among the many thousands of people who suffer from manic depression in Britain at the present time, there has only been and there is only one Spike Milligan. Manic depression, clearly, is not enough.

7

WOMEN AND
DEPRESSION

ONE of the most striking and consistent facts concerning depression, the most prevalent disorder in psychiatry, is that more women are affected than men. In a 1980 study by Goldberg and Huxley, the female:male sex ratios reported in three different clinical settings in two different areas of Britain were as follows (in each clinical setting the figure for Camberwell, in the South of England, is given first, followed by the figure for Salford, in the North): outpatients – 1.07:1 and 1.48:1; day patients – 2.05:1 and 1.06:1; inpatients – 1.35 and 1.02:1.

The problem with treatment-based studies is that the figures obtained are affected by such considerations as the willingness of men and women to seek help for ill-health, by the degree to which doctors recognize ill-health in men and in women and by the willingness of those doctors to initiate specialist referral.

To avoid these problems, researchers have conducted community surveys or sweeps. In 1957, a survey was undertaken of 750 families in a housing estate in Hertfordshire (Martin et al., 1957). The researchers took note of symptoms of depression reported by the estate dwellers but they made no attempt to formulate any diagnoses. Their reported prevalence rates indicated a clear female excess of self-reported depression, 'nerves' and sleep disturbance.

One of the most extensive and intensive community surveys was conducted by Paul Bebbington and his colleagues in Camberwell and reported in 1981. 800 people were screened and the final prevalence of psychiatric disorder was estimated at 6.1 per cent for men and 14.9 per cent for women. Women showed a higher prevalence of disorder in the age-groups 25-34 and 45-54 but in men there was no significant association with age. In both sexes, employment was associated with lower rates of disorder. It is important to note that virtually all the physical illness that was detected was mild in type.

Another and even more extensive study, conducted by Joanne Murray and her colleagues at the Institute of Psychiatry in London, involved a survey of over 6000 people representative of the population of West London. Here too a clear sex difference in the frequency of symptom reporting was found. Men were more likely than women to rate their health as good or very good (66 per cent compared with 54 per cent) and this sex difference persisted across all age groups.

The finding that women tend to report more psychological symptoms of distress than men is a consistent one. Eugene Paykel (1991), in a systematic review of the evidence, concluded that 'Depression in treated samples shows an approximately 2:1 female preponderance'.

But if we separate out the more serious forms of depression from the milder ones, does the female preponderance persist? No, it does not! The sex incidence of bipolar manic-depressive illness, for example, is approximately equal. Findings from Danish and American studies have suggested female:male ratios ranging from 0.5:1 to 1.3:1 and averaging out at 0.9:1.

This finding adds strength to the view that bipolar manic depression and possibly the more severe forms of unipolar depression are different from the milder forms of anxiety and depression that constitute the bulk of psychiatric disorders occurring in the community and general practice. The roughly equal sex difference supports too the argument that these severe forms of mood disorder are more biological in origin and that the female preponderance in mild to moderate depression suggests that these may be more psychosocial in origin. But are we any clearer about why women appear to suffer more mild and moderate depression than men?

POSSIBLE CAUSES

For the purpose of clarity, theories about possible causes of the apparent excess of mood-related disorders in women can be divided into biological theories and environmental theories. The biological group includes genetic and hormonal theories. The environmental category includes social stress, social supports and sex roles as possible causes.

Genetic factors

The argument in favour of a gene or genes operating in mood disorders, as we have seen in Chapter 4, is plausible and persuasive. The argument is strongest, however, when it comes to established bipolar manic depression and the more severe forms of unipolar depression. As we have seen above, these are not more prevalent in one sex. The evidence that a genetic component may play a role in the less severe forms of mood disorder, the forms which particularly afflict women, is far less convincing.

Hormones

As we have seen, the body rhythms of sleep, appetite, libido, temperature and hormonal secretion are all disturbed in depression. Researchers explore these changes in the hope of unlocking the secret of depression itself. The menstrual cycle is another body rhythm but one unique to one sex. There has, as a result, been much discussion of its possible role in explaining illness variations between the sexes, most notably variations in mental ill-health. Such medical interest has not been without benefit. The 'medicalization' of the menstrual cycle has, it could be argued, resulted in vaginal infections being recognized as caused by bacteria rather than demonic possession; puerperal psychosis (following childbirth) as a consequence of organic changes rather than misbehaviour; and menopausal symptoms the result of waning hormones rather than hysterical over-sensitivity.

However, there are problems. The most serious is the tendency to equate menstruation with disease. Consider, for example, the operation of hysterectomy. In the United States, it is the second-commonest operation after Caesarean section. One particular enthusiast in the late 1960s argued that:

> after the last planned pregnancy, the uterus becomes a useless, bleeding, symptom-producing, potentially cancer-bearing organ and therefore should be removed.

> (Wright, 1969)

The widely respected *Novak's Textbook of Gynecology* largely agreed. In its 1975 edition it noted that:

> Menstruation is a nuisance to most women and if this can be abolished without impairing ovarian function, it would probably be a blessing to not only the woman but her husband . . . thus one can make a rather convincing case for the value of elective hysterectomy and there seems definitely a trend in this community as well as in the country as a whole for this to be the procedure of choice.

Such views envisage each organ of the body purely in terms of narrow physical function. Medicine, within such a model, becomes the human equivalent of car mechanics. In addition, much human discomfort, unhappiness and distress is attributed not to an interaction of biological events and social psychological factors but to hormones. Doctors, and many women too, come to believe that whereas little can be done concerning psychological difficulties and social problems, there is often a pill, pessary or potion that promises relief. In the case of the menstrual cycle, the rhythmic ebb and flow of the hormones and the monthly bleed become simultaneously the suspected cause of all manner of physical and psychological complaints and the target of medical and surgical interventions.

18th and 19th century attitudes

That the medical profession, particularly in the 18th and 19th centuries, succumbed to the view of the menstrual cycle as a major factor in female pathology has been ably documented by a variety of historians, including Haller, Showalter, Shorter and Rosenberg. Women have long been seen as both the prisoners and the products of their reproductive systems. By the turn of the 19th century, the President of the American Gynecological Society was able to declare with confidence that the healthy woman is one who is sexually burned out!

> Many a young life is battered and forever crippled in the breakers of puberty; if it crosses these unharmed and is not dashed to pieces on the rock of childbirth, it may still ground on the ever-recurring shallows of menstruation, and, lastly, upon the final bar of the menopause ere protection is found in the unruffled waters of the harbor beyond the reach of sexual storms.
>
> (Engelmann, 1900)

The 'ever-recurring shallows of menstruation' exercised a fascination on doctors other than gynaecologists. 19th century physicians solemnly considered the enormous and largely negative implications of menstruation for women and society generally and issued appropriately apocalyptic warnings. The female sex, one physician explained in 1827,

> is far more sensitive than the male, and extremely liable to those distressing affections which for want of some better term have been determined nervous, and which consist chiefly in painful affections of the head, heart, side, and indeed of almost every part of the system.
>
> (Hall, 1827)

The intimate and hypothetical link between ovaries, uterus and nervous system was the logical basis for the 'reflex irritation' model of disease causation so popular in 19th century texts. It was accepted that any imbalance, exhaustion, infection or other disorder of the reproductive system could cause pathological reactions in other parts of the body. No organ, and certainly not the brain, was untouched. The brains of women, in the view of one senior French scientist in the late 1880s, Gustav le Bon, resembled those of gorillas more closely than those of men. Le Bon conceded that there were a few intelligent women around, but it was a grudging admission, for he went on to argue that such women were monstrosities, like a gorilla with two heads! In his classic text, *Functions of the Brain*, published in 1876, the celebrated British neurologist, Sir David Ferrier, argued:

> As the reproductive organs in women form such a preponderant element in their bodily constitution, they must correspondingly be more largely represented in

the cerebral hemispheres, a fact which is in accordance with the greater emotional excitability of women and the relatively larger development of the posterior lobes of the brain . . .

By the end of the last century it was being seriously suggested that there was a male and a female hemisphere in the brain. The male was said to be the left cerebral hemisphere, and was regarded as more stable, verbal and intellectual: the female was the right and was viewed as more excitable, intuitive and more readily exhausted. The medical historian, Anne Harrington, commenting on such ideas in 1987, observed somewhat wryly that once one has given the two hemispheres gender identities, the idea of cerebral dominance, whereby the left is characteristically seen to take precedence over the right on account of its being the location of the speech centre, 'becomes a rather apt metaphorical encapsulation of the social and economic relationship between the sexes in 19th-century Europe'.

Theories of female insanity were specifically linked to the biological milestones of the female life cycle – puberty, pregnancy, childbirth and the menopause – during which the mind could be weakened and the symptoms of psychological exhaustion and even insanity could emerge. So worried had physicians become concerning the alleged impact of woman's 'periodical ordeal' (a euphemism for menstruation), for example, that they began to express warnings regarding its effects on those women who had begun to invade traditional bastions of male supremacy, such as medicine and the medical school. One horrified physician wrote in 1869:

> One shudders to think of the conclusions arrived at by female bacteriologists or histologists at the period when their entire system, both physical and mental, is, so to speak, 'unstrung', to say nothing of the terrible mistakes which a lady surgeon might make under similar conditions.

(Irwell, 1869)

God knows what the poor man would have made of a female Prime Minister! Rejecting John Stuart Mill's proposal for female suffrage in 1867, *The Lancet* observed that a woman's place is in the home; in support of this sturdy proposition, the journal pointed to the fact that women's physical nature

> shows a comparative delicacy, the confirmation of structures and organs is less developed; there is less stength and vigour, and less fitness to encounter the obstacles of intercourse with the world.

Then, as now, women appeared trapped whichever way they moved. The traditional Victorian woman was constrained within an occupational role she neither accepted nor could find relief in. Fearful of the outside world of which she was still unsure, she languished in a state of constant nervousness, to judge from the records of physicians of the day. Because of the lack of diversification in women's work, they were seen to be the victims of 'habit fatigue'. A psychophysical change was said to occur that affected the centres of sensation in the brain and gave rise to feelings of depression, lassitude and tension.

The radical woman wishing to break out of this unhealthy domestic 'hot-house' could not apparently avoid the vulnerability to neurasthenia that appeared to accompany the more traditional feminine role. Indeed, her very efforts to immerse herself in the outside world only exposed her innate weakness all the more. Because a woman used her brain 'but little and in trivial matters', as George Beard, the American psychiatrist who 'discovered' neurasthenia elegantly put it, and because the capacity of her brain was but nine-tenths that of man, the efforts to change her lifestyle amounted to a futile challenge to her physical and mental constitution.

Indeed some went further and saw in a woman's efforts to change her social role evidence of mental instability itself. In a letter to *The Times*, the prestigious bacteriologist Sir Almroth Wright alleged that 'there is mixed up with the women's movement much mental disorder', a view that echoed those in a number of the newspaper's leaders, most notably that of 16th March, 1912. Under the heading 'Insurgent Hysteria', it described the 'regrettable by-products of our civilization' whose lack of mental balance provided the suffragettes with their recruits.

Victims of their biology

And with such a reductionist view came reductionist treatments. Ruth Bleier, in a powerfully polemical assessment of medical attitudes to women, reminds her readers of the widespread use and acceptance by the medical profession in the US of clitoridectomies and ovariectomies as modes of control of a woman's sexuality, mind and body throughout the last half of the 19th and the early 20th centuries. These were treatments for what male doctors diagnosed as hysteria, insanity, nymphomania, other sexual transgressions (contraception, abortion, orgasm) and dissatisfaction with women's 'normal' role within the family. Underpinning these diagnoses and treatments were a series of core beliefs: that women by virtue of their biology are always but a step away from hysteria, mental illness or criminality; that these biological tendencies lead to sexual transgressions and deviations from the social norms for middle- and upper-class women; that just being female was a disease. One consequence, Bleier points out, was that:

> Upper and middle class husbands and fathers handed over their fatigued, ailing, deviant or disorderly women to physicians, who became involved with their patients in a cycle of drug prescribing and operations, often removing one ovary and tube at a time – an approach that only served to make women more dependent, demanding and sickly. Many women, believing that ovaries and uterus were the source of their troubles, sickness or unhappiness, requested their removal themselves, according to gynaecologists of the time.
>
> (Bleier, 1984)

Many of these self-same arguments, albeit couched in more detached and scientific terms, can be heard today. Women are prone to psychological and psychosomatic complaints, so the argument goes, which is due to their hormonal make-up, their innate excitability, their lack of stability. Protagonists point to menstruation, pregnancy and the menopause as moments when women are especially vulnerable to depression, and conclude that it is their hormones and the biological, rhythmic cycle with which they are intrinsically linked that render them so vulnerable. Let us consider the evidence.

Previous attitudes to menstruation

The occurrence of physical and psychological changes during the time just before the onset of the msntrual flow was mentioned in the writings of Hippocratic physicians. Outside of the medical literature, there are references to premenstrual disturbances affecting health and behaviour. The French historian, Jules Michelet, for example, explained that for a period of 15 or 20 days out of every 28, a woman is 'not only an invalid but a wounded one'. The socially deviant heroine of August Strindberg's *Miss Julie* is explained by one of her servants: 'It's just her time coming on. She's always queer then.' Since Strindberg, a number of writers, including Anaïs Nin, Doris Lessing, William Faulkner and John Fowles, have made similar references to menstrually related alterations in mood and behaviour.

Not until 1931, however, did such alterations become identified as a medical syndrome. It was then that an American physician, Robert Frank, drew the attention of the New York Academy of Medicine to 'a large number of women who are handicapped by premenstrual disturbance of a manifold nature'. In the same year, the psychoanalyst Karen Horney published a paper, 'Die premenstruelle Verstimmungen', in which she explained the occurrence of premenstrual symptoms in terms of repressed sexual desire and power. Frank, a physician in the robust tradition, preferred faulty ovaries as the likeliest cause and prescribed ovarian irradiation as the chosen form of treatment!

For 30 years not a lot happened. There was some tinkering with the definition of the syndrome, which was hardly surprising since there was little agreement as to what symptoms constituted the premenstrual syndrome, what portion of the menstrual cycle was affected, whether symptoms promptly disappeared with the onset of menstruation and what possible causes were involved.

Origins of the premenstrual syndrome

Two developments appear to have contributed to an upsurge of interest in the late 1950s. The first was the growing application of new techniques to identify and measure the various hormones that wax and wane through the normal menstrual cycle. The second development related to the more sophisticated approach to the identification and quantification of psychological symptoms adopted in psychology and psychiatry.

By the mid 1970s an observer might have been forgiven for believing that an epidemic of premenstrual disorders was underway. Much of the energy behind the surge of interest could be traced to one individual, the redoubtable Katharina Dalton. Indeed so powerful a voice has Dr Dalton's been that one commentator, Germaine Greer, in a characteristically sharp essay written in 1981, suggested that it might be less confusing

> If we decided to follow the procedure usually adopted in such cases and named the syndrome after the woman who has devoted the last thirty years of her life to tracking it down and treating it, simply, the Dalton Syndrome.

In a series of papers and several influential books, Dalton mounted a massively persuasive case concerning the widespread nature of the premenstrual syndrome, its neglect by the medical profession and its grave physical, psychological and social consequences. Significant associations were claimed between the premenstrual phase of the menstrual cycle (the seven to ten days prior to the onset of the menstrual bleed) and such things as accidents, examination failure, crime, maternal illness behaviour, children's hospital admissions and suicide. The premenstrual syndrome was classically defined as the occurrence of a cluster of physical and psychological symptoms occurring during the seven to ten days leading up to the onset of the menstrual period. Dr Dalton widened this definition to include a very much larger number of symptoms and behaviours, including aggression, clumsiness and unpredictability.

The impact was dramatic. Some commentators, for example, demanded modification of the circumstances in which menstruating girls sat important examinations. Others insisted that warnings be circulated to women concerning the need for them to take special care while driving in the premenstrual phase. The reported prevalence rate of premenstrual irritability, tension and depression steadily rose, with several research groups reporting a significant majority of women in the child-bearing years to be afflicted.

Premenstrual syndrome: the dissenting voice

Yet there were some dissenting voices. In the United States, a sociologist, Mary Parlee, lamented the quality of the research, the uniformly negative approach to menstrual-cycle experience, the reliance on retrospective reporting, the lack of standardized measures of symptoms and behaviours, and the variation in definition of the syndrome employed.

While many of these methodological shortcomings have been addressed and overcome in the years that have passed, the original claims have remained remarkably persistent, despite the frailty of the foundations on which they rest. Few women and men realize, for example, that the claims linking premenstrual changes with serious crime, poor examination performance, suicidal behaviour and road accidents have never been substantiated.

Take what is potentially one of the most damaging claims – that a woman's ability to function intellectually during the premenstrual phase is impaired. Dalton's study of the intellectual performance of English schoolgirls provides the main supporting plank for this claim. The study involved an assessment of the effect of the premenstrual and menstrual phases of the cycle on the weekly grades of schoolgirls at a boarding school. A fall in the standard of school work during the premenstruum was found in 27 per cent, no change was found in 50 per cent and an actual improvement was found in 17 per cent. No statistical validation of the data was provided nor was the magnitude of any disimprovement revealed. Dalton also reported in a different sample that lower examination scores among English schoolgirls were noted during the premenstrual phase, but again no statistical data were reported (Dalton, 1960, 1968).

Since these studies, there have been several quite detailed and careful attempts to establish this negative effect of the premenstrual phase, with little success. In a particularly thorough effort, Walsh and his colleagues in 1981 studied the examination results obtained by 244 female medical and paramedical students in all examinations taken during one year and were quite unable to show any significant menstrually related effect on academic performance. Despite their negative findings, the authors just could not bring themselves to suggest that perhaps many of the other much-trumpeted claims concerning the negative impact of the premenstrual phase could do with a similar scrutiny. They preferred more cautiously to declare:

> In summary, although its effects are manifold and sufficient to cause both mental and physical distress in a large proportion of women, it seems that the menstrual cycle does not represent a significant examination handicap to the majority of female students.

It was, for all its careful qualifications, a brave statement, given the research efforts that had already gone into establishing links between the premenstrual phase and such variables as psychomotor activity, hormonal and other blood constituent levels, sensory threshold and central nervous system electrical activity. All these fascinating biological findings must after all mean something when it came to women sitting down and answering examination questions – yet to date there is substantial evidence to suggest that they do not. But one of the serious consequences of what has been termed the 'medicalization' of the menstrual cycle is that researchers are frequently tempted to assume a behavioural effect for an identified biological change, while neglecting to consider the possibility that such biological changes might be irrelevant or might be counteracted by other changes that have not been studied, discovered or recognized for what they are.

Within the medical literature of the time, such claims were accepted relatively uncritically, the few voices raised in doubt belonging in the main to psychologists and sociologists. One worried feminist observer of the discussion concerning the negative impact of the premenstrual phase was moved to write an anguished piece in a British weekly following two criminal trials (R v. Craddock; R v. English) in which the two female defendants successfully pleaded premenstrual syndrome as a defence against charges of aggressive behaviour and violence. (Dr Dalton appeared in both cases and gave expert evidence for the defence.)

Diminished responsibility through PMT?

Janet Radcliffe Richards, in her piece entitled 'PMT – an obstacle in the fight for female equality?' worries that the popularity of the diagnosis of the premenstrual symdrome might lead to a resurgence in the prevalence of deeply held prejudices about the inherent unreliability and instability of women. She attempted to reassure herself and her readers by emphasizing that 'only a tiny minority get into a state of diminished responsibility through PMT' (Richards, 1982).

Suggesting that fewer women than was originally thought suffer from the condition is one way of coping; recent prevalence estimates now reveal that only a tiny proportion of women are seriously mentally or physically affected by the phases of the menstrual cycle. Another way is to suggest that the very frequency of premenstrual symptomatology has quite different implications. Here is Germaine Greer commenting on this issue:

> Most women would readily agree with Dr Dalton that paramenstruum (the period of the menstrual cycle including the premenstrual phase and the menstrual period itself) is a time of vulnerability but that is not at all the same thing as giving up any attempt to control it. Even given the period of vulnerability, women get up to very little mayhem compared to men, who have no cycle at all. Perhaps the predilection of men for rapine and slaughter should be interpreted as meaning that men are premenstrual at all times.

Greer's observation is more than a debating point. All the major behaviours allegedly associated with the premenstrual phase are behaviours for which men are very much more noteworthy than women – aggressive and violent behaviour, road accidents and suicide. But her more important point concerns the way in which the medicalization of the menstrual cycle takes control over its effects away from women and places it in the hands of doctors. The last 30 years have seen a bewildering array of treatments advocated for the premenstrual syndrome; many of them, such as progesterone, bromocriptine, oestrogen implants, are not without potentially serious side-effects. In contrast, the literature relating to the psychological and social treatments of premenstrual symptomatology is considerably thinner. My own research colleagues, Roslyn Corney and Bob Newell, have shown that the use of behavioural treatment and relaxation does offer considerable relief to women who complain of premenstrual symptoms, and there is now growing interest in this whole area (Corney et al., 1990).

Prevalence figures in excess of 90 per cent were originally reported. That is to say, it was claimed that the vast majority of women in their active reproductive years were quite seriously handicapped by irritability, tension, depression and a variety of physical symptoms in the week prior to the onset of each menstrual period. However, whenever care has been taken to eliminate the common errors in estimating frequency, the true prevalence of severe premenstrual symptoms does not appear to exceed 10 per cent, and in most instances appears to be less than 5 per cent.

A very revealing and fairly typical illustration is provided by the experiences of one research study. Out of 254 women referred to a specialist service for premenstrual complaints, only 42 met the strict but now widely accepted operational criteria of established premenstrual syndrome. Yet when these 42 women were followed up over the menstrual cycle, only 26, or approximately 10 per cent of what was already a highly selected sample, had severe symptoms during the premenstrual phase and at no other time in the cycle (Steiner et al., 1980).

This is not to underestimate the impact of the syndrome on the 5 to 10 per cent of affected women in the active, reproductive phase of their lives. But it is important to recognize that an imprudent overestimation of the prevalence of the syndrome can and did very quickly rekindle old ideas concerning the allegedly innate vulnerability and instability of women due supposedly to the vagaries and variations of their reproductive system. The extent to which this can be self-fulfilling can only be guessed at. Persuade enough women that their ills and dissatisfactions are partly or entirely due to disturbances in their menstrual cycle and one consequence is what researchers continue to report, namely many more women claiming to have the syndrome than turn out on closer examination to do so.

The female sex hormones that are active in the menstrual cycle and vary during it (such as progesterone, oestrogen and prolactin) do affect and interact with the monoamines believed to be involved in mood disorder – serotonin, dopamine and noradrenaline (discussed in Chapter 4). For this reason, researchers are particularly interested in a possible link between premenstrual depression and depression itself. But thus far the results have been disappointing. Women who are vulnerable to depression are more likely to complain and be affected during the week leading up to their period. But for the majority of women the premenstrual phase is negotiated without undue psychological distress. It is, therefore, unlikely that premenstrual changes underpin the excess of psychological illness which women manifest compared with men during the mid-life phase.

Pregnancy and childbirth

What of pregnancy and childbirth? Depression during pregnancy is common. A study undertaken by Russell Blacker and myself in a North London general practice found a trend towards higher rates of depression in the first and third trimesters. This result was similar to that identified by Channi Kumar and Kay Robson in their 1964 study of pregnant women. But pregnancy is also a significant precipitating life event for men too! One study has reported that half of a sample of 50 manic-depressive men relapsed during or immediately after their wives' pregnancies.

Childbirth is strongly associated with mood change. Postnatal depression (PND) is the most common form of psychological distress after childbirth but the term is loose and tends to be used to cover three distinct conditions – 'baby blues', postnatal depression itself and puerperal psychosis.

In the days immediately following delivery, between two-thirds and three-quarters of mothers are affected by 'baby blues', or rapidly alternating highs and lows. The mothers swing from feeling euphoric and exceedingly happy to tearful and distressed. It lasts about 48 hours and clears up as rapidly as it began. The 'blues' are thought to be linked with the sudden and substantial hormonal changes which occur after childbirth. Similar shortlived changes of mood have been described post-operatively in men as well as women.

Postnatal depression affects between 10 and 30 per cent of mothers. It appears usually within six weeks of delivery, although occasionally later, and is marked by sleeping and eating difficulties, marked fatigue, inability to cope, loss of confidence and of self-esteem, and periodic feelings of despair. Contributory factors include difficulties coping with a newborn baby, marital conflict, financial strain, difficulty sleeping by virtue of breast-feeding demands and the presence of other small children.

The third and most extreme condition is puerperal psychosis. The majority of these psychoses are manic-depressive in type and occur within one month of delivery. The incidence rate is between 0.5 and 2 per 1000 deliveries. The risk in mothers who have had a puerperal psychosis with a previous pregnancy or who have had an episode of manic depression is substantially increased, perhaps to as much as one in ten. There is no clear association between puerperal psychosis and obstetrical complications, nor is the rate higher in those mothers for whom the pregnancy is unwanted.

Because the postpartum phase (after childbirth) is one of considerable hormonal change, there is much interest in the possibility that some abnormality of hormonal function, or some alteration in receptor sensitivity or neurotransmitter function, may be at work in manic depressions occurring at this time. Recent evidence from Ian Brockington and his colleagues in Birmingham does suggest that such psychoses as occur around this time are not related to recent life events, making a hormonal cause more plausible (Brockington et al., 1990). The problem is that, to date, there is little evidence that hormonal changes in women with puerperal psychosis differ from those in unaffected women during this same phase. If hormonal factors do play a part, it may be as precipitating factors in women predisposed to develop serious disorder for some other reason.

The clinical features of severe manic depression occurring in the post-partum phase are similar to those in orthodox manic depression save for a couple of exceptions. The puerperally depressed woman is often seriously deluded, believing her baby to be malformed, possessed, damaged or altered in some way; acting on such beliefs, she may attempt to kill her child, herself or both.

It has been suggested that parity (the fact that a woman has previously borne a child) might explain the sex differences in the prevalence of depression. The effect, however, does not appear to be related to the number of pregnancies a woman has had nor to whether the mother has to care for the children at home during the day. In certain social conditions, parity may be protective – in a 1989 New Zealand study, Sarah Romans-Clarkson found lower rates of depression in women with children than women with no children, for example. But most of the evidence does suggest that once a woman has experienced pregnancy she remains more susceptible to depression until around the age of the menopause. Clearly both biological and non-biological factors could be at work, and the role of both remains to be clarified.

The menopause

What evidence is there that women are particularly prone to depression at the time of the menopause? The evidence in favour tends to come from the findings of gynaecologists on the basis of studies of statistically dubious and unrepresentative samples of women attending their clinics. When properly controlled studies are undertaken, they provide little support for the widely held view that the menopause is a psychologically traumatic time for women and no evidence that it results in an upsurge of depression.

Dennis Gath and his colleagues at Oxford have reported a link between depression and menopausal symptoms such as flushes and sweats, but not between depression and cessation of menstruation. The issue revolves around the view that oestrogen deficiency is the cause of some depressions at this time. In many countries, oestrogen has been used to treat depression around the menopause but the results are unclear. Psychiatric symptoms around this time could, of course, reflect changes in the woman's role as her children leave home; her marital relationship changes; her own parents age, get ill and die; and she reassesses her own life.

In summary

Summarizing these findings, it would appear that hormones do not account for the mild to moderate depressions reported by women but may play a significant role in the major affective disorders seen around childbirth. Pregnancy, menstruation and the menopause do not appear to be particularly risky times for the development of depression although at these times established manic depressive illnesses may well relapse or worsen.

Environmental causes

Research into depression in the community has provided evidence that life events such as the death of a spouse or job loss, and chronic social stresses such as financial hardship, migration and low social class, are implicated as causes of depression. There is evidence too that social supports – friends, an understanding spouse or lover, an integrated community – may ameliorate or 'buffer' the effect of social stresses on health to reduce the liability to depression.

Social stress

There does not appear to be much evidence to support the view that one or other of the sexes experience more life events or adversity. It is still possible that women in general do experience more undesirable life events by virtue of their low social and economic status overall, since there is much evidence that women stil have less overall status than men, both at home and at work, and frequently earn less even when in comparable jobs. There is no evidence as yet to indicate whether women experience more chronic stress than men.

Social supports

It has been repeatedly claimed that casual, less intimate friends as well as intimate ones afford protection from developing illness and that psychological symptom levels probably vary with social support even when there is no serious life event present. It is therefore apparent that contacts with colleagues at work may also be supportive to the individual. It is argued that the housebound woman experiences relative isolation in the home, experiencing less frequent daily verbal exchanges with other individuals than does her male counterpart in the office. To date, the evidence is conflicting as to which of the sexes enjoys the greater degree of social support.

Sex roles

Much attention is currently being paid to the possibility that it is sex-role conflict that renders women more vulnerable to psychological ill-health. It has, for example, been suggested that sex differences in the early upbringing and social environment of men and women place a permanent stamp on the personality of the individual, thus affecting vulnerability to psychiatric ill-health in later life. Evidence certainly exists to support the notion of sex-stereotypic beliefs about male and female abilities. There is some evidence that these stereotypic beliefs, particularly as they relate to female abilities, encourage low self-esteem; but how far this phenomenon might account for the sex difference in illness rates remains to be assessed.

There have been surprisingly few studies that have attempted to compare illness rates in men and women after having matched them for certain crucial social variables related to sex roles and self-esteem – variables such as educational attainment, occupation, occupational opportunity, financial remuneration, personal autonomy and responsibility. A British researcher, Rachel Jenkins, has, however, attempted just such a study. She selected a sample of employed men and women drawn from a population of executive officers in the Home Office. The study used a number of tried and tested measures of psychological ill-health and social stess and involved 104 men and 80 women. She chose this sample because Home Office executive officers, male and female, are comparable in terms of age, educational background and achievement, occupational and social environment, and indeed occupational opportunities and promotion prospects. She found that there was no difference between the men and the women when it came to psychological ill-health in the sample in general (Jenkins, 1985).

An Australian researher, Kay Wilhelm, working in Sydney with a sample of teacher trainees, was similarly anxious to ensure that the men and the women she studied were comparable in terms of important social factors. Setting aside such dominant social elements would help establish the extent to which biological features do play a crucial role in any excess of psychological morbidity in women. Her sample, 350 in number, was scrupulously assessed and then reassessed five years later. The mean age of the group on entry into the study was 23 years (28 years on follow-up). Again, she found no difference between the male and the female teacher trainees in terms of their consulting for help with psychological symptoms although, interestingly enough, women were more likely to have sought help from a friend for depression. Medication for 'nerves' had been taken by 11.9 per cent of the females and 7.1 per cent of the males in the previous year. Scores on depression and self-esteem scales were the same for males and females (Wilhelm and Parker, 1989).

It may well be that as the samples age, the sexes will diverge and begin to show the familiar excess of mild to moderate depression in women over men. Such an excess could still have biological factors operating, but I am doubtful. What of the role of marriage, a social factor which exercises a differential effect upon the sexes? It has indeed been argued that if women are biologically more susceptible to mental illness than men, women should have higher rates of such illness in each marital category. In fact, the literature tends to suggest that, while married women do indeed have higher rates of psychological ill-health than married men, single women, the divorced and widowed do not have higher rates than their male equivalents. Indeed, this has led some to conclude that being married is a less stressful and more satisfying experience for men than for women in Western society.

Divorce is certainly stressful for both sexes but, from the mental health perspective, it appears to be particularly so for men. For example, the standardized patient consulting ratios by marital status for all psychiatric disorders is 95 for married men, 98 for married women, 143 for divorced men, 119 for divorced women.

In their report, *Breakdown and the Health of the Nation*, Dr Jack Dominian and his colleagues at the marriage research centre, One Plus One, provide substantial evidence in support of their thesis that marital breakdown has a more profound and damaging effect on men than on women. The relative risk of premature death is much higher in divorced men than divorced women. Divorced men have higher relative risks for a wide range of illnesses, and not just psychiatric ones, than divorced women. Divorced men have higher rates of mental-hospital admissions and higher rates of alcohol abuse.

All of this strongly supports the argument of those who insist that marriage is good for men and not for women. It may also be, of course, that divorce is particularly difficult for men because of major gender differences in the divorce process. First of all, as in much of Western Europe, women in England and Wales are the official instigators of divorce; 73 per cent of all divorce petitions are granted to them. In addition, women are much more likely to be granted custody of any children and possibly less likely to leave the matrimonial home. The 'active' partner in the divorce process is much less able to deny the fact of marital separation, a maladaptive coping mechanism associated with a greater chance of ill-health. This has been found in a study of the impact of divorce and separation on work and career, in which profound differences between men and women in terms of their repsonses to marital breakdown and the associated stress were found (Paul et al., 1990).

Spike Milligan's experience of marital breakdown confirms such a view. In 1957, his marriage to June Marlowe, which had lasted five years and had produced three children, broke up. June left home taking the children with her. Spike was in Australia when he received her letter, and on the ship home he took an overdose.

> I just couldn't take it, we were cut off at sea, I couldn't get to a telephone, we were crossing the Pacific, the next port of call would be Panama. I couldn't stand the tension so I did take a massive dose of sleeping pills. I think it was a token suicide but I had forgotten that I had invited the ship's doctor to come for a drink in my cabin. All I remember was a stomach-pump and he was saying 'How many did you take?'
>
> (Scudamore, 1987)

When he got back, the home was empty and June had filed for divorce. She had found another man. Spike decided to contest custody and, to his own surprise, he succeeded. Nevertheless, he has never ever really come to terms with this break-up. When depressed nearly 40 years later, he insisted to me that he had been primarily responsible, and the one area where he readily admitted to causing people pain was in relation to his children. To a very great extent, the agony of those days appears to have fuelled his enormous determination to ensure that his three young children would have as stable a life as possible. He was granted custody in 1960 and married Patricia Ridgeway in 1961. Spike Milligan, in common with most men, survived divorce by remarrying as soon as possible.

However, marriage may not be quite the simple psychological stress for women that some critics argue. More searching studies, attending to other factors – including social class, social isolation, poverty and the presence of children – have established that the relationship of marital status to ill-health is complex and varies among groups of different educational attainment.

The argument that employment protects women, single and married, from psychological ill-health is likewise complex. Some studies have found that women employed outside the home enjoy a clear advantage in terms of their mental health compared with women who are occupied full-time within the home. Others, however, have found that this simple finding is complicated by other factors, such as the duration of employment outside the home, the presence of a strong and intimate relationship and the level of educational attainment of the women concerned.

CULTURAL DIFFERENCES BETWEEN THE SEXES

Is it possible that the excess of women suffering from mild to moderate depression is an artefact? Perhaps it is due to the fact that women are much more prepared than men to express distress and dissatisfaction in the form of emotional symptoms such as anxiety and depression, whereas men – fearful of emotional expressiveness, which they associate with 'femininity' – express their distress and dissatisfaction in forms of 'acting out' behaviour (drinking too much, taking drugs, gambling, indulging in extramarital, promiscuous or criminal behaviour). Is it possible that aspects of being a woman have become 'medicalized' into illness, whereas aspects of being a man are elevated into a macho masculinity, the idealized manifestations of bodily and mental strength?

Several studies have indeed shown that it is culturally acceptable for women to be emotionally expressive about their difficulties while men are expected to bear their problems stoically and uncomplainingly. Some studies too have indicated that women are more likely than men to disclose intimate information about themselves, especially unpleasant feelings such as anxieties and worries. On the other hand, there is persuasive evidence that the higher rate of symptoms reported by women do actually reflect real differences in symptom experience between the sexes. They do not merely reflect a greater willingness on the part of women to discuss their problems with others.

And what of the possibility that the excess is due to a greater willingness of doctors to diagnose emotional problems in women? This popular explanation is not actually supported by research findings. There is no evidence that doctors of either sex are more or less partisan towards their own or the opposite sex when it comes to diagnosing depression.

CONCLUSION

The milder forms of mood disorder are more prevalent among females, according to most of the treatment studies, although rising rates of depression in men have been reported in four longitudinal studies. Despite a long, historical preoccupation with biological factors as a cause of the female excess of depression, there is little convincing supportive evidence. Rather, it appears that social and environmental factors, including difficulties pertaining to the role and the status of women, hold the key. There is no female excess when it comes to manic depressive or severe unipolar depressive illness; here women and men appear equally at risk. These facts lend support to the argument that biological factors common to both sexes play a significant role in manic depression and that social and environmental factors may be much less significant (Clare, 1985).

These findings are important. They suggest that when it comes to the depressions and anxieties experienced by women in the community and by women consulting GPs, we would be well advised to look carefully at the burdens borne by women in society at the present time, particularly young and middle-aged women, who are especially at risk. The role conflict experienced by so many women – torn between the demands and the expectations of marriage and family life on the one hand and occupational fulfilment and professional satisfaction on the other – is clearly a major factor in the psychiatric ill-health of large numbers of women at the present time. As for manic depression, women appear no more at risk than men, a finding that casts doubt on the tendency of some doctors to assume that a woman's psychiatric status is a direct reflection of her reproductive system.

8

THE TREATMENT OF DEPRESSION

ONE of the major difficulties affecting those of us who get depressed is that because of our apathy, loss of hope, sheer misery, feelings of guilt and self-reproach, and disinclination to bother people with what seems to be a hopeless case, we just do not believe there is any point in seeking help. Many of the accounts of suicide carried in the newspapers relate to such a state of affairs. Few people in the immediate circle of the suicide victim ever grasp the nature of what is happening or, if they do, have much idea of what might be done. Such deaths are tragic in this day and age because few people suffering from depression or mania need die. Suicide is preventable for the most part. It really is as simple as that.

It is often said, however, that depressed people don't want anything to be done. They don't believe others who try and reassure them that they will get better. They insist that the bleak vision they have of their own lives in particular, and of life in general, is true. They are extremely resistant to suggestions that all is not lost, that recovery can be achieved, that they will feel better, that they have felt better before.

It can be very difficult for friends and relatives emotionally caught up in the despair and despondency of the depressive. In these circumstances, the neutral yet sympathetic observations and responses of a doctor can be of considerable help. The skilled counsellor and doctor, in addition to being able to assess the severity of a mood change, can usually persuade a person to agree to treatment while avoiding arguments as to the effectiveness of any intervention.

Before detailing the many and varied treatments currently available for the treatment of depression and of mania, it is important to consider for a moment the importance of having someone who is there, prepared to listen, willing to support, able to indicate that he or she understands. In their magnificent book *Manic Depressive Illness*, Fred Goodwin and Kay Jamison reproduce a letter from an anonymous patient that eloquently testifies to the inestimable importance and worth of a good, caring, sympathetic, understanding therapist. It tends to get left out in animated discussions of pills and psychotherapy, diet, sunlight, cognitive manipulations. Here is what the patient wrote:

I remember sitting in your office a hundred times during those grim months and each time thinking, what on earth can he say that will make me feel better or keep me alive? Well, there was never anything you could say, that's the funny thing. It was all the stupid, desperately optimistic, condescending things you didn't say that kept me alive; all the compassion and warmth I felt from you that could not have been said; all the intelligence, competence, and time you put into it; and your granite belief that mine was a life worth living. You were terribly direct which was terribly important, and you were willing to admit the limits of your understanding and treatments and when you were wrong. Most difficult to put into words but in many ways the essence of everything. You taught me that the road from suicide to life is cold and colder and colder still, but – with steely effort, the grace of God, and an inevitable break in the weather – that I could make it.

                    (Manic-depressive patient, Godwin and Jamison, 1991)

That testimony says it all. The various treatments described in this chapter are in differing ways effective. The therapist described above enhances the effectiveness of all of them.

Given the multiplicity of theories, claims and findings concerning causation in depression, it is to be expected that there will be many treatments on offer. There are. For simplicity's sake, these can be divided into psychological treatments and physical treatments, although, in truth, such a sharp division is artificial and unnecessarily polarizing. Many treatments exercise psychological and physical effects. Many approaches to the treatment of mood disorders involve the use of both psychological and physical treatments. There is no intrinsic incompatibility between psychotherapy and drugs, for instance. These caveats should be borne in mind during the subsequent discussion of various forms of treatment.

PSYCHOLOGICAL TREATMENTS

Talking about feelings, doubts, guilt, remorse, may seem pointless. How can it possibly help? As the patient above warns, therapy can be patronizing, condescending, stupid. It can indeed be these things, but it can also be helpful. In the milder forms of depression, when the mood swing is not totally incapacitating, when the affected individual is just about able to sustain personal relationships and friendships, can carry on working, and has some (albeit reduced) level of enjoyment in life, then several sessions with a sympathetic counsellor may be all that is required to restore confidence and renew energy. Merely having a sounding-board against which problems can be bounced can make all the difference.

Often the sounding-board is the individual's GP; much general practice is about providing a listening ear. It is, of course, true that many GPs do not appear to have the time to provide such a facility. It is equally true that many find the time and as a consequence do much to ease milder forms of mood disturbance. In the course of reflection, useful advice, reassurance and guidance can be provided.

However, reassurance and a sympathetic ear are not enough for more severe forms of depression. So is there a role for more sophisticated forms of talking – for psychotherapy? A very common assumption is that it is necessary to get at the roots of depression and cure it, rather than merely treating it symptomatically with drugs or some other form of physical treatment; and that the best way to do this is to undergo a deeper form of therapy, one that involves taking the patient back to the earliest years and the earliest experiences by way of the earliest memories. We shall later examine the evidence for this assumption, but for the moment let us just consider what is meant by psychotherapy. After all, it is something of a rag-bag term, seeming to cover everything from a reassuring talk with your golf club bartender to daily psychoanalytic sessions with an expensive psychotherapist.

Psychotherapy

There are various forms of psychotherapy employed in the treatment of psychiatric disorders, but they all have several features in common. These features include an intense, confiding relationship which occurs in a healing setting, is founded on some rationale of therapy and involves a therapeutic procedure.

The many forms of therapy that share these features can be grouped into those which provide support (the supportive psychotherapies), those which attempt to teach the individual new patterns of behaviour and social functioning (the re-educative psychotherapies) and those which aim to dismantle the old and rebuild a new personality (the reconstructive psychotherapies).

Supportive psychotherapy

This is as variously defined as it is widely used. It has been described as a form of psychological treatment given to patients with chronic and disabling conditions, for whom basic and fundamental change is not seen as a realistic goal. Such psychotherapy aims to promote the patient's best level of psychological and social functioning (given the persistence of a disabling condition, such as chronic depression), the bolstering of self-esteem and confidence, the prevention of relapse and, in certain circumstances, the transfer of the source of support from professionals, such as doctors and counsellors, to the individual's family or friends.

Supportive psychotherapy can also be used with reasonably healthy people to ensure that they stay healthy. The Royal College of General

Practitioners in Britain emphasizes in its training the importance of providing support in enabling individuals to negotiate what are termed 'psychosocial transitions' – particular life events and challenges which are known to provide and produce psychological reactions such as depression. Take an event like imminent retirement or the expected demise of an aged, sick and much-loved spouse or relative. The objectives of supportive therapy include the minimizing of the impact of the anticipated event by rehearsing expected feelings and experiences, the provision of protection and relief from responsibilities during the change or bereavement, the encouragement of the expression of emotions and talking through the anticipated difficulties, and the provision of support for the individual's attempts to seek out new directions in life.

In the case of depression, there is much hope that such anticipatory guidance might help people who are vulnerable to depression because of genetic or family reasons, or because they have a history of previous depressive episodes, to avoid becoming depressed. But such support can also help individuals who are already depressed and who are waiting for the full therapeutic effects of other treatments, such as antidepressants, to occur. Supportive psychotherapy involves listening, reassuring when appropriate, explaining and enabling people to express their feelings. In truth, a great deal of medicine, social work, nursing and psychology involves supportive psychotherapy. Many of these professionals provide it in blissful ignorance of the fact that that is indeed what they are doing. Sometimes, with a little more training, they would do it with much more sophistication and effect.

Supportive psychotherapy, however, has little to offer more serious forms of mood disorder. Talking to, listening to, reassuring and advising Spike Milligan in the depth of a depression or at the height of a manic swing would be largely a waste of time.

Re-educative therapy

So what about attempting to change his attitudes and teach him new and more positive patterns of behaviour by the use of re-educative forms of psychotherapy? There is particular interest at the present time in one particular re-educative psychotherapy, namely cognitive behaviour therapy.

Depressed people tend to express their profound gloom and misery by way of repetitive intrusive thoughts reflecting low self-esteem, self-reproach and pessimism. 'I'm a failure' is a common statement. So is 'Everything I do is useless'. Spike Milligan, when depressed, commonly says what he said to me one melancholic day in the autumn of 1990 when we were discussing this book: 'I feel I have no future. I can only think about the past. The present is unbearable.'

This very common kind of cognitive abnormality seen in depression is termed 'cognitive distortion'. The subject's view of reality is impaired. Aaron Beck, the founding father of cognitive behaviour therapy, has described four forms: arbitrary inference, selective abstraction, overgeneralization and magnification-minimization. Arbitrary inference is the process of forming an interpretation of a situation, event or experience when there is no factual evidence to support such an interpretation. Such arbitrary judgements tend to reflect and accentuate underlying low self-esteem, self-reproach and denigration. Selective abstraction is the process of focussing on details taken out of context, ignoring everything else and forming conclusions on the basis of the selected detail. Overgeneralization occurs when a general conclusion is drawn from a single instance. Magnification and minimization are errors of evaluation so gross that they constitute distortions.

The fundamental thrust of cognitive behaviour therapy is to counter these negative thoughts or cognitions. The cognitive therapist aims to train the depressed patient to recognize the negative way in which he or she automatically responds to everyday stresses and happenings and how this amplifies his or her feelings of worthlessness and hopelessness. By training people to challenge their own negative thinking and to consider alternative, more positive and rational explanations, the cycle of repetitive negative thinking, which is such a cardinal feature of depression, is broken.

Beck has helped pioneer an elaborate range of strategies to assist in the development of what is a self-control procedure. They include the verbal challenging by patient and therapist of distorted and negative thoughts and the modifying of negative basic assumptions. For example, take Spike Milligan's tendency, when depressed, to interpret the shortcomings and failings of others as a slight or insult to him. Other people's unpunctuality, an irritant to him at the best of times, becomes a deliberate and calculated slur when he is depressed. Selective abstraction is at work. Or again, when depressed, he is unable to sparkle at a dinner party. He feels guilty and interprets innocuous signs and happenings as evidence that he is letting other people down and affecting their enjoyment. He magnifies the extent to which others notice, and minimizes the fact that he has actually coped well and more than pleased his host.

Cognitive therapy, in these instances, would attempt to help Spike stand back from his interpretations and examine and correct them objectively by reasoning. The therapist would try to help him distinguish appropriate from inappropriate responses and reasonable from unreasonable interpretations. Therapy would also be directed at distracting him from brooding on depressive thoughts – in Spike's case, nostalgic thoughts about the past, India and his children.

Spike Milligan, in common with many depressed individuals, is given to overgeneralization. As already mentioned, the fact that his wartime friend took umbrage over an inconsequential joke is elaborated by Spike, when he is depressed, into a statement about human unreliability and fatuity in general. Therapy focusses on this and other errors of logic, and the therapist points them out repeatedly to the patient to encourage him or her to recognize and correct them in everyday life.

Additional strategies have been developed to help patients combat the inactivity, fatigue and feelings of social inadequacy that are a common feature of depression. For example, an activity schedule can be constructed involving a gradual return to activity appropriate to the person's interests and severity of depression. Tasks are developed to enable the sufferer to test and challenge irrational ideas – the approach being, 'Let's find out what happens if you try to do this.' The sufferer is encouraged to keep a diary of thoughts and moods with the aim of identifying the repetitive intrusive thoughts that help to worsen the depressed mood. Such negative thoughts include, 'I am never going to get well,' 'I cannot cope,' and 'I am a complete burden to others.' The patient is encouraged too to examine the evidence for and against these depressed beliefs, with the aim of increasing awareness of the extent to which thinking is distorted. The therapist may also note the occurrence of positive events and draw these to the attention of the patient in an attempt to disrupt the pattern of negative thinking.

Cognitive therapy commonly involves between 15 and 20 one-hour therapy sessions over a period of about three months. There are now several studies showing that, in the case of unipolar depression of mild to moderate severity, it is every bit as effective as drug treatment and may even be more effective in preventing a recurrence. Patients who appear to respond particularly positively are those who score highly on tests of self-control, that is to say patients who when well typically rely on their own resources rather than on those of others to solve their own problems.

To date, however, there is no convincing evidence of its efficacy in more severe forms of depression and manic depression. In severe forms – and Spike Milligan's illness is a case in point - the depth of depression makes any testing of assumptions and contemplation of alternative modes of reasoning impossible, at least until some relief of the depression has been achieved through other forms of therapy.

A major question-mark opposite this form of therapy concerns the relationship between negative thoughts and depression. The theory suggests that the thoughts occur early in the chain of events that culminate in depression. However, there is evidence that they are merely the symptoms or effects of the depressed mood – ie it is a case of thinking the depressing thoughts because one is depressed, rather than a case of being depressed because one thinks depressing thoughts. Once the depression has cleared, the tendency to see the world through a glass darkly, to indulge in self-blame, to interpret neutral events in a depressed manner, begins to clear too. Recovered manic-depressive individuals seem no more likely to display distorted and depressed thinking than individuals who have never been depressed.

Cognitive behaviour therapy is often criticized for being merely a symptomatic treatment, dealing with and trying to alter the way that people behave, respond and see the world without getting to the bottom of why they have developed such negative ways of thinking and patterns of behaviour in the first place. Many people intuitively believe that getting to the bottom of a problem such as manic depression involves 'deep' psychotherapy of the kind that is popularly associated with psychoanalysis.

Reconstructive psychotherapy

Psychoanalysis is certainly the definitive reconstructive psychotherapy. Its ultimate goal is to reduce the force of irrational strivings and impulses and bring them under conscious control. In addition it aims to increase the range and flexibility of the various forms of psychological defences which enable us to function reasonably effectively and to dissect out our personalities, identifying and eliminating the flaws and maldevelopments. The key defining concepts of psychoanalysis are:

- free association
- interpretation
- transference.

Psychoanalytical technique consists essentially of instructing and helping the patient to express his thoughts and feelings as freely and in as uncensored a form as possible, of interpreting what the patient says and the various difficulties encountered in the therapy, and of analysing and explaining the patient's attitudes and feelings towards the therapist. The approach rests on the psychological theories concerning the origin of psychiatric disorders formulated by Freud and his followers. Crucial concepts in Freudian theory are:

(1) the unconscious, the idea that there exists mental activity of which the subject is unaware but which nonetheless exerts a dynamic effect on his behaviour
(2) resistance, the idea that consciousness resists the emergence of unconscious impulses into consciousness
(3) transference, through which the patient transfers his past emotional attachments, usually involving parental and sibling figures, to the psychoanalyst. The analyst becomes a substitute for the parent or sibling.

Transference may be either positive or negative; in positive transference, the patient loves the analyst and wishes to obtain love and satisfaction from him or her, whereas in negative transference the patient views the analyst as unfair, unloving and rejecting. Interpreting the transference helps make the patient aware of the fact that, for example, his infatuation with the analyst is not related to the analyst as a person but is simply a reflection of previous emotional entanglements and particularly emotional experiences in childhood. Indeed, in psychoanalytic psychotherapy, regression to childhood is necessary for the resolution of conflicts that are seen to have their roots in the earliest years of life.

Psychoanalysis is expensive and time-consuming – ideally it is conducted at least five times weekly, each session lasting 50 minutes. It was not always time-consuming, however. Many of Freud's earliest psychoanalytical treatments were quite short. Bruno Walter, the celebrated conductor, described in his autobiography how he underwent a six-session therapeutic programme, while Ernest Jones recalled that in 1908, in a single four-hour session, Freud was apparently able to elucidate the psychodynamic origins of the composer Gustav Mahler's sexual impotence with his wife, and relieve it. In recent years, as pressure has grown for the development of less expensive and less time-consuming therapies, a number of modified approaches have emerged.

One of the features of psychoanalytic psychotherapy is the relative inactivity of the therapist. It is the patient who is expected to do the talking, the therapist remaining, in Gilbert Ryle's words, 'personally opaque and unrevealing and relatively silent'. It differs from cognitive therapy in being aimed primarily at altering the personality and resolving key conflicts while paying relatively little attention to symptomatic relief. There have, however, been approaches which utilize both psychoanalytic and cognitive principles, and enthusiasts insist that such mixed therapies are effective.

Effectiveness of psychotherapy

Unfortunately, the evidence that psychoanalysis or brief forms of psychodynamic psychotherapy (forms of psychotherapy that rely heavily on Freudian and post-Freudian theory but have evolved more active methods of therapy and intervention and demand less in time and expense) are effective in treating depression is not particularly convincing. It has certainly proved difficult to demonstrate. Only in the past 15 years have appropriately sophisticated attempts been made to discover whether such a costly treatment actually works. More detailed analyses have been required to make sense of the studies. And the conclusion? No single convincing demonstration that the benefits of psychotherapy exceed those of less complex and expensive therapy or indeed of no therapy at all in the treatment of depressive illness.

The debate over the effectiveness of psychotherapy has been one of the stormiest in the history of psychiatric research. Part of the reason has been the fact that the more complicated a therapy is, and the more global and fundamental its aims, the more difficult it is to establish whether it works.

For example, testing a pill that is claimed to lift mood is relatively straightforward. Testing a therapy that includes the personality and training of a therapist, a varying frequency and expense of sessions and a variety of therapeutic techniques; that is used to treat all sorts of patients and that is supposed to change their lives in a fundamental way – testing that is a scientific nightmare. How do you assess change? Suppose the patient is more depressed, has lost his family, job and financial independence but insists that he now understands himself better – is that improvement? Can the treatment be judged a success? Or, alternatively, suppose the patient feels better and behaves better but has given up on everything that appeared to overwhelm him – job, spouse, family – can treatment be judged a failure? And if the therapy has been underway for many years, how does one rule out the possibility that such changes as have occurred would have taken place anyway, given the fact of growing older and wiser?

To side-step such enormous theoretical and practical difficulties, as well as to develop a more pragmatic, effective, feasible and testable form of psychotherapy, a group of researchers in the United States, headed by Myrna Weissman and Gerald Klerman, have developed a more simple form of psychotherapy, which they have termed Interpersonal Psychotherapy (IPT). In this form of psychotherapy, emphasis is placed on current interpersonal relationships and on strategies to improve the individual's personal and social relationships in the 'here and now'. Intense exploration of the individual's past life and experience is avoided. Psychodynamic interpretations based on Freudian and post-Freudian psychoanalytic theory are avoided. The main goal of therapy is to help the individual identify, understand and solve problems in his or her current life and develop more constructive and positive ways of coping and relating to others. Klerman and Weissman (1984) have laid out the rationale for this approach in some detail and have provided systematic and detailed guidelines concerning its use and aims.

What is interesting about IPT is threefold. First, it represents a major shift away from the identification of psychotherapy with psychoanalysis or psychodynamic psychotherapy. Second, it is defined in a way which allows for its effectiveness to be tested. Third, it was specifically designed to be used in the treatment of unipolar depressions of mild to moderate severity.

When the powerful American National Institute of Mental Health (NIMH) decided to study the effectiveness of psychotherapy in the treatment of depression, it was decided to design a study in which cognitive therapy and interpersonal psychotherapy would be compared with antidepressant drug therapy. It was a multicentre trial. 250 depressed patients were allocated to one of four treatment groups receiving

(1) weekly sessions of cognitive therapy for 16 weeks, or
(2) weekly sessions of interpersonal psychotherapy for 16 weeks, or
(3) full therapeutic doses of an antidepressant for 16 weeks, or
(4) a placebo (ie inert pill) for 16 weeks

The benefits of the control treatment – the placebo plus visiting the doctor, reassurance, etc – were considerable. The specific treatments, however, were statistically superior. Whereas 40 per cent of the patients recovered with the placebo, 60 per cent were judged to be recovered with the active treatments. In terms of the most severely depressed patients, antidepressant therapy was the most effective, followed by interpersonal psychotherapy and cognitive therapy (Elkin et al., 1989). It is interesting to note that a decade earlier, Myrna Weissman and her colleagues at Yale had shown that combining interpersonal psychotherapy with antidepressant psychotherapy benefited depressed women to a significantly greater extent than treating them with either of these treatments separately (Weissman et al., 1979).

So important was the NIMH study regarded in the United States that Daniel Freedman, editor of the journal in which it appeared, the prestigious *Archives of General Psychiatry*, issued an editorial note summarizing and highlighting the findings. His conclusions were that for the more severely depressed, standard antidepressant drugs remain the treatment of choice. Interpersonal and cognitive forms of psychotherapy are helpful as additional strategies.

Another respected commentator in this field, Australian psychiatrist Gavin Andrews, reviewing the evidence for the usefulness of psychotherapy in the treatment of depression, comes to similar conclusions. Drugs are clearly effective. Cognitive therapy and simpler forms of psychotherapy are less effective but have a role to play. As for complex, expensive, time-consuming psychotherapy, there is little evidence of therapeutic benefit at the present time. His conclusions at the end of an extensive review in 1991 of the evidence carried out for the journal *Current Opinion in Psychiatry* concerning the efficacy of the cognitive form of psychotherapy versus psychodynamic forms are remarkably honest and sobering:

Until sufficient controlled trials have been completed to show that dynamic psychotherapy is effective, cognitive begaviour therapy is to be preferred in terms of effectiveness and cost. I do not think we meant things to happen this way, and certainly until faced with the literature provided by this journal, I did not think the evidence for dynamic psychotherapy was so bleak. But as Lewis

Thomas said of research, 'You either have science or you don't, and if you have it you are obliged to accept the surprising and disturbing pieces of information, even the overwhelming and upheaving ones, along with the neat and promptly useful bits. It is like that.'

It is indeed like that. Psychotherapy is helpful in severe depression but only in association with antidepressant medication. Cognitive forms of psychotherapy and reality-based interpersonal forms appear superior to psychoanalysis or psychoanalytically derived forms of psychotherapy. Simple reassurance and guidance are of little help in the treatment of severe depression or manic-depressive illness.

PHYSICAL TREATMENTS

For centuries, physicians and patients have sought pharmacological relief for depression, and an extraordinary array of drugs, herbs and medicaments have been tried. Until the development of the antidepressants, none has been effective. One drug that did give hope was the stimulant amphetamine. Amphetamine increases alertness and self-confidence and produces a euphoria and resistance to fatigue, but these are transient effects which wear off rapidly and result in a profound post-treatment depression. Dependence is also a problem and, in a minority of people, severe paranoid reactions can occur.

In 1956, Dr Nathan Kline working at Rockland State Hospital was impressed by the effects on mood of a drug called iproniazid, which at that time was being used to treat tuberculosis. Kline started to give it to depressed patients and was impressed by the results. The drug belongs to a class of drugs called monoamine oxidase inhibitors (MAOIs) still in use today.

That same year, Dr Roland Kuhn and his colleagues in Switzerland, searching for a drug to relieve psychotic symptoms in severely ill patients, developed imipramine. When they tested it in schizophrenia they found it relatively ineffective. But they did note that depressed schizophrenics became less depressed. Imipramine belongs to another class of compounds, the tricyclic antidepressants (TCAs), which to this day remains the mainstay of pharmacological treatment of depressive illness.

It was formerly believed that antidepressant drugs worked by their ability to increase the availability of monoamines, such as noradrenaline and serotonin, at receptors on neurones in the brain. In the case of the TCAs, this was done by blocking the re-uptake of these neurotransmitters from the synaptic cleft, and, in the case of the MAOIs, by slowing the metabolism of the monoamines inside the neurone so that the level builds up (see Chapter 4). However, quite how these drugs work remains unclear. Antidepressants are known to have other effects on other important receptors, and they may also exercise a direct effect on the regulation of circadian rhythms.

The tricyclic antidepressants

These drugs are so-called because they are chemically composed of three linked chains to which a side-chain is attached. Their antidepressant properties depend on the central ring structure, while their potency and sedative properties depend on variations in the side-chain. When a fourth ring is added, they are called tetracyclic. Imipramine and amitriptyline are the two oldest and most commonly used, but many other tricyclic and tetracyclic drugs have been produced. These do not differ greatly in terms of their therapeutic effects, although their different range of side-effects is sometimes useful for the clinician to consider when choosing a particular one.

Tricyclic antidepressants are the first line of physical treatment in depression and are particularly effective in patients with physical symptoms such as sleep disturbance, loss of appetite and physical slowness or agitation. Their main disadvantages are two-fold. First, they rarely begin to exercise a therapeutic effect until between two and four weeks following onset of treatment. Secondly, they can produce disagreeable side-effects which, in the initial stages, are difficult for patients to tolerate.

The delay in effect can lead many patients to discontinue therapy before it has had a chance to take effect. Discontinuation is more of a problem with the older forms of tricyclics, particularly because of unwanted effects such as sedation, blurring of vision, dry mouth and constipation. Such side-effects also mean that many patients resist any increase in dose to appropriate therapeutic levels. As a consequence, patients often fail to respond to the drug because they simply are not getting enough. The newer tricyclics, every bit as effective as imipramine and amitriptyline, appear less likely to cause such side-effects and are much better tolerated.

Improvement in sleep is usually one of the first benefits noted with tricyclic antidepressant therapy. Within six weeks considerable improvement is usually apparent, and by twelve weeks most patients have recovered. Approximately 70 per cent of patients respond to treatment with the first antidepressant prescribed for them. A further proportion, some 10 to 15 per cent, will respond on being switched to another drug, but this leaves up to 20 cent of patients resistant to conventional antidepressant therapy. During his most recent depressive episode, Spike Milligan was one of this 20 per cent!

But there are still ways in which antidepressant effects can be obtained in many of these non-responding patients. Adding thyroid hormone to TCAs produces a positive response within one to two weeks in about 25 per cent of non-responders. The mechanism of thyroid potentiation is unclear. Adding lithium (see below) in doses between 600 and 1500 milligrams daily has also been reported to improve response. This appears to have stimulated a response in the case of Spike Milligan's most recent mood swing. Some non-responders to TCAs respond when switched to NAO inhibitors. Some are effectively treated with a combination of TCAs and MAOIs. And some require ECT for relief.

Once the depression has lifted, many patients are anxious to discontinue taking the drugs. At the present time, many people are worried about drugs and dislike remaining on them, particularly when they feel well. The problem is that, in many instances, depressed patients promptly relapse when they discontinue their antidepressant medication. It has been estimated that the relapse rate in patients who discontinue antidepressant therapy within one year may be as high as 65 per cent – the likelihood of relapse varies greatly with the severity, the past history and the type of depression. Early treatment intervention does appear to shorten the length of the illness episode.

Many depressed individuals appear to benefit from maintenance treatment, ie taking between one half and two-thirds of the therapeutic dose for several months after they have recovered to prevent relapse. More recently, researchers in Philadelphia have studied outcomes in patients maintained on full therapeutic doses of antidepressants for up to three years, some of whom were also in receipt of interpersonal psychotherapy. These researchers concluded that patients maintained on a full dose of tricyclic antidepressants (in this study, 200 milligrams of amitriptyline daily) for three years had a significantly better outcome than patients treated for shorter periods of time and with reduced doses. Monthly interpersonal psychotherapy did seem to lengthen the time between depressive episodes in patients who were not receiving active medication. This study very forcefully raises the possibility that patients who respond to tricyclic antidepressants and relapse when medication is discontinued or reduced, but remain well while maintained on full therapeutic doses, may have to remain on full doses in antidepressants for many years and indeed in some instances for life if they wish to avoid repeated relapse.

But what about side-effects? The commonest side-effects can certainly be distressing, but many do ease with time. The newer antidepressants, including dothiepin, mianserin, and lofepramine, are better tolerated. These are particularly useful in the treatment of depression in the elderly, in the light of their relative lack of unwanted effects on the heart.

Many of the side-effects are well-tolerated by younger patients but are particularly aggravating to more elderly sufferers. Postural hypotension is a case in point. On standing up, the patient's blood pressure falls briefly but sharply. It is a response inherent to most TCAs. Younger patients tolerate it; older patients often do not. For example, a retrospective American study of 100,000 elderly patients was conducted for the purpose of relating the incidence of hip fracture to treatment with psychotropic medication (drugs used in the treatment of psychiatric disorders). The results of this study showed that about 0.7 per cent of patients aged between 65 and 74 years fracture a hip each year. The incidence rises to 2 per cent in the over-75 group. But a hip fracture occurred three times as frequently in those elderly patients prescribed a tricyclic antidepresant. At the present time there is much interest in such new antidepressants as fluoxetine and fluvoxamine (see below), which appear to have much less effect on blood pressure.

The need for safe antidepressants for use in the elderly is underlined by the fact that depression, as we noted in Chapter 3, is common and serious. Another major issue at the present time is the suggestion that depression occurring for the first time in old age might be a risk factor for dementia and that adequate treatment might delay or even prevent dementia occurring. But proper treatment of depression in the elderly is only possible with safe drugs that possess a low number of side-effects and that do not cause confusion, poor brain blood flow or negative effects on memory and concentration.

There is another serious problem with tricyclic antidepressants. They are potentially lethal in overdose. Ten times the normal therapeutic dose of one of the older tricyclics, such as amitriptyline, can cause death, mainly through its effects on the heart. In 1986, of the 4000 suicides committed in England and Wales, 300 were accomplished by overdose with TCAs. In the United States, TCAs are the most common agents used for suicide and are responsible for over 2000 deaths each year.

The frequency of side-effects, the slow onset of therapeutic action and the potential toxicity of TCAs are all reasons for the search for a safer, more effective and more acceptable antidepressant to continue. In recent years, a number of new antidepressants including fluvoxamine, fluoxetine and sertraline have been introduced and more are on their way. These drugs appear to act by way of selective inhibition of serotonin uptake from the synaptic cleft and are thus termed 'selective serotonin re-uptake inhibitors' (SSRIs). While there is still argument as to their superiority as antidepressants over more established tricyclics such as amitriptyline and imipramine, they are becoming popular (one, fluoxetine, is now the most commonly prescribed antidepressant in the US) because of their reportedly lower rate of serious side-effects. It is too early to say that they represent significant advances on the established 'first generation' of antidepressants, but the signs are hopeful.

Monoamine oxidase inhibitors

This group of drugs inhibits or slows down the process whereby the enzyme monoamine oxidase breaks down the neurotransmitters believed to play a key role in the maintenance of normal mood (see Chapter 4). They appear to possess anti-anxiety as well as antidepressant effects, and clinicians have reported them to be useful in the treatment of depression with marked anxiety, phobic anxiety states and anxiety disorders with panic attacks. One, tranylcypromine, has a stimulant effect similar to that of amphetamine, which may account for part of the reputation gained by the whole group in the treatment of depression.

MAOIs are used to treat depressions in which certain 'atypical' features are said to occur, such as the presence of marked anxiety, increased sleep and appetite, and worsening of mood in the evening rather than the morning.

Side-effects of the MAOIs include drowsiness, headache, weakness, fatigue, dry mouth and constipation. Less frequently, agitation, nervousness, blurred vision, difficulty urinating, sweating, rashes and increased appetite are reported. Occasionally, mania can be precipitated. Rare side-effects include convulsions.

The major problem with the MAOIs, however, results from the fact that they prevent the breakdown of tyramine (a substance present in cheese and other foods) and of other amines found in certain medicines (including cough mixtures and laxatives). The resultant build-up of tyramine in the body can cause a dangerous rise in blood pressure (the 'cheese reaction') leading to a stroke or even death. Early symptoms include a severe, usually throbbing headache. Tyramine-rich foods and medicines must be strictly avoided while taking MAOIs and for 14 days after treatment stops. Not surprisingly, these dietary restrictions have made them unpopular drugs with some doctors and patients.

All patients prescribed MAOIs are given a treatment card, to be carried at all time, listing the foods which contain high levels of tyramine and which should be avoided. These include extracts of meat and yeast (Bovril, Oxo, Marmite), broad bean pods, smoked or pickled fish, hung poultry or game, and cheeses (particularly camembert, brie, stilton, gorgonzola, cheddar and some processed cheeses). Chianti, some other red wines and some beers, including low-alcohol and even alcohol-free varieties, may also cause reactions.

A number of drugs, including adrenaline, noradrenaline, amphetamine, fenfluramine, as well as cough medicines containing certain amines, are affected by MAOIs and should not be given simultaneously. Certain drugs used to treat blood pressure, anthistamines, local anaesthetics, opiates, barabiturates and insulin can also be involved in dangerous interactions. Combinations of MAOIs and TCAs should only be administered under careful medical supervision.

It has since been discovered that there are two types of monoamine oxidase, termed MAO-A and MAO-B. It has been suggested that depression is due to a deficiency of monoamines in the central nervous system, especially those metabolized by MAO-A. Selectivity refers to the ability to block either the MAO-A or MAO-B. The early MOAIs were not selective, whereas the new forms are selective inhibitors of MAO-A in man. Not merely are they selective but their effects are readily reversible, which means that the interaction with tyramine is much less likely to occur. As a result, the newer form of MAOI is termed a RIMA (Reversible Inhibitors of MAO-A). Preliminary studies do suggest that these new MAO inhibitors may be as effective as TCAs, but it is early days yet. If true this will be an important step forward. The RIMA-type antidepressants appear to have fewer side-effects, work rapidly and constitute a low risk in overdose. At present, patients prescribed such antidepressants are advised that they can eat a broad diet but should still be careful of foodstuffs rich in tyramine.

The question of addiction

Because of the considerable publicity generated by the discovery of the fact that the benzodiazepine group of tranquillizers can be addictive, many depressed patients, their relatives, members of the general public and journalists writing on health matters appear to believe that antidepressants are addictive too. In the MORI poll conducted for the Royal College of Psychiatrists and published in early 1992, 46 per cent of respondents erroneously classed antidepressants as 'very addictive', a figure not far short of the 56 per cent who correctly placed tranquillizers in the same class. A further 32 per cent of respondents regarded antidepressants as 'fairly addictive' (29 per cent so classed tranquillizers).

Neither the tricyclic antidepressants nor the monoamine oxidase inhibitors, except the amphetamine-like tranylcypromine, cause dependence. The fact that many people believe antidepressants are addictive is a major reason why so many depressed patients are reluctant to take them and why so many relatives, friends and acquaintances spend so much time persuading depressed patients who are taking antidepressants to stop taking them. It is worth repeating: antidepressants are not addictive.

That is not to say that someone taking them can just stop the drugs immediately without experiencing side-effects. Withdrawal should be gradual over two to four weeks. Otherwise, sudden withdrawal can cause nausea, vomiting, loss of appetite, headache, giddiness, chills and insomnia. But if withdrawn rapidly or slowly, antidepressants do not produce the craving desire for the tablets and the inability to cease taking them that are such obvious and distressing features of a drug-dependent state.

Lithium

Lithium salts were initially used in the treatment of gout and as a substitute for salt for patients with heart disease needing to take a salt-free diet, although both these uses have been abandoned. In 1949, John Cade, an Australian psychiatrist, discovered that lithium appeared to exercise anti-manic effects and could prevent the occurrence of mood swings. That the discovery was accidental is an understatement. Cade was actually following up a theory of his own concerning the cause of mania, namely that in some way the substance urea was involved. To test his theory he decided to inject guinea pigs with urea and the only way he could do this involved combining lithium and uric acid in the form of lithium urate. Instead of becoming 'manic', the guinea pigs became quite markedly lethargic. Cade wondered whether lithium might have some calming effect on mood so he administered lithium carbonate to ten manic patients and recorded exceedingly positive results.

Mogens Schou, a Danis psychiatrist, further studied the drug and concluded that indeed lithium did possess potent preventative properties and could counteract one of the major hazards of manic-depressive illness, namely its tendency to recur. Lithium is currently prescribed in the form of lithium carbonate or lithium citrate.

The discovery of lithium's anti-manic properties, in the view of some psychiatrists, was earth-shattering. Ronald Fieve, a prominent American psychiatrist specializing in mood disorders, terms its arrival 'the Third Revolution' in psychiatry. (In Fieve's view, Pinel's freeing mental patients from physical restraints and Sigmund Freud's discovery of psychoanalysis constituted the first two psychiatric revolutions.)

Revolutionary or not, lithium has proven to be a major advance in controlling relapse in hitherto intractable manic-depressive individuals. Currently it is used to prevent reccurrence of mania and depression, to treat acute episodes of mania and, more recently, to treat resistant depression, particularly in combination with tricyclic antidepressants.

What is particularly interesting about lithium is that it is a naturally occurring element and not a synthesized drug. It does not induce dependence and there is no withdrawal syndrome on cessation of its use. Proponents of its use also argue that it is helpful in the treatment of some forms of alcohol abuse, aggressive behaviour and premenstrual tension, but the evidence is conflicting. Lithium does not 'cure' mood swings, but it does appear to prevent them from occurring.

Unfortunately, it may take up to a year to exercise its full effect, and many patients are reluctant to try it for that long. Indeed, failure to take lithium is the commonest reason why relapse occurs. Failure to take enough is another factor. Lithium is a substance which only exercises its clinical effect between a narrow range of levels in the blood – normally between 0.5 and 1.3 millimoles per litre (where a millimole is a measure of the amount of substance in body fluids). Below 0.5 millimoles per litre lithium has no therapeutic effect. Above 1.3 millimoles per litre, lithium starts to cause undesirable effects.

To establish the dose which will produce a therapeutic level in the bloodstream, it is necessary to take a blood test just after commencement of treatment, then regularly until the appropriate blood level has been reached and maintained and then at three- to six-monthly intervals to ensure that the level does not markedly change. It is usual to have the blood test some twelve hours after the last dose of lithium.

Lithium side-effects include a mild hand tremor, increased thirst, increased urination, occasional metallic taste in the mouth, nausea and abdominal cramps. Such side-effects usually subside three to four days after the commencement of treatment. If they persist it will be necessary to reduce the dose. In some patients on lithium, the thyroid gland swells and underactivity of the gland may occur, necessitating either discontinuation of lithium or the addition of a small amount of thyroid hormone. Lithium can also produce weight gain – usually as a consequence of the consumption of high-calorie drinks to assuage the thirst that can be a troubling feature of lithium therapy. Patients are better advised to drink water or a low-calorie alternative if they wish to avoid weight gain.

Lithium is filtered from the blood by the kidneys and partly reabsorbed. Dehydration causes lithium levels to rise. Left unchecked, this can cause problems if the lithium level rises above safe limits. Patients with pre-existing kidney disease shold not be prescribed lithium. Lithium itself can cause kidney damage but the doses need to be consistently high for this to occur. It is wise, however, to check kidney function every six months in patients who are on long-term therapy.

Women who take lithium during the first three months of pregnancy risk deformities of heart and major blood vessels in their babies. The risk being greatest during the early weeks of pregnancy, women of child-bearing years are usually advised to take contraceptive precautions if lithium is being prescribed. Manic-depressive women who wish to become pregnant are advised to discontinue taking lithium. After the first three months of pregnancy, there is no longer a risk to foetal development and the medication can be restarted.

Toxic effects are related to dose. They include poor co-ordination of limb movements, muscle twitching, and slurred speech. Vomiting, diarrhoea and confusion follow as the blood lithium concentration increases. Coma and convulsions can occur and, if untreated, death. Lithium must be stopped and a high intake of fluid provided. The commonest causes of such toxicity include: (1) taking too many lithium tablets (either accidentally, or as part of a suicide attempt); (2) the loss of salt from the body (due to physical illness such as fever, nausea, vomiting, diarrhoea or dehydration, dieting or fasting, low-salt diets, the use of diuretics or some pain relievers, or excessive exercise and sweating), or (3) kidney disease.

To avoid the troublesome thirst associated with lithium use, patients are encouraged to drink several extra glasses of water daily. To reduce any tremor, patients are advised to avoid caffeine or other stimulants; if it still persists, the drug may have to be discontinued.

There is convincing evidence that lithium reduces the risk of relapse in manic depression although quite how effective it is is still controversial. Proponents quote studies which suggest that as many as 75 per cent of patients suffering from recurrent manic depression have an excellent response and do not experience further severe mood swings. Critics doubt that lithium has been so effective but concede that for a significant number of patients it does increase the period between relapses and may modify and reduce the severity of any relapses that occur.

Compliance is a major problem. It has been estimated that about 25 per cent of manic-depressive patients discontinue taking lithium against medical advice (Jamison et al., 1979). One reason is that patients, on recovery from ill-health, erroneously conclude that the medication is no longer needed. Another reason is side-effects. Women tend to stop because of urinary frequency or weight gain. Men are more troubled by tremor and impaired memory. Compliance has been found to be higher in patients with stable marriages where the partner assumes a supportive and at times supervisory role. It may also be improved in patients receiving adjunctive psychotherapy or cognitive behaviour therapy.

Lithium is a maintenance medication, and most patients prescribed it can expect to take it for years, perhaps indefinitely. Some patients have been taking the salt for almost 20 years with no ill-effects. There is substantial evidence that well over half of those patients who do discontinue lithium maintenance relapse within six months.

Quite how lithium works is unclear. It does exercise effects on the monoamines and on the regulation of sodium and potassium within the cells and body fluids, and these may in some way be related to its therapeutic effects.

Recently, a number of other drugs, including the anticonvulsant drug carbamazepine, have been found to be helpful is reducing relapse in manic depression. The combination of lithium and carbamazepine is sometimes more effective than either drug alone.

Following his most recent episode of depression, Spike Milligan has joined the large number of individuals who suffer from recurrent manic depression and who now take lithium. Initially, he worried about taking the drug particularly because of its reported effects on the thyroid and kidneys and because of his age. However, acquainting himself with the available literature reassured him that properly administered, supervised and monitored, lithium prophylaxis is one of the safest therapies in medicine. He has had several severe depressive swings over the past decade. Lithium offers him the possibility of freedom from relapse. But, in his case, lithium, in combination with tricyclic antidepressant therapy, appears to have lifted a depression which had lasted over a year and which had defied antidepressant therapy, which had resisted ECT and which threatened to sink Spike into a slough of terminal despondency.

Electro-convulsive therapy (ECT)

Spike's experience illustrates how some forms of severe depression do not respond even to ECT. However, this treatment still holds an important place in the list of treatments available for the treatment of depression.

'There is scarcely a more controversial or more widely used treatment in contemporary British psychiatry than electroconvulsive therapy – ECT.' I wrote this statement 16 years ago in a book entitled *Psychiatry in Dissent*, when I reviewed in some detail the arguments about ECT that raged at that time. It remains true today. There is evidence that ECT is used somewhat less – the controversy and the development of safer and more varied antidepressants may have contributed to this fall in popularity. But ECT remains an important treatment for individuals suffering from severe depression.

I am often asked whether I give ECT. When I answer that I do if there are clinical indications, I invariably encounter a hostile response, a reaction that suggests I am some kind of Frankenstein, a fiendish Caligari blowing the minds of my helpless patients when I can think of nothing better to do. People who regard themselves as rational observers of the human condition and open to reasoned argument go glazed around the eyes and their expression adopts that closed, intolerant look. Nothing I can say can change their minds. They know that ECT is barbarous. After all, does it not consist of shocking, jolting, electrocuting the brain?

The most arresting public images of ECT have been derived from the cinema. One of the earliest portrayals of the treatment was in *The Snake Pit* (1948), described by Krin and Glen Gabard in their critical view of the American cinema's portrayal of psychiatry:

ECT is made to appear grotesque by means of camera angles and orchestral crescendos on the sound track. To emphasize the excruciating pain of the process, the film focuses on the contraption forced into the mouth of the victimized patient (Olivia de Havilland) as if it were a bullet that cowboys bite during an operation on the prairie with only a slug of whiskey for an anaesthetic. (Gabard and Gabard, 1987)

Despite the melodrama, the film did actually portray ECT as an effective treatment. After a few sessions, the patient improved. However, the anti-psychiatric mood of the 1960s and early '70s resulted in a more hostile and malevolent portrayal of the treatment.

In Milos Forman's *One Flew Over the Cuckoo's Nest* (1975), for example, electroconvulsive therapy was administered without anaesthesia to a recalcitrant patient, the message clearly being that the procedure was not a benign therapy but a sadistic punishment. In *Frances* (1982), ECT was again used by a punitive and destructive buffoon of a psychiatrist to humiliate and control a patient who is clearly very much saner than he is. In both films, psychiatry is but an extension of society's need to control dissent, invalidate criticism, eliminate creativity, stifle imagination. ECT doubles as a particularly horrible instrument of torture and a 'scientific' procedure whereby the individual can be rendered psychologically sterile.

Is there evidence that cinematic images of a treatment such as ECT affect public attitudes towards it? There is no systematically accumulated evidence that I am aware of – but I am not the only psychiatrist who has had to correct the notions of ECT held by patients and their relatives and obtained from media such as the cinema. Gabard and Gabard themselves describe patients revoking their consent to ECT and revising their views of the safety of psychiatric hospitals and the integrity of their doctors as a consequence of seeing films such as *Cuckoo's Nest* and *Frances*.

But what is the truth about ECT? Why are we still relying on a treatment that appears to consist of little more than giving the body's most sensitive, most subtle, most exquisitely complex organ a jolt of electricity to shock it into order?

The story of the discovery of ECT resembles the story of so many of the effective treatments available to psychiatry. Yet again, it was discovered by accident. Ugo Cerletti, a psychiatric research worker in Rome in the 1930s, was investigating the changes in brain tissue produced by convulsions in animals. At this time it was thought that there was some kind of 'biological antagonism' between epilepsy and schizophrenia such that sufferers from one were unlikely to suffer from the other. This led to the suggestion that if epileptic-type convulsions could be induced in schizophrenics perhaps they might improve.

Cerletti, having perfected in animals the induction of convulsions by passing a current of 70 volts through the brain between two electrodes, decided to try it in man. The patient chosen was an incoherently gibbering 'catatonic schizophrenic' from northern Italy found wandering in a Rome railway station by the police. He appeared confused, was quite unable to provide the simplest information about himself and expressed himself in a severely thought-disordered fashion. David Impastato, who has given a detailed account of this first therapy session, describes what happened next:

> The patient was brought in, the machine was set at one-tenth of a second and 70 volts and the shock given. Naturally, the low dosage resulted in a petit mal reaction. After the electric spasm, which lasted a fraction of a second, the patient burst into song. The Professor [Cerletti] suggested that another treatment with a higher voltage be given. The staff objected. They stated that if another treatment were given the patient would probably die and wanted further treatment postponed until the morrow. The Professor knew what that meant. He decided to go right ahead then and there, but before he could say so the patient suddenly sat up and pontifically proclaimed, no longer in jargon but in clear Italian: 'non una seconda' [not again, it will kill me]. This made the Professor think and swallow but his courage was not lost. He gave the order to proceed at a higher voltage and a longer time; and the first electroconvulsion in man ensued.

> Impastato (1960)

The first ECT was administered in 1938. Over the next 20 years it gradually became established as the major physical treatment in psychiatric practice. The original belief that it would be effective in schizophrenia was never confirmed. Instead, it became clear that ECT appeared to exercise a most remarkable effect on depressed mood. Attention was paid to what constituted the appropriate number and frequency of induced convulsions, the optimal strength and type of current, the most suitable part of the head to which to apply the electrodes, and the psychiatric conditions for which it seemed most appropriate.

The development of a group of drugs capable of briefly paralysing muscles (curare, gallamine, succinylcholine) and of short-acting anaesthetic agents (thiopental, methohexital) meant that ECT could be administered with reasonable safety, few side-effects and a minimum of discomfort. The muscle relaxant ensured that a fit could be induced without a concomitant and massive spasm of the muscles. (Such spasms occur with induced as well as epileptic seizure and, if severe enough, are capable of causing fractures of the spine.) The anaesthetic relieved the patient's understandable anxiety during the treatment and much of his post-treatment anxiety as well.

The administration of ECT

The patient is instructed to abstain from food for at least four hours before treatment, to rule out any danger of vomiting while under the anaesthetic (a normal precaution taken before any procedure requiring an anaesthetic). The patient lies on a bed or couch with the pillow removed and the usual precautions (eg removal of false teeth, spectacles) observed. He or she is then given an intravenous injection of a short-acting anaesthetic (usually methohexital sodium) and, through the same needle, a dose of muscle relaxant (usually suxamethonium).

Within 15-20 seconds of the injection, slight rippling of the muscles under the skin can be seen (muscle fasciculations). These serve to indicate that muscle paralysis is imminent and the anaesthetist takes over respiration of the patient by way of a face mask and a pressure bag. When the fasciculations have ceased and the patient is well oxygenated by way of the mask and bag (skin colour good, blood pressure and pulse steady), the shock can be safely administered.

Two electrodes, dampened with a bicarbonate solution to prevent skin burns at their points of contact, are applied to the anterior temporal areas of the scalp (at each side of the head, above and in front of each ear). A gag is inserted in the patient's mouth to prevent the tongue from being accidentally bitten (the gag so sinisterly portrayed in *The Snake Pit!*).

Modern ECT machines deliver a string of high-voltage, very brief, direct current pulses, about 60-70 pulses a second, which results in a 'modified' convulsion, as evidenced by mild tonic-clonic movements in the facial muscles and in the muscles of the hands and feet. After the convulsion, the gag is removed and the patient is turned on one side. The anaesthetist maintains an oxygen supply until the muscle relaxant wears off (this occurs within several minutes of its having been given) and the patient starts to breathe on his own. Within five to 20 minutes the patient gradually returns to full consciousness although he or she may feel sleepy and indeed may sleep for up to an hour after treatment. The usual course of treatment consists of between six and 12 treatments, given at a rate of two to three treatments per week.

Does it work?

The debate in the mid-'60s and the belief that ECT was being given too frequently and for all manner of conditions, not merely depression, together with the publicity surrounding the film *One Flew Over the Cuckoo's Nest*, resulted in a more energetic attempt by the psychiatric community to establish the effectiveness of ECT in a more scientific manner than had hitherto been tried. Several carefully constructed and conducted trials were undertaken comparing 'real' ECT, administered as described above, with 'simulated' ECT, in which anaesthetic and muscle relaxant were administered and electrodes applied but no electricity applied. Patients were rated 'blind' – ie by raters who were not privy to whether the patient had received the 'real' or 'simulated' variety. These studies confirm that for severe depression ECT is effective, is at least as good as antidepressant drugs and acts more rapidly. It is the induced convulsion which appears to bring about the antidepressant effect.

But how does ECT work if work it does? Interest centres on the possibility that ECT acts on those neurotransmitters believed to hold the key to the cause of severe depression. ECT certainly affects these monoamines, but in complicated ways, and it has not hitherto proved possible to produce a coherent explanation. Another possibility is that ECT works by its effects on those centres in the brain that regulate the circadian rhythms, rhythms which, as we have seen, are upset in depression. Interest too has focussed on its effects on those hormones whose secretion is altered in depression. What *does* seem clear is that there is no evidence that ECT works by punishing the patient or by abolishing memory. Recovered patients more often than not have as sound a memory for the events leading up to their depression whether they received ECT or whether they didn't.

Side-effects

Mention of memory, however, does raise the issue of side-effects. Before discussing them it is worth pointing out that ECT is a remarkably safe treatment. Remember that the expected mortality from depressive illness by suicide is 10 per cent in five years, and up to 15 per cent in 10 years. Remember too that suicide often occurs by means of antidepressants prescribed for the depression in the first place. Mortality from ECT has been estimated at less than five per 100,000 treatments. Furthermore, studies have shown that, in the three years following ECT administration, mortality from suicide is lower than in those treated inadequately with antidepressants or given neither drugs nor ECT.

The common side-effects of treatment are headache and mild confusion. Some patients also complain of muscle aches in the jaw, neck or shoulders. Such symptoms quickly clear. Most patients are mildly confused immediately after treatment but it usually clears within 12-24 hours.

Occasionally, however, patients report that they lose patches of memory for remote events (as distinct from recent events) for up to several weeks after ECT. During this time they may experience difficulty forming new memories. More subtle testing does show in a small number of patients memory defects which persist for up to six months after treatment. At present it is not possible to say whether there is a subgroup of patients in whom ECT produces some longer-term defects, but there are individuals who have had ECT many times who insist that their memory has not recovered and remains impaired months and even years after treatment. Complicating the issue still further is the fact that memory impairment and concentration difficulties commonly occur in depression, and assessing any additional effects of ECT is not made any easier by this fact.

Who benefits most from ECT?

Given that the few deaths from ECT that have occurred have been as a result of cardiac failure, coronary thrombosis or heart irregularities in those with a pre-existing susceptibility, it might be thought that ECT would not be a treatment used in elderly depressives. In fact, ECT is a highly effective and safe treatment of severe depression in elderly patients. Antidepressants in such patients are often not tolerated. Appetite and fluid-intake changes often mean that such patients are poorly nourished and need urgent treatment and a speedy response. The dangers of suicide are even more pressing. ECT in such patients is often dramatically effective.

Spike Milligan has had ECT on a number of admissions to hospital. During the writing of this book he underwent a course of six. His view of the procedure is prosaic – 'an anaesthetic and I'm asleep. I wake up when it is all over, with a headache like a hangover. In a few hours I am as I was.' The course of treatment in his case eased the depression somewhat, for which he was thankful, but it took a few further months of antidepressant therapy and the addition of lithium for full recovery to occur. Spike is critical of the adverse comments about ECT and sees the therapy as having been useful for many fellow-sufferers from depression and manic depression.

One of the problems with ECT is that, like penicillin, it became somewhat over-prescribed. It is the fate of effective treatments. Having found ECT effective in cases of severe depression and acute mania, clinicians began to try it in less severe forms of mood disorder, in depression associated with alcohol abuse, in anorexia, in schizophrenia, in paranoid illnesses, even in personality disorder where depression was suspected of playing some aggravating role. Inevitably, such indiscriminate use helped bring the treatment into disrepute. Today, the Royal College of Psychiatrists in Britain and the American Psychiatric Association in the US have formulated tight guidelines concerning the use of ECT, and there is evidence that the treatment is used more circumspectly and judiciously. Most psychiatrists reserve ECT for the following categories of patients:

- Severely depressed patients who are a particular risk for making determined suicide attempts
- Severely depressed patients with psychotic symptoms, where ECT is thought by many clinicians to be the treatment of first choice.
- Depressed patients who are intolerant of antidepressants or whose illness is particularly resistant to drug therapy or who themselves do not wish to take antidepressant drugs
- Depressed patients who have shown a prompt response to ECT in the past

- Patients with puerperal (post-childbirth) psychosis who respond particularly well to ECT
- Depression in the elderly where ECT may be safer than antidepressants.

ECT is a much misunderstood treatment. Vilified by critics who in truth often know little about it, it is praised by many patients who have found it a lifeline to recovery. In view of the alarmist reports of ECT regularly published in the press and elsewhere, it is worth reading the account of ECT published in 1965 in the *British Journal of Psychiatry*. It was written, anonymously, by a psychiatrist who had received a course of treatment for depression. The account is a clear and dispassionate one of how the treatments were given, the memory disturbance experienced, and the response of his depression to the shocks. He ends his account with the hope that it will help to:

> dispel the myth that ECT is a terrifying form of treatment, crippling in its effects on the memory and in other ways. The technique is today so refined that the patient suffers a minimum of discomfort, and the therapeutic benefits are so great in those cases where it is indicated that it is a great pity to withhold it from mistaken ideas of kindness to the patient.
>
> (Anonymous, 1986)

Light treatment

The possibility that exposing depressed individuals to artificial bright light might help alleviate their symptoms, particularly those symptoms showing a seasonal variation, has led to the development of phototherapy (light treatment). Clinical trials involving this have shown that between 60 and 70 per cent of patients with winter depressions do improve significantly with phototherapy. It is now clear that to be effective:

- Phototherapy requires light several times brighter than that of typical indoor environments.
- Phototherapy is effective whatever time of day it is administered, although some patients do show a better response when the therapy is applied in the morning.
- Phototherapy is more effective when given for at least two hours every day; a dose of four hours' exposure is most effective.
- The effective strength of the light stimulus appears to be in the range of 2,500-3,500 lux at a distance of three feet.
- The treatment effects of phototherapy are mediated by the eye and not the skin.

Response to phototherapy is rapid, slight improvement being experienced within one or two days and maximum improvement commonly occurring within one week. The problem is that relapse is equally rapid when treatment is discontinued. Norman Rosenthal, who has undertaken most of the research in relation to this form of therapy, does claim that starting phototherapy in late summer appears to prevent winter depression in patients with a previous history of Seasonal Affective Disorder.

Does any kind of light work? No. For example, patients do not respond to yellow light of ordinary intensity. Then again, a study comparing phototherapy administered through the eyes with that administered through the skin found that even though patients expected to benefit from both conditions, they responded only to the treatment administered through the eyes.

How might phototherapy work? Current interest is focussed on the seasonal variation in levels of substances such as melatonin and serotonin. Serotonin levels clearly vary with the season. They also vary in response to phototherapy. Interpretation of these findings is difficult but they do suggest that light treatment may influence serotonin metabolism. To date that is about all that is known.

Tranquillizers

Drugs have been used to relieve anxiety for centuries. This century has seen the rapid development of anti-anxiety drugs. Most of the drugs commonly prescribed during the first half of the century – drugs such as the bromides, chloral hydrate and the barbiturates – were potent, addictive and lethal in overdose.

In 1960, chlordiazepoxide (Librium), the first of a new class of anti-anxiety drugs, the benzodiazepines, was introduced. It was quickly followed by diazepam (Valium) and a dozen or more related compounds. They appeared effective, without significant side-effects, and overdose did not result in death. Between 1965 and 1970 prescriptions for these drugs in England and Wales rose by 110 per cent, compared with a 19 per cent increase for all psychiatric drugs. By 1970, when the number of prescriptions topped 12 million a year, the 'benzodiazepine era' had arrived. It peaked in 1979 when just over 30 million prescriptions were written in Britain. Then, as concern about abuse, dependence and addiction increased, prescribing fell. By 1987, prescriptions had fallen to 25 million.

Tranquillizers were originally introduced as a treatment of anxiety. However, many studies, particularly in general practice, have shown that they are commonly used to treat depression. For example, Myrna Weissman and Gerald Klerman (1977) studied 150 depressed women who had responded to tricyclic antidepressants and who had received eight months of maintenance treatment as part of a clinical controlled trial. When followed up, between one and four years after the trial had ended, the women were more likely to have received a tranquillizer than an antidepressant when they sought medical help. Similar findings emerged from another community survey, in which Weissman and her colleagues (1981) found that episodes of major depressive disorder in the community were more likely to be treated with tranquillizers than with antidepressants.

But do tranquillizers work in depression? They are certainly ineffective in cases of manic depression and severe unipolar depression. In milder depression they may exercise some benefit through relief of associated symptoms of anxiety, thereby enabling the affected individual to regain control of his or her life and set about remedying the situation, thus relieving the depression. In general, however, tranquillizers are not an appropriate treatment for mood disorders. Quite why doctors, in particular GPs, persist in prescribing them is not clear. But their relative safety in overdose, especially when compared with antidepressants, may lead GPs to prefer to prescribe them in cases where suicidal activity is feared.

REFERRAL TO THE PSYCHIATRIST

At any one time, as we have seen, about one in 20 people are depressed. Yet only a fraction of these are ever referred to a psychiatrist. Referral is for the most part decided by the patient's general practitioner. Reasons for referral are often divided into those pertaining to the patient ('patient-centred') and those pertaining to the doctor ('GP-centred'), although the division is by no means absolute.

Patient-centred reasons include:

- uncertainty about the diagnosis
- failure of the diagnosed depressed patient to respond to counselling and antidepressants
- suspicion that an underlying physical disease may be present, eg dementia, malignancy, Parkinson's disease, thyroid disease
- suspicion that an associated psychiatric condition is present, complicating the clinical picture and making treatment difficult, eg alcohol abuse, anorexia nervosa, obsessive compulsive disorder
- severity of illness – perhaps the commonest reason for referral; suicidal or psychotic patients or patients unable to cope in their own domestic situation and who require asylum and rest as well as effective and swift relief and treatment.

GP-centred reasons include:

- pressure from the patient or relatives requesting a specialist opinion concerning diagnosis and/or treatment

- anxiety on the part of the GP in the face of worrying, angry or unpredictable behaviour by the patient.

At present, many patients are reluctant to be referred to see a psychiatrist and are often shocked by the very suggestion. Seeing a psychiatrist raises the whole issue of stigma. Patients assume that referral means that they are 'mad', 'out of control' or even 'dangerous'. Public perceptions of psychiatrists don't help either. Popular and contradictory stereotypes of the psychiatrist as mad, dangerous, omnipotent and useless abound.

In the MORI poll conducted on behalf of the Royal College of Psychiatrists, respondents were asked who they would talk to if they felt depressed. A substantial majority (60 per cent) identified the general practitioner whereas only 2 per cent identified the psychiatrist. Part of the GP's task in referring appropriate patients to see psychiatrists involves correcting misconceptions concerning psychiatrists and explaining what referral can offer.

CONCLUSION

An objection often raised is that the treatment of mania or depression, particularly treatment with drugs, only treats the symptoms. The real cause of the illness remains obscure or indeed is covered up instead of being revealed. Much depends on the word 'cure'. Those who object appear to use it to mean the permanent removal of symptoms. So, because depression is often recurrent, the removal of the symptoms is not seen as a cure but just symptomatic relief.

Yet most treatments in medicine remove symptoms without guaranteeing immunity from further episodes of illness. This is as true of antibiotics in tonsillitis, or digoxin in heart failure, or analgesics in arthritis, as it is of antidepressants in depression. The actual causes of many diseases remain to be established, yet effective treatments are available – one thinks of diabetes, ulcerative colitis, asthma, rheumatoid arthritis.

The argument about the effectiveness of treatment is often put in terms that suggest that, while drugs and ECT are symptomatic, psychotherapy is curative. Again, this is highly simplistic. Not merely is there no evidence whatsoever that any of the psychotherapies can bring about permanent change in depression, mania or manic depression, there is positive evidence that insofar as these psychological therapies are effective it is by virtue of their ability to enable patients to cope better with their mood disorder. In other words, both forms of therapy – physical and psychological – can be condemned or praised as 'merely symptomatic'. My own view is that when we know much more about the way in which mood disorders develop we may find ourselves in possession of treatments with a greater degree of effectiveness. Until that day, we have to make do with the treatments that are available, are tested and are in the great majority of cases reasonably effective.

9

DEPRESSION – HOW
TO COPE

*F*INDING the factors which play a role in causing depression holds out the possibility of doing something about it. Knowledge, after all, is power. Ignorance only serves to deepen the sense of helplessness that afflicts people who are profoundly depressed and the relatives and friends who, despairingly and helplessly, watch. The first two cardinal pieces of advice to sufferers and their families and friends are:

(1) Depression is treatable
(2) We can do something about it

THE ROLE OF RELATIVES AND FRIENDS

Hitherto depression has been a mysterious condition. Sufferers and others have, in the absence of knowledge, trusted to common sense. Hence non-sufferers, well-meaning and earnest, suggest that depressed people 'look on the bright side', 'count their lucky stars', 'pull up their socks' and they exhort them to show backbone and fight. Sufferers themselves thrash around in desperate attempts to identify factors responsible for their state. They sometimes draw conclusions and make changes which, far from easing the depression, only serve to make it worse. So the first piece of advice to relatives and friends of sufferers is: Do not tell someone who is seriously depressed to 'pull themselves together'. When someone is mildly depressed, perhaps feeling a little sorry for themselves and seeking pity and concern from others, there may be something to be said for encouraging them to distract themselves from pessimistic thoughts and to engage in activities which in the past have helped them feel better. When people are recovering from being profoundly unwell such encouragement has a place, too. But when someone is particularly low and feeling utterly worn out and without hope, to respond by suggesting they shape up and snap out of it is not just crude but cruel.

The evidence on treatability of depression has been reviewed in Chapter 8. Effective treatment is available. Sympathetic support can and does make a difference. But what can we, in the everyday situation, do about it? In this chapter we examine the answers as they apply to someone who is depressed, to the sufferer's friends and relatives, to the health-care professionals and to the public. All of us can benefit from learning about depression.

The first thing we can all do is to become better informed about what depression looks like. We should suspect that someone may be depressed if there is a sudden change in mood, behaviour or general ability to work, relax, mix. Someone who starts to sleep badly, to be irritable, to find it difficult to laugh or enjoy the things that formerly interested and stimulated him or her, who seems out of sorts, unhappy, lacking in zest, who begins to drink too much, may very well be depressed. If such a state persists, say for more than a week or two, then don't say nothing. Say you are worried and would like to help. Ask whether anything is the matter. If the individual indicates that there is, but that you are not the right person to tell, encourage him or her to see someone more suitable.

Any one of us suffering from depression for the first time will be puzzled as to what is happening to us. The tiredness, loss of interest, the draining away of zest, the loss of appetite, the difficulty sleeping and, most distressing of all, the nagging sense of pain which often persuades sufferers that there is something physical, something going wrong with their body. Now, as we have seen, something 'physical' may indeed be going wrong – depression is as much a physical disorder as it is a mental one. A diagnosis of depression is not a pseudo-diagnosis, made because a doctor cannot find anything really wrong. Depression is itself a real disorder with clear-cut and consistent signs and symptoms. So, the first and foremost step that any one of us, sufferers or otherwise, can take is to learn as much about mood disorders as possible. To help us there are now a number of excellent, simply written and informative books and pamphlets available. (See page 204)

But how do depressed people cope? What can we learn from those, like Spike Milligan, who have to live with the reality that from time to time their mood will become seriously depressed despite all their best attempts to prevent this happening? This is what Spike Milligan said to me when I asked him how, during his most severe period of depression in 1991, he had kept absolute despair at bay:

> I kept telling myself that I had felt like this before and the storm had passed. I kept trying to remember good times, the times when my children were small, the times when I made people laugh, the times when I myself laughed. I couldn't always manage it. Sometimes life just looked to bleak. But I kept at it. Now I am back and it's gone.

So what Milligan did is to remind himself that he was indeed suffering from depression and that he would eventually come out of it. This is far from easy for someone experiencing their very first attack nor is it easy when the depressed mood is extremely low. Everyone who has been seriously depressed describes on recovery just how difficult it is when you are depressed to imagine yourself feeling any other way.

Spike's effort, however, is one that relatives and friends can reinforce. Gently reminding the depressed person that he or she will get well and not to despair may not seem helpful at the time. It may even provoke an angry dismissal and an accusation that you don't know what depression is like, but it is worth persevering. Encouraging someone not to lose hope is not to be equated with an ignorance of what is involved. Quite the contrary. You can continue to encourage hope while simultaneously making it clear that you do recognize how wretched the person must feel and how difficult it must be for them to maintain hope.

So how did Spike cope with his depressive swings in earlier days? His agent and close friend, Norma Farnes, told me how it went:

> He was more traumatized by it then than he is now. He used to go to bed more often and the mood seemed deeper. He would go to bed, take his drugs, self-medicate himself all the time and for two, three, four, five days you wouldn't hear from him. He used to sleep at his office during his illness periods. He never went home. He didn't want his children to see him in those days – of course the kids were very much younger. I was actually here [in the London office] all the time and he would take himself off to his room at the top of the building and you would never hear from him. He'd be locked up there and then he would come out very quietly and thank you for everything and that would always be the sign that things were getting better! Because in normal life he didn't thank you for anything. That's not a criticism – it was simply a case of 'get on with what you have to do'.

Many seriously depressed people avoid social contact and withdraw into themselves, unable to handle the give-and-take of human relationships. What should their relatives and friends do? Should they leave them alone and wait until time and treatment ease the pain? Or should they try and jolly them out of their misery?

There comes a stage in depression when all drive goes, any residual ability to lift the mood even slightly disappears and the issue of whether friends and relatives can jolly the patient along becomes academic. Now the depressed person becomes a member of what American novelist William Styron has memorably called the 'walking wounded'. He coined this term, he says,

> For in virtually any other serious sickness, a patient who felt similar devastation would be lying flat in bed, possibly sedated and hooked up on tubes and wires of life-support systems, but at the very least in a posture of repose and in an isolated setting. His invalidism would be necessary, unquestioned and honourably attained. However, the sufferer from depression has no such option

and therefore finds himself, like a walking casualty of war, thrust into the most intolerable social and family situations. There he must, despite the anguish devouring his brain, present a face approximating the one that is associated with ordinary events and companionship. He must try to utter small talk, and be responsive to questions, and knowingly nod and frown and, God help him, smile. But it is a fierce trial attempting to speak a few simple words.

(Styron, 1991)

Spike Milligan's depressions have reached a severity warranting admission on only a handful of occasions. On many other occasions, however, his own method of coping mimicked what would have happened had he been hospitalized – sedation, sleep, withdrawal from social contact. This is what severe depression requires.

Before it reaches that level of severity is there anything that can be done if you feel depressed and unhappy and just cannot seem to be able to lift it? The first and simplest piece of advice for someone worried about becoming depressed is 'Don't bottle things up'. If you have had some bad news, a major upset, a serious loss, if you feel trapped by a disastrous decision or an impossible job, try to tell others how you feel, what has happened, what it means to you. If there are people too close to you who you feel could not cope or understand, then tell someone who may well be a little more detached and able to contain what you say without feeling an irresistible need to make you feel better. Telling how you feel may have to occur several times. Often a good cry helps, although in the more severe forms of depression you may not be able to cry – a sign that things are really serious.

Spike, when very ill, could not face those nearest to him. This is common. And those closest to a seriously depressed person often find it equally difficult to cope. Shelagh, Spike's present wife, waits patiently for the mood to pass, recognizing that there is little she can do other than be there while Spike struggles to survive. Paddy, Spike's second wife, found coping more difficult. Norma Farnes described what would happen:

She used to walk away from Spike's depression. She would go into terrible eating binges. She would come in here [to the office] and cry. She had a weight problem anyway. I recall when Spike was really ill, she came here one day and wept and said 'I might as well go and live in the fridge'. Spike would stay here and I would give her daily reports. When he got bad she would get miserable, too.

It can be exceptionally difficult for patients to communicate how they feel to their nearest relatives. There is a desire to avoid causing pain and anguish, a wish to avoid being a burden. For their part relatives can find the presence of a depressed family member profoundly distressing. Relatives can feel threatened and hurt to find that a loved one feels suicidal. They feel they must have failed the depressed person in some way. Often relatives resort to jollying along the depressed person, pointing to the good things in his or her life, unwittingly adding to the sufferer's guilt and self-reproach. Spouses, relatives, friends are emotionally involved and hence emotionally affected. Almost invariably they are tempted to rush in to reassure instead of letting the persn just tell it how it is. This is one reason why it is so often easier and more helpful for sufferers to talk to outsiders, such as a trained counsellor or a sympathetic GP.

Most of Spike's friends stay away. A few stay in touch. But some, according to Norma Farnes, are just too embarrassed.

> You say 'Spike is not well' and they say 'Oh Dear!' What the fuck does that mean, 'Oh Dear'? You know I never hear people saying 'Is there anything we can do?'

Spike himself described something similar.

> When I was first ill no-one seemed to notice. I was screaming inside, hurting and hoping someone would do something. Maybe I would have told them to mind their own business but I don't think so. I think I would have said 'Thank God'.

But is there anything that Spike's friends can do? Norma Farnes points out:

> Well they might ring him up and just listen to him. He needs people. All you have to do is go upstairs and sit with him, hold his hand. He needs people. He needs to know that there is someone there. Because he feels so alone. He feels, or at least I think he feels that he is not well and that only he can cope with it. The truth is, however, that he actually cannot cope with it and in the early stages he only copes by screaming and shouting.

Her comments are mirrored by Spike's responses when I asked him how an understanding person might cope with a depressed friend.

> Immediately he'll reach out emotionally and say 'What can I do to help? Let me sit and talk to you a while'.

So the advice is consistent – don't underestimate listening. We don't do it often and it does not come easy. But it is absolutely invaluable to many a depressed person and can make a great deal of difference. Refraining from giving trite advice does not mean abdicating the task of persuading the depressed person of the need to keep going, that suicide is not acceptable, that sooner or later the misery will pass. Over and over again patients on recovery tell me how vital, how life-saving can be the dogged, patient, unrelenting, devoted insistence on the part of lovers, family, friends, admirers that the sufferer's life is worth something, that the mood disorder will pass, that they will be saved.

How else can one help a depressed person to cope? Suggest that he or she seeks expert advice and suggest this after you have listened to what they have had to say. Do not rush in with such a suggestion within minutes of someone saying they feel ill, depressed, out of control, tired or whatever. Hold it until you are sure that the person involved believes that he or she has given a good account of what seems to be happening. Advice given then will stand a very much better chance of being taken. In the case of a manic individual, the advice may not be taken. You may then have to bring someone, such as the GP or a trusted friend, to help you.

What many of us fear is that during a conversation with someone who is depressed they may reveal that they are suicidal. The important thing is not to panic nor indeed to argue. Instead, you would be better advised to acknowledge that you recognize how desperate the person feels and suggest that help should be sought. Acknowledge, too, that you recognize that the depressed person may not see any point in such help. Put the emphasis instead on the need to understand what is going on.

It is important not to underestimate the relief that can occur when help is offered. Yes, it may be rejected but that is no reason for not suggesting that it be sought. Frequently depressed and indeed manic individuals readily agree to contact a counsellor or a GP. However, relatives and others close to the depressed person procrastinate and become flustered instead of making plain their anxiety and concern.

A reason why people are often hesitant about offering help is that someone who is depressed may appear changed in one or more ways. People who have interviewed Spike Milligan when he is depressed and who may never have known him any other way often describe him as misanthropic, angry, bitter, unforgiving, even humourless. When depressed, many of us become more unattractive than usual. People who can only see disaster, who fear the worst, who believe the worst about themselves and their fellow-men, are rarely stimulating companions. This is one of the reasons why people who are depressed become socially isolated even if they were not that at the outset. Those who are not depressed can find depression corrosive, infectious even. One way to cope is to remember that the side of the person you see is just that – one side. Every one of us, however, is multidimensional, multifaceted. However, the depressed person recognizes and shows but one side. Don't get taken in.

People close to the depressed individuals – spouses, relatives, friends – often remark on physical changes which appear to occur with the onset of the illness. Indeed these physical alterations can often be the first signs of a relapse. This is what Norma Farnes said about Spike:

> There would be warning signs. He hunches his shoulders. A physical sign. He sits down and puts his hands between his knees and crouches down. His face changes and it is not so much that he gets bags under his eyes as he gets sort of purple discolouration down either side of his face. And he goes a dreadful ashen colour. His eyes change. It is difficult to describe but they just do.

A crucial piece of advice therefore to anyone who has a depressed loved one is not to give up hope. Sometimes when a loved one seems incorrigibly depressed and suicidal and the illness seems intractable, spouses, parents, children, friends begin to lose heart. Depression has been described as a 'blue plague'. It is not infectious in the true sense of the word yet it can 'spread' in one sense. Resisting the temptation to share the bleak and dismal vision of the depressed person can be surprisingly difficult yet it is vital that you do so. Many a depressed person has testified on recovery how important it was to have known that others close to him or her had not lost heart, even though at the time relatives and friends had no inkling that their responses, behaviour and attitude were in fact making any impact whatsoever.

Finally, there is one important piece of advice concerning therapy: you should not tell people who are being prescribed medication that they should stop taking drugs. People are often strongly inclined to do this on the grounds that drugs are bad for you, they can be addictive, they block out important experiences or they are 'merely' symptomatic treatment. Remember: depression is a dangerous, potentially lethal disorder. Ordinarily, untrained people do not go around telling others what drugs they should take. Diabetics are not told to stop taking insulin (another symptomatic treatment which often needs to be taken for life) nor are patients with heart failure usually encouraged to discontinue taking their digoxin because it could poison them! Yet regularly people who know little about depression or mania pronounce on the foolishness of taking antidepressants or lithium with a confidence worthy of an experienced pharmacologist. If someone asks your advice concerning treatment, suggest they discuss the issue with their doctor or therapist or take a look at one of the recommended books on the subject.

Many people do have very firm views on drugs and heartily disapprove of people taking them 'unnecessarily'. But before expressing views on the subject of medication it would be well to learn a little bit about what may be involved. A common misunderstanding about antidepressants, for example, is that they are addictive. They are not. A Royal College of Psychiatrists' pamphlet, published in 1992, puts this issue squarely:

These [antidepressants] are not tranquillisers although they may help you feel less anxious and they are not addictive either. They are very effective at getting depressed people back to normal and they need not usually be taken for more than a few months. Your doctor would want to see how you are getting on, adjust the dose and to ask you about any side-effects.

THE ROLE OF PROFESSIONALS

Thus far we have considered the role of relatives and friends in helping the depressed person to cope. What can the professionals do? Throughout Spike Milligan's career as a sufferer from severe depression, only a handful of doctors, nurses and other therapists appear to have made much of an impact on him. One, a Dr Joseph Robson, who practised hypnotherapy, appears to have been important for a while. However, it does not appear to have been his therapy (hypnosis) which made the difference so much as his personality. He took the time to relate to Spike, to understand what made him tick, to get behind the mask. He first began treating Spike in 1955 when *The Goon Show* was in full swing.

Spike was vague when I asked him about Dr Robson. He seemed to find it difficult to recall quite what it was that the doctor actually did. The description provided by Pauline Scudamore in her biography of Spike suggests that his approach blended relaxation and hypnosis but what actually endeared him to Spike was his empathy, his lack of pomposity and his honesty.

Whatever the therapeutic approach, the two elements required of any professional involved in the treatment of depressed individuals are a thorough knowledge of the condition and a profound desire to help. Many lack both. Some want desperately to help but they don't know what they are doing. Others know a great deal but appear unable to indicate their care and compassion to the patient. Sadly the accounts provided by many depressed people concerning the psychiatrists and GPs they encountered during the course of their illnesses do not always give grounds for confidence.

Again and again I hear patients extolling the virtues of doctors, therapists, counsellors, social workers and nurses who exhibited the qualities described by the anonymous patient quoted at the beginning of Chapter 8 – 'compassion and warmth', 'intelligence, competence and the time you put into it and your granite belief that mine was a life worth living'. Patients appreciate directness, simplicity, frankness in the setting of a caring and committed relationship. It is sometimes argued that one of the disadvantages of the biological approach to psychiatric disorder is that it causes some doctors to ignore and dismiss the content of the patient's mind, on the grounds that the trouble has little to do with how they think or feel but rather with their brain enzymes or their hormonal flows. Yet no real understanding by the doctor of how the depressed individual feels, and no real commitment by the patient to what the doctor says, can take place in a therapeutic relationship which lacks mutual trust, confidence, respect and emotional warmth.

The do's and don't's for those whose professional occupations put them in the front line when it comes to detecting and treating mood disorders are straightforward. At all times therapists should endeavour:

(1) to learn as much as possible about the current state of knowledge relating to mood disorders;

(2) to develop the relevant skills needed to detect depression, to communicate with depressed patients and to initiate effective treatment;

(3) to appreciate the anxieties of the individual person confronted by depression, its mysteries and its extraordinary effects, anxieties which in turn relate to the widespread ignorance of the disorder, the entrenched stigma surrounding all forms of psychiatric disorder, the persistent suspicion concerning psychiatry and the current doubts and hostility regarding psychiatric drugs and psychiatric hospitals.

Is there anything that we can do to avoid getting depressed in the first place? For example, given that the role of genetic influences in some forms of manic depression is, as we have learned, considerable, what can we possibly do about that? Now some critics, most notably the psychotherapist Dorothy Rowe, have attacked the emphasis on a genetic role in manic depression because it appears to render the sufferers powerless, unable to do anything about their illness other than passively to accept what their doctors tell them. In her book *The Depression Handbook* (1991), Rowe is critical of biological researchers such as Colin Blakemore in Britain and Donald Klein and Paul Wender in the United States who argue that genetic factors play an important and crucial role. These biological psychiatrists, declares Rowe,

are saying that whenever we fall into despair, doubt our own worth, regret our actions, rage against our fate, what we are saying and feeling are of no more importance than red spots in measles.

The biological psychiatrists take great satisfaction in relieving parents of the guilty feeling that they personally have 'made' their offspring depressed, that they have by their own actions caused depression to occur in their children. But, objects Rowe, if parents cannot be blamed if their children turn out badly, they can hardly be praised if they turn out well! She powerfully argues her case for the role of early childhood experiences in the genesis of depression. She would, I feel sure, be especially interested in Spike Milligan's early experience of loss and of the impact of his parental dysharmony in making sense of his illness. She despairs of the geneticists' apparent blind dismissal of the importance of such experiences. And why do they do this?

The reason for this blindness is the ambition of those men who wish to impose on others their belief that the mind is no more than a machine and that our sufferings are no more than the malfunction of a machine. In doing so, these men acquire power, prestige and money, and they deny their awareness of their own experience of living and their own responsibility for the lives that they lead.

However, whether there is a role for genetic factors in depression is an issue independent of whether biological researchers do or do not behave in the way that Rowe suggests. If there is a genetic role there is a genetic role and all our protests, objections and criticisms of the fact will not alter it one whit.

When in the deepest pit of his depression Spike Milligan spoke of his fear that he might have passed on the gene or genes to one or more of his children. There is nothing to be gained by questioning or ignoring the role of genes. The evidence of a genetic role is persuasive. We have to live with it. One can, however, acknowledge a genetic role in depression without suggesting that individual sufferers can do nothing about it. Klein and Wender, for example, argue that the powerful role of genes in cases of manic depression is distressing but insist that

> an awareness of genetic tendency helps a concerned parent or the vulnerable individual to detect the illness when it is beginning to develop. Early detection can mean proper treatment. The depressed child, adolescent or young adult may be spared unnecessary pain and the sometimes cumulative and far-reaching difficulties that stem from depressive illness.
>
> (Klein and Wender, 1988)

Accepting a role for genes in depression may seem unnecessarily reductionist, defeating and itself depressing. Spike Milligan, however, accepts the fact that there is a genetic role. So what can be said to him? What do I say to him? I say what I would say to any person who suffers from manic depression or any other form of serious depression, namely that genes do appear important but are rarely important enough. Other factors are important too – life events, stress, the presence or absence of supportive relatives and friends, a strong personality. Whatever the genetic role it is important, too, to recognize that progress has been made in terms of treatment.

And what about early childhood experience? Some biologists, it is true, do appear eager to discount any role for such experience in severe depression. Yet it is as foolish of experts to discount early experience as it is for Rowe to dismiss the genetic evidence. It does help to explore early experiences but it does not help if that becomes an end in itself, or indeed if it becomes a search for a scapegoat, a way out. Sufferers can, of course, become the prisoners of a past they do not understand and have not explored. But they can also become prisoners of that same past if they conclude, as some do, that because their past is fixed and unchangeable so the consequences of it, including personality and illness, are fixed and unchangeable, too.

But talking about the past, indeed talking about anything, as Spike Milligan made plain, is difficult for someone who is severely depressed. To demand of a depressed person that he or she talk and explore is often to expose them to unnecessary additional pain and suffering. Talking about symptoms and feelings can, of course, be helpful but exploring and confronting the possible reasons for being depressed takes energy and motivation and is well-nigh impossible when seriously depressed.

People when depressed often thrash around and struggle to identify a possible cause of their depression. They may identify problems in their job, their marriage, their living conditions, their financial situation, or whatever. On recovery they may recognize that what appeared to have been a problem when they were depressed is no problem at all. Now if the depression appears to be connected with a particular problem then of course it is perfectly reasonable, indeed sensible that such a problem be explored. Psychiatrists, however, have learned from experience about the need to warn patients and their relatives to avoid making decisions, particularly irreversible decisions, until recovery has occurred. Sufferers can, for example, resign from jobs while depressed, only to regret such a decision bitterly on recovery.

Is there anything else that a person can do? What about diet? The general advice is that you should eat a good, balanced diet even if you do not feel like eating. Fresh fruit and vegetables are recommended. The problem, however, is that people who are severely depressed do not eat, lose weight and can run low in important vitamins which in turn can lead to or aggravate depression.

Resist the temptation to drown your sorrows. Despite a widespread belief to the contrary, alcohol actually depresses mood. In the initial stages it may provide temporary relief but invariably you end up feeling more depressed than when you started drinking. Worse, alcohol aggravates sleep and appetite disturbances and interferes with your ability to seek help and solve problems. Some people get exceedingly worried about not sleeping. Indeed, worrying about not sleeping is a common reason why people find it difficult to get off to sleep. Listening to the radio, watching television, reading a book can all help by distracting you from worry. However, persistent difficulty falling or staying asleep are reasons for going to see your doctor for advice and help.

Another piece of advice, to be found in the helpful pamphlet on depression prepared by the Royal College of Psychiatrists for its Defeat Depression Campaign, is that someone who begins to feel depressed should try and avoid dwelling on the past. Depressed people tend to have selective memories – they can usually only recall painful memories. Spike Milligan is especially prone to brooding on past experiences, on irreversible changes, on the remorseless passage of time. When he starts to feel depressed, nostalgia becomes physically painful:

> There are a number of things which go towards my depression. One of them is that I am completely ridden in nostalgia. I get sad when my children aren't children any more. I get depressed that I am old . . . A simple drive through London on my way to the BBC and I see all the sites where I used to be a young man, houses in which my friends used to live, the dance hall where I used to play in the band, the site where I used to work in a launderette, all these reminders non-stop, all the time. And it haunts me, the past, it haunts me. It preys on my mind. I turn on the radio and it suddenly plays a tune, say Glenn Miller's 'Moonlight Serenade', and straightaway it takes me back. Yes it's all gone, Glenn Miller is dead and the band is split up and I am not young any more. It has all come to an end. The nostalgia does that to me.

Spike becomes so exquisitely sensitive to nostalgia when depressed that he has to discipline himself not to look at old mementoes of his children's childhoods, even at photographs. He told me that his father similarly avoided the past. Once Spike found a sheaf of letters and a collection of remarkable family photographs in a desk and said to his father: 'There are lots of bits and pieces in your desk. Why don't we get them out and have a look?'

He said, 'No son, it makes me very sad'.

It now makes Spike sad too and, when low, he struggles to avoid confronting the very mementoes, the bric-a-brac, the artefacts, the childhood toys, clothes and possessions which, when he is well, he accumulates with a scrupulous and dedicated zeal.

Spike Milligan's own experience of depression, like every individual case history, is unique. No two stories are the same. But he has described vividly what it is like to feel depressed and he has known depressed moods of such severity that he has doubted that he would ever get better. He has, too, been misunderstood and shunned. In Spike I have seen a man crippled by an illness every bit as much as if he had suffered a stroke, or had an infectious disease, and stigmatized and misunderstood every bit as much as if he had Aids. Many, overwhelmed by the burden not merely of depression, but of the ignorance, misunderstanding and prejudice that surround it, succumb and kill themselves. In the years of his illness Spike Milligan has come close.

Towards the end of 1991, as the book was taking its final shape, he suddenly improved. Why this happened remains unclear. Perhaps the illness episode had come to its natural end, as depressive episodes fortunately often do. Perhaps he had come to terms with his mother's death. Perhaps the addition of lithium to his antidepressant therapy had made a difference. Spike Milligan's experience of the relapses and remissions of his illness is similar to that of the hundreds and thousands of his fellow-sufferers. He survives partly because of his innate dogged determination, partly because of the support and understanding of his wife, children and his close friends and partly because he has learned a great deal over the years about his illness and its effects.

Coping with depression is not easy. But the message of this book is that the burden can be eased. It helps to know what can be done and what is being done. It helps to know that one is not alone, whether one is a depressed or manic sufferer experiencing the swings of mood or a relative or friend struggling to make sense of what is happening. Fortunately there are now organizations and support groups in existence which have as their major aim the provision of information, advice and support to sufferers of depression and their families and friends.

Spike Milligan and I both hope that the account of depression contained in this book, an account of mood disorder in general and the account of one sufferer in particular, may go some way towards dispelling some of the myths, ignorance and fear surrounding what is a common and debilitating experience. For some it can prove an ultimately rewarding experience – one that they will on recovery insist has sensitized them towards the cruelties and injustices of life, that has reminded them of the true worth of human love. In December 1991, confronted by Spike Milligan restored once more to his humorous, generous, exuberant self, I asked him whether he thought there had been any value for him in being seriously depressed. This was his reply:

I see no value in my having been depressed. I see no value in my having been depressed. It is a dreadful scourge which has caused me terrible pain, caused my first wife much distress and my children much unhappiness. It is a disease, no question of that, and one which like all the others demands to be understood and relieved. Yes, of course I have learned who my true friends are and who can stay by me in my worst times – but that is no justification for what is a dreadful scourge. It does help to know there are others and that slowly people, including doctors, are beginning to learn something about it. But it has been around an awfully long time, a lot of people are suffering and it is about bloody time we took it seriously.

SUGGESTED READING

Winokur, George, *Depression: The Facts*.
Oxford: Oxford University Press, 1981.
A clear guide to depression by one of America's leading psychiatric researchers. Dr Winokur has spent a lifetime clarifying the nature and prevalence of depression, the way it presents and the best ways to treat it.

McKeon, Patrick, *Coping with Depression and Elation*.
London: Sheldon Press, 1986.
An Irish psychiatric colleague, Dr McKeon directs one of the largest mood disorder clinics in the world. His experience led him to found the highly successful support group AWARE which provides information, advice and help for sufferers from mania and depression and for their relatives.

Styron, William, *Darkness Visible*.
London: Jonathan Cape, 1991.
This is a remarkable, compelling and stark account of a descent into depression by a renowned American novelist. Styron writes from the inside. His account has been dramatically yet accurately described as 'an unprecedented journey into depression'. This slim volume does indeed describe depression as it is and as Spike Milligan and hundreds of thousands of other describe it.

Fieve, Ronald R., *Moodswings*.
London: Bantam Books, 1976.
A confident, forward-looking account of depression by a psychoanalytically trained American psychiatrist who has since come to acknowledge the powerful contribution made to the disorder by biological factors and biological treatments.

Johnson, F. Neil (Ed.), *Depression Brief*.
Hove, East Sussex: Lawrence Erlbaum Associates.
This is a quarterly journal aimed at health-care professionals who deal with depressive illness and related conditions and who wish to be kept up with the latest developments. It is of particular interest to psychiatrists, GPs, social workers, psychotherapists, counsellors and members of various voluntary organizations. Its style and content should appeal to sufferers and family members and friends.

Royal College of Psychiatrists, *Depression*, 1992.
This is a 14-page pamphlet which neatly and attractively highlights the main facts of the illness. It has been produced for the Defeat Depression Campaign organized by the Royal College of Psychiatrists and the Royal College of General Practitioners.

There are many other books and pamphlets available on the subject, not to mention the regular stream of articles and essays written in newspapers and magazines and emphasizing different aspects of the condition. The important point is that information and facts are now widely available. There is no longer any real reason for ignorance. Given the common occurrence of depression we should all know something about it – certainly we should know how to find such information quickly.

SUPPORT GROUPS AND ORGANIZATIONS

GREAT BRITAIN

ASSOCIATION FOR POST-NATAL ILLNESS
25 Jerdan Place, Fulham, London SW6 1BE

A nationwide telephone support scheme for those with post-natal depression. Their publications include leaflets and a booklet on post-natal depression.

BRITISH ASSOCIATION FOR COUNSELLING
37a Sheep Street, Rugby, Warwickshire CV21 3BX
Tel. 0788 578328

A national body which provides information about local counselling services and individual counsellors during office hours.

DEPRESSIVES ANONYMOUS
36 Chestnut Avenue, Beverley, Humberside HU17 9QU
Tel. 0482 860619

An organization run as a source of support for sufferers; complementary to professional care.

THE MANIC-DEPRESSION FELLOWSHIP
13 Rosslyn Road, Twickenham, Middlesex TW1 2AR
Tel. 081 892 2811

A network of local self-help groups for sufferers and their families. Produces a useful and informative regular newsheet. Spike Milligan is Patron.

MIND
22 Harley Street, London W1N 2ED
Tel. 071 637 0741

The major voluntary organization in the mental health field. Publishes a wide variety of literature on all aspects of mental health. Provides advice and advocacy and has a reputation for civil rights concern.

RELATE (Marriage Guidance Council)
Herbert Gray College, Little Church Street, Rugby CV21 3AP

The major organization in the UK concerned with marital difficulties, stress and breakdown.

THE SAMARITANS
17 Uxbridge Road, Slough, Berks. SL1 1SN
Tel. 0753 32713

A national organization offering support to those in distress who feel suicidal or despairing and need someone to talk to. There are 184 branches in Britain, open 24 hours a day, every day of the year. The telephone number of your local branch can be found in the telephone directory.

SANE (Schizophrenia A National Emergency)
Tel. 071 724 8000

A recently formed voluntary organization aiming at providing an information and support resource to sufferers from schizophrenia, their families and friends. SANE has raised a substantial sum of money to found a research unit specifically charged with advancing knowledge not merely of schizophrenia but of major depressive illness too. A telephone helpline exists providing information, advice and support concerning schizophrenia and severe depressive illness in particular and mental illness in general.

IRELAND

AWARE
Fenian Chambers, 37-38 Fenian Street, Dublin 2
Tel. Dublin 719711 and 775423 ext 629

The major voluntary organization in the Irish Republic concerned with mood disorders, AWARE provides support group meetings for sufferers and their families, provides factual information through literature, audio visual material and public lectures and promotes research into the biological, phsychological and social aspects of depression. Its head office is in Dublin but it has regional offices through Ireland. An AWARE Depression Helpline is a listening service which operates between 10 am and 4 pm, Mondays through Fridays and is manned by trained volunteers based at St Patrick's Hospital in Dublin.

GROW
11 Liberty Street, Cork and
50 Middle Abbey Street, Dublin 1
Tel. Dublin 734029

A community-based mental health movement which provides information and advice and organizes support groups for sufferers of psychiatric disorder and their relatives.

THE MENTAL HEALTH ASSOCIATION OF IRELAND
Mensana House, 6 Adelaide Street, Dun Laoghaire, Co. Dublin
Tel. Dublin 2841166

The major mental health organization in Ireland, it provides help, advice and information, holds national and local conferences and strives to raise the visibility of mental illness within the community.

THE NORTHERN IRELAND ASSOCIATION FOR MENTAL HEALTH
Beacon House, 84 University Street, Belfast BT7 1HE
Tel. 0232 28474/5

The equivalent organization to MIND in Britain and the Mental Health Association of Ireland in the Irish Republic.

INDEX

SHREWSBURY COLLEGE OF ARTS & TECHNOLOGY
RADBROOK COLLEGE

Telephone 01743 232686 Ext 642

To Renew Book Quote No:
and last date stamped.